The Ethics of Exodus

THE ETHICS OF
EXODUS

RABBI DR. ABBA ENGELBERG

KODESH PRESS

© Abba Engelberg 2016

ISBN: 978-0692589380

All rights reserved. Except for brief quotations in printed reviews, no part of this publication may be reproduced, stored in a retrieval system, or transmitted in any form or by any means (printed, written, photocopied, visual electronic, audio, or otherwise) without the prior permissions of the publisher.

The Publisher extends its gratitude to
Chaim Orent for assistance with this project.

Published & Distributed by

Kodesh Press L.L.C.
New York, NY
www.KodeshPress.com
kodeshpress@gmail.com

TABLE OF CONTENTS

INTRODUCTION 11

SHEMOT 18
   ANTI-SEMITISM IN EGYPT 20
   PARTICIPATION OF WOMEN 25
   THE EVENT AT THE LODGING PLACE 28
   SUMMARY 31

VA'ERA 33
   THE GENEALOGICAL TEXT 35
   ANALYZING THE GENEALOGY: SEVEN QUESTIONS . . . 37
   SUMMARY 56

BO 58
   WAS PHARAOH DESERVING OF PUNISHMENT? 61
   WAS PHARAOH DEPRIVED OF HIS FREEDOM OF CHOICE? . 63
   SUMMARY 79

- **BESHALLACH** 80
  - THE SHORTAGE OF WATER AT MARAH: THREE QUESTIONS . 83
  - THE SEA SHORE: UNDERSTANDING THE WORDS *VA-YASSA MOSHE* ("AND MOSES LED ISRAEL") 86
  - WERE THE BITTER WATERS OF MARAH A PUNISHMENT? . 97
  - CONNECTING THE SECOND PART: "THERE HE MADE A STATUTE AND AN ORDINANCE FOR THEM" 101
  - HOW COULD THE ISRAELITES' BEHAVIOR HAVE DEGENERATED SO FAST? 104
  - SUMMARY 106

- **YITRO** 107
  - WAS JETHRO RIGHTEOUS? (R. ELAZAR VS. R. YEHOSHUA) . 111
  - DID JETHRO ARRIVE BEFORE OR AFTER THE TORAH WAS GIVEN? (IBN EZRA VS. RAMBAN) 117
  - DID JETHRO VISIT TWICE AND STAY THE SECOND TIME? (RAMBAN VS. IBN EZRA) 123
  - JETHRO CONTRASTED TO OTHER BIBLICAL CHARACTERS . 126
  - SUMMARY 131

- **MISHPATIM** 132
  - THE CONCLUSION OF *YITRO*: G-D-ORIENTED LAWS . .133
  - THE FIRST VERSE OF *MISHPATIM*: TRANSITIONING TO CIVIL LEGISLATION 136
  - THE MAIN BODY OF *MISHPATIM*: CIVIL LEGISLATION . 142
  - SUMMARY 155

- **TERUMAH** 157
  - WHAT FORM DID THE CHERUBIM TAKE? 159
  - WHAT IS THE DIFFERENCE BETWEEN THE CHERUBIM AND THE GOLDEN CALF? 160
  - WHAT ROLE WAS PLAYED BY THE CHERUBIM? 163
  - MIRACULOUS EVENTS AND THE CHERUBIM 166
  - SUMMARY 173

- **TETZAVEH** 175
  - WHY IS THE NAME OF MOSES ABSENT FROM THIS PORTION? . 176
  - WHY IS THE DESCRIPTION OF THE GOLDEN ALTAR DELAYED? 193
  - SUMMARY 210

KI TISSA 212
   THE GOLDEN CALF IN TANNAITIC, AMORAIC,
      AND MIDRASHIC LITERATURE 213
   THE SIN OF THE GOLDEN CALF ACCORDING
      TO THE CLASSICAL COMMENTATORS 229
   SUMMARY 243

VAYAKHEL 246
   WOMEN'S DONATIONS TO THE TABERNACLE 246
   THE WOMEN WERE REWARDED FOR THEIR GENEROSITY . 253
   SUMMARY 267

PEKUDEI 270
   ACHIEVING THE HIGHEST LEVEL OF REPENTANCE . . . 271
   THE IMPORTANCE OF UNITY 273
   SUMMARY 285

FIRST OVERVIEW: THE INTELLECTUAL
   DEVELOPMENT OF THE JEWISH NATION 287
   THE SEVEN NOAHIDE LAWS 287
   ADDING MORE MITZVOT AT MARAH 291
   THE GIVING OF THE TORAH AT MT. SINAI –
      WHAT WAS GIVEN AND WHAT WAS RECORDED? . . . 300
   FREQUENCY OF TORAH READING 305

SECOND OVERVIEW: TABERNACLE-ORIENTED PORTIONS . 310
   RAMBAN – (ALMOST) EVERYTHING IS IN ITS PROPER ORDER . 311
   RASHI: "THERE IS NO EARLIER OR LATER IN THE TORAH" . 321
   THE VIEW OF RAMBAN ON SACRIFICES AND THE TEMPLE . 330

APPENDIX I: BIBLICAL BACKGROUND FOR
   UNDERSTANDING R. TZADOK HA-KOHEN 336
   MIDRASHIC EXPLANATION OF THE BIBLICAL EPISODE . 339

APPENDIX II: FUNCTIONARIES IN JEWISH SOCIETY
   IN TEMPLE TIMES (A MISHNAH) 343
   SOURCES FOR THE MISHNAH 346
   THE IMPORTANCE OF A GOOD NAME 346

APPENDIX III: INCENSE AND THE PRIESTLY MISSION . . 350
    INCENSE AS A REMEDY 350
    INCENSE AS A SYMBOL 352

APPENDIX IV: ARBITRATION IN JEWISH
    LAW – MOSES VS. AARON 355
    THE TALMUDIC DISCUSSION 355
    RASHI VS. TOSAFOT 360

APPENDIX V: THE DESTRUCTION OF THE
    TEMPLE WAS IN RETRIBUTION FOR KILLING A PROPHET . 365
    REVIEW OF SOME BIBLICAL EVENTS 365
    TALMUDIC AND MIDRASHIC SOURCES
        RELATING TO THE KILLING OF ZECHARIAH 371
    THE DESTRUCTION OF THE FIRST TEMPLE 373

APPENDIX VI: WHAT HAPPENED TO THE HOLY ARK? . . 377
    THE LATER KINGS OF THE KINGDOM OF JUDEA . . . 377
    TALMUDIC DISPUTE REGARDING THE FATE OF THE ARK . 379
    THE HIDDEN TEMPLE GATES 387

SOURCE MATERIAL 389
COMMENTATORS 395

Introduction

Organization of the Book of Exodus

The Torah, or Five Books of Moses, has been divided into 54 weekly portions. Since the Jewish year varies in length from 50 to 54 weeks, it is possible to review the entire Torah every year by reading one, and sometimes two, portions per week, which is the current practice in the synagogue.

The book of Exodus deals with the following three topics:

A. enslavement and exodus from Egypt (Exod. 1:1-15:21)
B. the giving of the law (Exod. 15:22-24:18)
C. the Tabernacle (Exod. 25:1-40:38).

Exodus contains eleven of the 54 weekly portions, and the Hebrew names of these portions serve as the chapter titles in this book. The Hebrew names are chosen from the introductory words of the weekly portion, and do not necessarily reflect its content. The table below provides the non-Hebrew reader with the translation of the Hebrew names and the insignia of the topic that it deals with.

The Ethics of Exodus

	Hebrew Name	Literal Translation	Contents
1	*Shemot*	The names of (the Children of Israel)	A
2	*Va'era*	And I appeared (to Abraham, Isaac, and Jacob)	A
3	*Bo*	Go (to Pharaoh)	A
4	*Beshallach*	When (Pharaoh) expelled (the nation)	A/B
5	*Yitro*	Jethro	B
6	*Mishpatim*	Ordinances	B
7	*Terumah*	A donation	C
8	*Tetzaveh*	You shall command (the Children of Israel)	C
9	*Ki Tissa*	When you count (the Children of Israel)	C
10	*Vayakhel*	When (Moses) assembled (all of the congregation)	C
11	*Pekudei*	(These are the) accounts of (the Tabernacle)	C

Introduction

Questions Arising from the Weekly Portion

In this book, various insights will be offered in regard to questions concerning the content and import of the events described in Exodus, such as those listed below, with the relevant portion enclosed in parentheses:

1. Was the wife of Moses spiritually on the level of the matriarchs? (*Shemot*)
2. Would G-d have threatened the life of His holy messenger Moses? (*Shemot*)
3. What can be learned from the genealogical lists that appear in the Bible? (*Va'era*)
4. Why is the name of Miriam, the sister of Moses, absent from the genealogical listing? (*Va'era*)
5. Why was Pharaoh punished if it was G-d who hardened his heart? (*Bo*)
6. How could the nation that witnessed the splitting of the Red Sea be so ungrateful and complain at every opportunity? (*Beshallach*)
7. Was Jethro an outstanding convert on the level of Ruth, or otherwise? (*Yitro*)
8. Are the many laws presented after revelation arranged in any logical sequence? (*Mishpatim*)
9. What is the difference between the golden calf, which was an abomination, and the Cherubim, which were holy? (*Terumah*)
10. How could Aaron the High Priest have participated and accelerated the construction of the golden calf? (*Ki Tissa*)
11. Why did the women contribute more to the Tabernacle than the men? (*Vayakhel*)

12. How could the Tabernacle atone for the sin of the golden calf? (*Pekudei*)
13. Was the entire Torah given at Mt. Sinai, or just the Ten Commandments and the basic outline of the 613 commandments? (First Overview)
14. Was the Tabernacle part of G-d's original plan, or was it a reaction to the sin of the golden calf? (Second Overview)
15. What happened to the Holy Ark? (Appendix VI)

Of course, many of these questions have already been asked by the classical and later Biblical commentators, and I have quoted and explained their answers to the best of my ability. I have also added my own ideas when I thought I had something to contribute to the discussion.

Ethical Lessons Based on the Weekly Portion

As I did in *The Ethics of Genesis*, I will present some of the logical and ethical dilemmas that may arise when studying the book of Exodus. Some of the questions dealt with are listed below, with the relevant portion enclosed in parentheses:

1. What is the underlying cause of anti-Semitism? (*Shemot*)
2. What is the first instance of women being proactively involved in leadership? (*Shemot*)
3. Does G-d grant man freedom of choice? (*Bo*)
4. Does absolute morality exist independent of revelation? (First Overview)
5. What is the Jewish attitude to carnal love? (*Terumah*)

Introduction

6. Do women outshine men with regard to certain attributes? (*Vayakhel*)

The reader will probably identify with many of the ethical predicaments dealt with in these pages and will have many intriguing thoughts on the subject matter that would serve as a welcome contribution to the analyses presented here. If reading this book will stimulate people to contemplate these ethical quandaries, I will have achieved my goal.

According to the Midrash, the Torah and the Jewish nation were created before the universe. The import of this Midrash is that Israel's *raison d'être* is to abide by the laws of the Torah. Since the nation of Israel is meant to be a light unto the nations, G-d must have intended the Torah to play a prominent role in the overall world scene. It is thus not surprising that soon after the creation of man, attempts to channel mankind in the proper direction were initiated with the advent of the seven Noahide laws, and continued in a stream of small doses until revelation, when the Torah was transmitted to Moses in its entirety. Even with regard to the latter claim, varying opinions appear in the Talmud. Because the transmission process spans many weekly portions (*Bo*, *Beshallach*, *Yitro*, *Mishpatim*, *Ki Tissa*, and *Pekudei*), the entire topic is handled in "First Overview: The Intellectual Development of the Jewish Nation."

Another discussion point that relates to a series of portions in the second half of Exodus is whether the Tabernacle was part of G-d's initial plan for the nation of Israel, or whether it became a necessity only as a result of the sin of the golden calf. If the latter assumption is true, how is it that the portion of *Terumah*—which details the contributions, structure, and vessels of the Tabernacle—precedes *Ki Tissa*, which is where the story of the golden calf unravels? The classical views on this topic are presented in the "Second Overview: The Tabernacle-Oriented Portions."

In order to enable an in-depth discussion of some of the weekly portions, it was necessary to present a more comprehensive examination of certain philosophical, ethical, and halachic issues in a series of appendices, whose contents and relevance are listed below:

"Appendix I: Background for Understanding R. Tzadok ha-Kohen" elucidates an incident concerning King David as described in the book of 2 Samuel, which serves as the basis for R. Tzadok's explanation of why the name of Moses does not appear in the portion of *Tetzaveh*.

"Appendix II: Functionaries in Jewish Society in Temple Times" notes that one of the functionaries was the high priest, whose activities were intimately connected to the golden altar. This point is used to explain why the description of that altar appears in the portion devoted to presenting the priestly garments, and not previously when describing the other furnishings of the Tabernacle.

"Appendix III: Incense and the priestly mission" provides a description of the priestly function, and explains how incense helped fulfill it.

"Appendix IV: Arbitration in Jewish Law: Moses vs. Aaron" deals with the apparent compromise that Aaron made with the nation in connection with the golden calf.

"Appendix V: The Destruction of the Temple Was in Retribution for Killing a Prophet" presents Aaron's possible reasoning in allowing the Children of Israel to proceed with their plan to manufacture an idol.

"Appendix VI: What Happened to the Holy Ark?" discusses the disappearance (and preservation) of the Ark toward the end of the First Temple, as well as the burial of the Temple

Introduction

gates—in connection with the portion of *Terumah* which describes the Ark that was constructed for the Tabernacle and eventually placed in the First Temple.

In preparing this material, I have based myself on the Talmud and Midrash, as well as the many commentaries that have been written from the Middle Ages until the present. To give the reader an idea of the scope of the material upon which the book is based, I have included a glossary of sources followed by a list of the authorities quoted in *The Ethics of Exodus*. Since the title Rabbi appears frequently, I have abbreviated it using the letter "R." I have also used "b." to denote *ben*, meaning "son of." BT is an abbreviation for Babylonian Talmud, while JT signifies Jerusalem Talmud.

I would like to take this opportunity to thank my loving wife Ruthie, who made many insightful comments, in addition to proofreading the entire book.

I fervently hope that this book will be of benefit to those who read it.

Abba Engelberg
Jerusalem, 2016

Shemot

In the portion of *Shemot,* the reader is introduced to two elements that have characterized Jewish existence from the time of the exodus until modern times. The first is (unfortunately) anti-Semitism, which occurred initially when the King of Egypt imposed a corvée on the Children of Israel for the purpose of building cities in which his valuables were to be stored, not because such storage facilities were an absolute necessity, but to afflict them with their burdens (Exod. 1:11). When the king realized that forced labor did not sufficiently dampen their spirits, he decided to worsen the conditions of their employment. At first they were supplied with bricks, but as time progressed they were only given straw. They were then told to collect the sand which they would beat into mortar using their hands and feet, and so manufacture bricks (Ramban on Exod. 1:11). Finally, they were not even supplied with straw, so they had to collect on it their own. Nevertheless, they were required to produce the same number of bricks as in the past (Exod. 5:7-8).

The second characteristic element that is emphasized in this portion is the intimate relationship between G-d and Israel. G-d appears to Moses from within the burning bush (*sneh* in Hebrew, which may be related to the word "Sinai"), where revelation, the essence of which is receiving the Torah, is foreseen: "When you have brought forth the people out of Egypt, you shall serve G-d upon this mountain" (Exod. 3:12). The first hint of the extension of the seven Noahide laws by means of the 613 *mitzvot* of the Torah thus appears in the portion of *Shemot*.

In this chapter, the first element—Egyptian anti-Semitism—will be discussed, while the second element—the process of revelation—will be described in detail throughout the book of Exodus.

Another item which will be noted in dealing with the portion of *Shemot* is the role of Israelite women during the period of Egyptian slavery and its aftermath—the exodus from Egypt. In the book of Genesis, the matriarchs were referred to with the greatest respect, and many acts of loving-kindness (*chesed*) were attributed to them, as manifested, e.g., by the behavior of Rebecca at the well (Gen. 24:18-20). Additionally, they experienced many miracles, such as the continual burning of the Sabbath candles from one Sabbath eve to the next in the households of Sarah and Rebecca (Rashi on Gen. 24:67). Sometimes women became objects of desire by tyrants and bullies such as Pharaoh (Gen. 12:15), Abimelech (Gen. 20:2, 26:10, and Rashi there), and Shechem (Gen. 34:3). In other cases, their actions were not especially considered to be praiseworthy, e.g., Sarah's laughter upon hearing that she would become pregnant at an advanced age (Gen. 18:12), and later her attitude toward her maidservant Hagar (Gen. 21:10). This is also seen in the behavior of both Rachel and Leah in connection with the mandrakes which Reuben had brought to his mother (Gen. 30:14-16), and Rachel's theft of the *teraphim* from her father Laban (Gen. 31:19).

In spite of the women's innate involvement in many of the events described in Genesis, their function was not essential to the dénouement of the plot. Neither did they play a central role in many of the philosophical dilemmas and weighty decisions described, such as the destruction of Sodom and Gomorrah (Gen. 31:19), the sacrifice of Isaac (Gen. 31:22), or the descent to the land of Egypt (Gen. 31:45). Unlike Jacob's sons, his daughter Dinah was not included in the blessing Jacob bestowed before his demise (Genesis 49), clearly because she was not to be the progenitor of one of the tribes. In the book of Exodus, the situation will change.

Anti-Semitism in Egypt

Three questions will be addressed with respect to anti-Semitism, specifically:

1. What is the first recorded source of anti-Semitism?
2. What are the mechanics of anti-Semitism, i.e., how have enemies of the Jews traditionally gone about arousing, inculcating, and propagating anti-Semitism?
3. What is the underlying cause of anti-Semitism?

Answering the First Question: What Is the Source of Anti-Semitism?

On the basis of the Biblical story, it is quite clear that Pharaoh's main motivation was pure anti-Semitism and not the utilization of cheap labor, since one who wants more male slaves would be expected to encourage their birth, rather than suppress it. In the words of Esther:

> If we had only been sold as men- and women-slaves, I would have remained quiet; since then [our] suffering

would not have been worth [as much as] the damage it would have caused the king [by the loss of free slave labor] (Esth. 7:4).

Pharaoh's decrees revealed his true intentions, as stated in the following verse:

And he said, "When you attend the Hebrew women and see them giving birth, if it's a boy, kill him; but if it's a girl, let her live" (Exod. 1:16).

Answering the Second Question: What Are the Mechanics of Anti-Semitism?

With regard to the verse concerning Pharaoh's plans for dealing with the Hebrews, the Bible states: "Let us be wise in dealing with them, lest they multiply, and in the event of war they too will join our enemies and they will fight against us and leave the land" (Exod. 1:10).

Rashi interprets the words "and leave the land" in two ways. One explanation is that the Hebrews will leave by force, against the will of Pharaoh. This interpretation is consistent with the Midrash which says that Pharaoh's astrologers had deduced that the savior of Israel would suffer misfortune through water, and that is why Pharaoh, at a later stage (Exod. 1:22), decreed that every male baby (even Egyptian) should be cast into the river, thus preventing their savior from delivering them from bondage (*Exod. Rabbah* 1:18).

The second explanation interprets the words "and they will fight against us, and leave the land" to mean that the Israelites will fight the Egyptians and cause the expulsion of the Egyptians. It was a thought so dreadful to Pharaoh that he was unable to enunciate it unequivocally, but had to formulate it in a much milder form, as if it were the Israelites who were to be expelled. This explanation fits well with the view of Chizkuni (on Exod. 1:16) that Pharaoh wished to weaken the future Israelite army by murdering its potential soldiers.

It is possible that both interpretations are valid. The classical pattern of anti-Semitism has always been to initially generate a fictional fear, such as that Jews control all of the world's capital, or that they use the blood of Gentile infants in baking *matzah* for Passover. The second stage is to inculcate members of the younger generation with these false accusations when they are too young to verify them, so that they develop an emotional repugnance to Jewish people. The third stage is for the local population, when they come of age, to actively persecute Jewish people. Even though they are capable of checking the facts at this stage, after having been brainwashed in their youth, they no longer have an inclination to do so.

Similarly, Pharaoh initially spread the rumor that the Israelites were planning to revolt, displace the locals, and exile the Egyptians, thus generating consternation (based on the second explanation). After arousing fear and eventually disgust in the populace, he incited his subjects to seek revenge by oppressing and abusing them as slaves and preventing them from emigrating (the first explanation).

Answering the Third Question: What Is the Underlying Cause of Anti-Semitism?

In addition to presenting the first occurrence of anti-Semitism, this portion alludes to its cause. The second chapter of Exodus contains the following verses, which relate to the adolescence of Moses:

> 11 And it came to pass in those days, when Moses was grown up, that he went out to his brothers and looked on their burdens; and he saw an Egyptian smiting a Hebrew, one of his brothers. 12 And he looked this way and that way, and when he saw that there was no man, he smote the Egyptian and hid him in the sand. 13 And he went out the second day and, behold, two men of the Hebrews were striving together; and he said to him that did the wrong: "Why do you smite your friend?" 14 And he said: "Who made you a ruler and a judge over us? Are you thinking of killing me, as you killed the Egyptian?" And Moses feared, and said: "Surely the thing is known" (Exod. 2).

These verses reflect quite clearly Moses' empathy with his brethren during the time of their suffering. Beyond relating to the specific victims of Pharaoh's malevolence, his actions highlight his pro-active resistance to tyranny and brutality. It is not coincidental that Moses behaved in this manner. Quite the contrary—because Moses possessed these qualities, he was chosen as the archetype of what Israel is meant to achieve in this world.

Rashi (on Exod. 2:13) states that the two adversaries mentioned were Dathan and Abiram, the same pair that later disregarded Moses' command not to store manna (the G-d-given heavenly food which sustained the Israelites in the desert for forty years) overnight (Exod. 16:19-20) and joined in the rebellion led by Korah (Num. 16:1). With regard to the words "And Moses became afraid" in verse 14, Rashi quotes the Midrash (*Tanchuma Exod.* 10) which states that Moses was distressed, not because of his own precarious situation, but because he saw that among the Israelites there were wicked men—men who did not appreciate his efforts to instill justice and protect the victims of tyranny. Such being the case, Moses feared that the Hebrews were perhaps not even worthy of being redeemed themselves, and certainly not capable of serving as a model for the rest of mankind to emulate.

Rashi proceeds to cite the Midrashic explanation of Moses' statement at the end of verse 14: "Surely the thing is known." The Midrash (*Exod. Rabbah* 1:30) explains that what suddenly became known to Moses was the sinful behavior that caused Israel to be singled out, more than any of the other seventy nations of the world, to be oppressed by the crushing servitude imposed by Pharaoh. The transgressions of Dathan and Abiram consisted of their disregard for the requirement to love one's neighbor, and the lack of a sense of responsibility for, and participation in, the destiny of Israel.

From the behavior which caused Moses to fear that perhaps Israel was not worthy of redemption, one can deduce what was in fact the prerequisite for that redemption—namely, a well-developed sense of morality. Clearly, such was the purpose of the enslavement experience, which G-d had already planned for the Jewish nation from the time of the covenant between G-d and Abraham (Gen. 15:13). One may assume that the experiment succeeded and that the majority of the Israelites, with the exception of Dathan and

Abiram, developed caring, moral, and empathetic personalities, and so were indeed worthy of redemption.

A potential cause of anti-Semitism has now been identified. Israel presented a superior standard of moral behavior, which stood out even as they were enslaved. The Egyptians, similar to many Gentiles in future generations, could not meet the moral standard displayed by the Israelites, so they preferred to obliterate the messenger, namely—the Children of Israel.

Participation of Women

As previously mentioned, in the book of Exodus the role played by women undergoes a transformation. Women play a pivotal role starting from chapter 1, where the Hebrew midwives circumvented Pharaoh's orders to kill the male babies by claiming: "Hebrew women are not like Egyptian women; they are vigorous and give birth before the midwives arrive" (Exod. 1:19). The names of the midwives given in the Biblical text are Shiphrah and Puah, but the Talmud explains that these appellations actually refer to Jochebed and Miriam (BT *Sotah* 11b), in keeping with the tendency of the Midrash to minimize the number of different characters appearing in Biblical stories.

However, not only Jochebed and Miriam helped build the nation, but all of the women contributed. When their husbands returned from work completely exhausted, the women had to use all of their wiles to stimulate their husbands to have relations with them. The Talmud says that they would bring fish and warm water to the fields in order to pamper and refresh them, and as a result of this display of love and concern, their husbands' desire was rekindled and they were able to procreate (BT *Sotah* 11b). Since it was dangerous for the women to be seen when their pregnancy was close to term, being that male children were meant to be cast into the river, the women had to give birth in the fields. G-d sent heavenly beings to serve as midwives and to wash and straighten the limbs of the newborn. The infants were miraculously fed and sustained in the fields, hidden from the Egyptians, and they returned to their homes only after they were grown.

In addition to saving the lives of many newborn, the altruistic behavior of Jochebed and Miriam served as a positive influence on all of the Children of Israel, including Amram, Jochebed's husband. According to the Talmud, when Amram, father of Miriam and Aaron, heard Pharaoh's decree to cast all male babies into the river, he divorced his wife, in order to prevent wanton loss of life (BT *Sotah* 12a). All of the men of Israel followed in his footsteps, since he was known to be the greatest sage of the generation. His young daughter, Miriam—according to the Midrash (*Exod. Rabbah* 1:13), she was only five years old at the time—gave him a lesson in belief in the Almighty by saying:

> Father, your decree is harsher than that of Pharaoh. Pharaoh's decree was limited to the male babies, while yours prevents the birth of females as well. Pharaoh's decree deprives the male children of life in this world, while yours deprives them of life in both this and the next world [every soul created is entitled to life in the next world, independent of the quality or length of life in this world]. The decree of the wicked Pharaoh may or may not transpire, but yours, being that you are so righteous, will certainly come to be (*Exod. Rabbah* 1:13).

The wisdom of the young Miriam laid the basis for the eventual exodus from Egypt and receipt of the Torah on Mount Sinai. When Amram realized how much pain he had caused his virtuous wife Jochebed, he comforted her by holding a ceremony on the occasion of the renewal of their vows that rivaled their original wedding in pomp and splendor.

The following verse describes the revival of Amram's marriage to Jochebed: "And there went a man of the house of Levi [Amram], and he took to wife a daughter of Levi [Jochebed]" (Exod. 2:1).

The Talmud asks with regard to the words "there went a man": Where did he go? The answer given is that he did not physically go anywhere. Rather, he followed the advice of his daughter, i.e., Miriam's stricture was taken seriously by Amram. A great man accepts advice from any person, independent of age, sex, race, or religion.

Jochebed was rewarded for her unflinching loyalty to her husband by giving birth to Moses, which was accompanied by miracles that highlighted his future spiritual mission. The Talmud deduces that Jochebed was 130 years old at the time, noting three points (BT *Sotah* 12a):

1. Jochebed was born as the family of Jacob passed through the walls upon their arrival in Egypt;
2. the bondage in Egypt lasted 210 years;
3. Moses was 80 at the time of the exodus.

Subtracting 80 from 210 gives 130, Jochebed's age when she gave birth to Moses. Thus, the first miracle was that she was rejuvenated, and her body developed the signs of youth once more. At birth, it was discovered that Moses was already circumcised, and the house filled with light. Jochebed understood that her son was destined to be a prophet and a leader.

The Ethics of Exodus

The Event at the Lodging Place

A mystical incident involving Moses' wife, Zipporah, occurred after G-d requested that Moses return to Egypt in order to participate in the redemption of the Israelites from slavery. The following verses describe the event that took place on the way to his destination:

> 24 And it came to pass on the way at the lodging-place, that the Lord met him and sought to kill him. 25 Then Zipporah took a flint, and cut off the foreskin of her son, and cast it at his feet; and she said: "Surely a bridegroom of blood you are to me." 26 So He let him alone. Then she said: "A bridegroom of blood because of circumcisions" (Exod. 4).

Regarding these verses, a number of questions may be posed.

First Question: Who Did G-d Seek to Kill, and Why?

The Talmud offers an answer to this question:

> Rebbe said: G-d forbid that Moses would have been lazy with respect to circumcision, but he reasoned thus: If I circumcise [my son] and leave [immediately to fulfill my mission to Pharaoh], I will endanger his life, as it is written, "And it came to pass on the third day, when they were sore" (Gen. 34:25). If I circumcise him and wait three days, G-d has commanded: "Go, return [without delay] to Egypt" (Exod. 4:19). Why then was Moses punished? Because he busied himself first with the inn, as it is written, "And

it came to pass on the way, at the lodging-place" (Exod. 4:24). Rabbi Simeon b. Gamliel said: Satan did not seek to slay Moses, but the child (BT *Nedarim* 31b-32a).

The Talmudic commentator R. Nissim of Gerona (the *Ran*, 1320-1376) explains that according to Rebbe, when Moses arrived at the inn, he should have immediately circumcised his son. Even though he was not yet in Egypt, the remaining trip was short enough that it would not endanger a recently circumcised baby. Moses was thus punished because he did not fulfill the command at the moment that it became possible to do so. According to Rabbi Simeon b. Gamliel, the angel (or Satan) sought to kill the baby himself, based on the Talmudic saying, "Small children are punished for their fathers' sins."[1]

Abarbanel (on Exodus 4) rejects the Midrashic approach, and claims that Moses was not guilty of belittling the circumcision ritual. In his view, the Talmud ascribes his error to the fact that he engaged himself in earthly matters, i.e., busying himself with the inn, instead of secluding himself in order to rise to the degree of holiness requisite for communicating with the Almighty. Both circumcision and lodging arrangements were distractions that diverted him from his sacred duties. Zipporah was aware of his mission, and she lovingly devoted herself to handling all of the menial duties required to sustain the family.

Which baby was not circumcised? Logically, one would assume that it was the younger son Eliezer, who is first mentioned in the Biblical portion of *Yitro* (Exod. 18:4), the older son, Gershom, having been born soon after Moses and Zipporah married (Exod. 2:22). According to Rashi, Moses separated from his wife and children upon arrival in Egypt, after his brother Aaron convinced

---

1. BT *Shabbat* 25a, and Rambam (*Teshuvah* 6:1) rules accordingly.

him that there were enough problems for those Israelites already trapped in Egypt, and bringing in another young family would only complicate matters. Moses and his family were only reunited sometime after the splitting of the Red Sea, when Jethro arrived with them from Midian (Exod. 18:2 and Rashi there). Combining the previously cited Talmudic view with Rashi's explanation, it can be assumed that Eliezer was born a few days before the family departed for Egypt or, according to Abarbanel (on Exodus 4), on the way to Egypt.

In contrast to the view that the endangered son was the newborn Eliezer, a Midrashic interpretation implies that it was the older son who was endangered:

> At the time when Moses said to Jethro give me your daughter Zipporah in marriage, Jethro said to him: "Accept this condition which I request of you, and she is yours to wed." He said to him: "What is it?" He said to him: "The son whom you have first will be devoted to idol-worship—from there on, for heavenly worship," and he accepted it upon himself.[2]

Since the first son had not been circumcised, it was on his account that death was being threatened.

Second Question: How Did Zipporah Know the Source of the Problem?

Rashi explains that the Almighty provided a strong clue to Zipporah as to the cause of the problem: "The angel became a kind

---
2. *Mechilta de-Rabbi Yishmael, Yitro,* tractate Amalek, *parashah* Aleph.

of serpent and swallowed him from his head to his thigh [then spitting him out], and then again swallowed him from his legs to that place. Zipporah thus understood that this happened on account of [the delay in] the circumcision" (Rashi on Exod. 4:24, based on BT *Nedarim* 32a and *Exod. Rabbah* 5:8).

Third Question: At Whose Feet Was the Foreskin Cast?

With regard to the words in verse 25, "Zipporah... cast it at his feet," the Jerusalem Talmud presents a dispute concerning to whose feet the verse relates. One view is that it refers to the feet of Moses, and it was as if she impatiently said: "Here is the foreskin which *you* were actually supposed to remove." Another view is that the foreskin was cast at the feet of the angel, as if to say: "Here is the foreskin. You have performed your mission and may thus leave" (JT *Nedarim* Ch. 3).

This Talmudic difference of opinion may be traced to varying views as to whether Zipporah was righteous from the very start and was able to appreciate the significance of Moses' mission, or whether her initial personality was flawed, in which case it is quite possible that she would have spoken to Moses in a petulant manner. Moses nevertheless chose to marry her because he realized that in the proper environment, she could develop into an outstandingly virtuous human being who was indeed fit to be his wife.

Summary

In the first portion of the book of Exodus, the Israelites transitioned from a free tribe to a persecuted and subjugated minority living in

Egypt. At the end of the portion they are still very much enslaved, but there is a glimmer of light, because, in the words of the Bible, G-d has seen the affliction of His people and heard the cries of pain as a result of the cruelty of their Egyptian taskmasters (Exod. 3:7). G-d has not only become aware of the situation, but He is also preparing to extricate the Jewish nation from their agony. In this portion, He has taken the first step by choosing the leader who will take them out of Egypt toward the Promised Land. The next portion opens with a more detailed description of the redemption from slavery that the Almighty has planned for the beleaguered nation.

Va'era

In the portion of *Va'era*, the Torah proceeds with the description of the exodus from Egypt. However, before it does so, the continuum is broken by a genealogical list of the major participants, beginning with the enumeration of the descendants of Reuben. In this chapter, rather than continue the exegesis of the exodus story, which will be examined in depth in the coming portions, a relatively minor topic will be dealt with, namely lessons which may be learned from the way the genealogy is presented.

Perhaps the Torah Is Not Particular about Details

It is known that the Sages gave serious consideration to every word of the Torah. The Talmud states: "Simeon Imsoni... interpreted every *et* [an article of speech which focuses attention on the noun which follows] in the Torah" (BT *Pesachim* 22b), while R. Akiva is said to have expounded upon each jot and tittle heaps and heaps of laws (BT *Menachot* 29b). It is possible to extract many lessons from the same word, as is implied by the saying: "The Torah possesses seventy faces" (*Num. Rabbah* 13:16). It is even possible to learn from each of various contradictory Midrashic interpretations, since the focus is not as much on the historical details as on the perspective of the author, as expressed in each Midrash.

If the Torah recorded the length of a person's life, the Rabbis assume that it was done for a reason. For example, when Jacob prepared a pottage of lentils, Rashi comments:

> On that day Abraham died, so that he should not see Esau his grandson going forth to a wicked life, and this would not be the good old age that G-d had promised him (Gen. 15:15). Therefore, G-d shortened his life by five years, for Isaac lived one-hundred and eighty years, and this one [Abraham, lived only] one-hundred and seventy-five [years], and Jacob was cooking lentils as the [traditional] first meal served to the mourner [his father Isaac] (on Gen. 25:30).

One might conjecture that perhaps there was no Divine intervention, just that Abraham's allotted time had elapsed. The *Siftei Chachamim* rejects this possibility by noting that with respect to Abraham, it says that he died "old and satisfied" (Gen. 25:8), while concerning Isaac, the Bible says that he died "old and satisfied in his days" (Gen. 35:29). This indicates that Abraham did not live out the number of days initially allotted to him.

Adopting this approach, the potentially monotonous family tree presented in *Va'era* will be analyzed, and a number of ethical lessons will be deduced, based on such minor details as the choice of which people and tribes were included; who was described in great detail and who was glossed over; and even why some descendants are referenced with an introductory phrase, while others are not. Were the derived ideas intended by the Author and perceived by the prophet Moses? Perhaps not, but they certainly

Va'era

reflect the opinions of the exegetes by whom they were proposed, and being that G-d's knowledge is infinite, He may certainly have foreseen such interpretations.

The Genealogical Text

The list starts by naming the descendants of Reuben, Jacob's firstborn. "These are the heads of their fathers' houses: the sons of Reuben the firstborn of Israel: Hanoch, and Pallu, Hezron, and Carmi. These are the families of Reuben" (Exod. 6:14).

Next, the Torah lists the names of the children of Simeon and Levi. All of the citations are from chapter 6 in Exodus:

> 15 And the sons of Simeon: Jemuel, and Jamin, and Ohad, and Jachin, and Zohar, and Shaul the son of a Canaanite woman. These are the families of Simeon. 16 And these are the names of the sons of Levi according to their generations: Gershon and Kohath, and Merari. And the years of the life of Levi were a hundred and thirty seven years.

At this point, instead of continuing horizontally by listing the children of the remaining brothers, the text extends the family tree vertically by detailing the names of the third generation of Levi, but only of Levi—in other words, the sons of Gershon, Kohath, and Merari:

> 17 The sons of Gershon: Libni and Shimei, according to their families. 18 And the sons of Kohath: Amram, and Izhar, and Hebron, and Uzziel. And the years of the life of Kohath were a hundred and thirty three years. 19 And the

sons of Merari: Mahli and Mushi. These are the families of the Levites according to their generations.

Once more, after presenting the names of the third generation (the sons of each of Levi's sons), instead of listing the fourth generation descendants of each member of the third generation, Scripture does so only for the third generation descendants of Kohath (Amram, Izhar, and Uzziel; for some reason the children of the third son of Kohath, Hebron, are not enumerated):

> 20 And Amram took Jochebed his father's sister as his wife, and she bore him Aaron and Moses. And the years of the life of Amram were a hundred and thirty and seven years. 21 And the sons of Izhar: Korah, and Nepheg, and Zichri. 22 And the sons of Uzziel: Mishael, and Elzaphan, and Sithri.

Continuing to narrow the genealogy, instead of listing all of the children of the fourth generation of Kohath, Scripture proceeds to list the descendants (fifth generation) of only two of them, Aaron son of Amram, and Korah son of Izhar:

> 23 And Aaron took Elisheba, the daughter of Amminadab, the sister of Nahshon, as his wife, and she bore him Nadab and Abihu, Elazar and Ithamar. 24 And the sons of Korah: Assir, and Elkanah, and Abiasaph; these are the families of the Korahites.

The genealogy concludes by mentioning the name of the son of Elazar the son of Aaron—the sixth generation: "And Elazar, Aaron's son, took for himself one of the daughters of Putiel as a wife, and she bore him Phinehas" (Exod. 6:25). The situation is summarized in the following tables:

Table 1: *This table shows two generations of Reuben and Simeon, and three of Levi:*

1	Reuben	Simeon	Levi	Levi
2	sons	sons	Gershon	Merari
3			sons	sons

Table 2: *The following table shows the descendants of Levi through Kohath. Specifically there are three generations to Hebron, four through Uzziel, four through Amram to Moses, five through Izhar, and six through Amram by way of Aaron to Phinehas. Among other items, the symmetry of the genealogical tree will be discussed.*

1	Levi	Levi	Levi	Levi	Levi
2	Kohath	Kohath	Kohath	Kohath	Kohath
3	Amram	Amram	Izhar	Hebron	Uzziel
4	Aaron	Moses	sons, Korah		sons
5	sons, Elazar		sons		
6	Phinehas				

ANALYZING THE GENEALOGY: SEVEN QUESTIONS

A number of questions (some of which have been alluded to previously) arise with respect to the aforementioned list:

1. Why does the list appear at this point, interrupting an earnest discussion between Moses and the Almighty concerning

whether he is indeed suitable to serve as the leader of the exodus from Egypt?[3]

2. Why is the list discontinued after detailing the children of Levi, the third of the twelve tribes?
3. Why are only two generations of Reuben and Simeon specified, while three and more are listed for Levi?
4. Why is the description of the descendants of Levi alone (verse 16), in contrast to the other lists, preceded by the introductory phrase: "And these are the names of the sons of Levi"?
5. Why does the length of life appear for some of the family members (Levi in verse 16, Kohath in verse 18, and Amram in verse 20), but not for others?
6. Why are the sons of Hebron not listed, while the sons of the other three sons of Kohath are included?
7. Why is Miriam the sister of Moses not included among the children of Amram in verse 20?

Answering the Seven Questions

The First Question: Why Does the List Appear in the Middle of a Conversation with G-d?

Rabbi Samson Raphael Hirsch (Exod. 6:14-30) relates to this question, and explains that the genealogy was required for two purposes. First, it was important to demonstrate that Moses did not fall from heaven and was not a god, but was a normal person who matured in a natural fashion just like everyone else. It was

---

3. The discussion starts in verse 9, is interrupted by the genealogy in verses 13-28, and continues with verse 29, all in Exodus 6.

therefore important to describe the family tree from his ancestors down to Moses. On the other hand, the opposite fear also existed, namely that one might think that Moses did not have any outstanding qualities, and perhaps anybody could have played his role—speaking with G-d and leading the nation. It was therefore important to record the names of members of a number of the tribes, and also the names of other branches of the extended family, in order to show that Moses was chosen from among all of them because he excelled. He was possessed of superior attributes that made him qualified to lead the nation through the most significant period in its history. It was important to show the Jewish nation that they were being represented by an aristocratic multi-talented individual, and also to warn Pharaoh not to relate disdainfully to Moses and Aaron, because they were Israel's authentic leaders.

Malbim (Exod. 6:14) considers the list to be necessary in order to show the Hebrews themselves, as well as the world at large, that Israel's leadership was chosen and implemented in an intelligent and participatory manner. He notes that sound management is based on three vital elements. First, the leader must be wise. Moses had escaped from Egypt at a young age and worked as a shepherd, and Aaron, as a member of the tribe of Levi, was exempt from hard labor. Both had much free time available to develop their intellect. Second, the leader must not have ulterior motives or seek personal benefits in accepting the position. Their ages and seniority are stressed because older people are not as prone to petty jealousies, greed, deceit, or prevarication. Finally, it is essential that an auditing and advisory committee be established in order to suggest alternative policies before any particular one is implemented, and in order to analyze the results of the chosen initiative post-factum. Malbim proceeds to suggest that Moses was constantly being overseen by many of those mentioned in the genealogy. For example, as is evident from the story of Korah (Numbers 16), Moses had been observed all along by Korah and the descendants of Pallu (also known as Pelet): On, Dathan, and Abiram (Num. 16:1; 26:8-9), who eventually rebelled against him. From the events described in Num. 25:1-15, and especially the Midrashim thereon, it is likely that the tribe of Simeon, as well as the zealot priest Phinehas, had been gadflies for many years, each in his own way, and their names are also mentioned in this portion.

Abarbanel looks upon the dynastic list as a means of honoring Moses and Aaron (Exod. 6:14). He states that just as Scripture honored Abraham by enumerating the previous generations (although his righteousness would have been contrasted with their wickedness; Gen. 11:10-27), so Moses and Aaron are honored by naming their illustrious ancestors—Abraham, Isaac, Jacob, Levi, Kohath, and Amram.

The Second Question: Why Is the List Discontinued after Enumerating the Children of Levi?

Rashi (on Exod. 6:14) explains that the list ends with the genealogy of Levi because the text wishes to focus on the leaders who emanated from that tribe—namely Moses and Aaron. If that is the case, why were the tribes of Reuben and Simeon mentioned at all? Ramban (on Exod. 6:14) explains that the Torah was considerate of the feelings of the members of Reuben, and did not want it to appear as if their tribe was being deprived of its primogeniture. The

Midrash[4] offers the following four reasons why the generations of only Reuben, Simeon, and Levi were listed:

1. These tribes were more particular about the lineage of the women they married, in terms of both family and personality.
2. These tribes did not engage in idolatry at any time during their enslavement in Egypt.
3. These tribes had informally served as the leaders of the other tribes in Egypt.
4. These tribes were worthy, in spite of the fact that their father Jacob reproached them when he parted from his children before his death (Gen. 49:3-7). Perhaps Jacob's tone had been overly harsh, and it was the Bible's intention to stress that he had referred to passing flaws, and in the overall picture, these tribes were no less meritorious than the others.

Kli Yakar is of the opinion that it was not in fact pre-ordained that the leaders were to be chosen from the tribe of Levi. He describes the process as follows:

> He searched Reuben first, to see if there was to be found in that tribe an appropriate person for this mission, just as the prophet Samuel examined the children of Jesse serially [when choosing a king for Israel]… so, here, did He wish to choose from among the children of Reuben and Simeon, but He did not find anyone suitable, until He examined the tribe of Levi and encountered Moses and Aaron, after which it was no longer necessary to search.[5]

---

4. *Num. Rabbah* 13:8. The fourth reason is also quoted by Rashi in Exod. 6:14.
5. Exod. 6:14. Abarbanel on this verse is of the same opinion.

Alshich (Exod. 6:25-26) goes even further in stating that the search actually encompassed all of the tribes. G-d sifted through all possible candidates just as a person sifts through a handful of sand looking for a gem, which of course turned out to be Moses. Once he had been chosen, his placement within the house of Jacob was explicated.

Based on the various commentaries, the following moral values may be derived:

1. consideration for the feelings of others,
2. provision of equal opportunities to all people,
3. rewarding those who are meritorious,
4. compensating those who have been wronged in the past.

The Third Question: Why Are Fewer Generations Specified for Reuben and Simeon than for Levi?

Based on Rashi's approach, since the purpose of the genealogy is to trace the origin of Israel's leaders, clearly it is necessary to list all of the generations until one arrives at Moses and Aaron. Ramban (Exod. 6:14) notes that adding the phrase "according to their generations" for the descendants of Levi exclusively teaches that the members of that tribe alone were virtuous in the third and fourth generations. The only righteous descendants of Reuben and Simeon were the first two generations—those who entered Egypt. Seforno (Exod. 6:14) explains why this was the case. He notes that Levi outlived all of the brothers. He was able to serve as a positive influence on the later generations of his family, an opportunity not available to his brothers. Seforno feels that Scripture means to stress the important role that grandparents and even great-grandparents play in educating future generations.

Rabbenu Bachya (Exod. 6:14) explains why the fifth generation is delineated in the line of Korah, and the sixth in the line of Aaron. He says this section lists the names of six prophets, all from the tribe of Levi: Aaron, Moses, and Phinehas (Elijah, according to the Midrash), and three sons of Korah: Assir, Elkanah, and Abiasaph. These six are among the forty-eight prophets listed in *Seder Olam Rabbah*—the traditional almanac of Jewish historical events. The Torah describes more generations[6] when referring to righteous people, concerning whom there is greater interest.

THE FOURTH QUESTION: WHY IS LEVI'S LIST PREFIXED WITH AN INTRODUCTORY PHRASE?

The *Shlah*[7] explains that Levi was already aware that the Children of Israel would be enslaved, since it had been predicted in the covenant between G-d and Abraham (Gen. 15:13). He was also familiar with Egyptian protocol, and thus realized that his tribe, being clerical in nature, would not be subjugated. Nevertheless, Levi wished to empathize with his brethren by assigning names to his children that reflected their suffering. To highlight this special effort on his part, the list of his descendants is opened with the leading phrase: "And these are the names of the sons of Levi." The *Shlah* supplies the following explanation of the names of the children of Levi:

---

6. The Torah describes more details in general—see the Abarbanel quoted in answering the fifth question.
7. *Derech Chaim Tochachat Musar, Va'era* 19.

Gershon: derived from the Hebrew word *ger*, meaning "stranger," to indicate that they were strangers in a foreign land.

Kohath: derived from the Hebrew *kehut*, meaning "setting on edge," since their teeth were set on edge due to their enslavement.

Merari: derived from the Hebrew *maror*, meaning bitter, reminiscent of the phrase: "And they made their lives bitter with hard service" (Exod. 1:14).

The *Shlah* points out that Levi's behavior demonstrates the importance of sympathizing with the public in their distress, even when one is not personally affected. In a similar fashion, the Almighty tells Moses: "I AM THAT I AM" (Exod. 3:14), which the Talmud interprets as follows:

> The Holy One, blessed be He, said to Moses: Go and say to Israel: I was with you in this servitude, and I shall be with you in the servitude of other kingdoms. He [Moses] said to Him: Lord of the Universe, let us not mention future suffering at this early stage. Thereupon the Holy One, blessed be He, said to him: Go and tell them: **I am** has sent me to you (BT *Berachot* 9b).

The Midrash (*Exod. Rabbah* 3:6) explains that Moses had misunderstood G-d, who had not meant to relate to future persecutions, so as not to cause additional anguish. G-d had rather intended that information to remain privy to Moses, who would discreetly empathize with the Children of Israel based on his knowledge of their future suffering. Levi is thus seen to be acting in a G-dly manner.

Va'era

The Fifth Question: Why Is Longevity Mentioned for Only Some of Those Listed?

Rashi (on Exod. 6:16) answers this question on a one-to-one basis. With regard to Levi, he says:

> Why are Levi's years mentioned? To tell us how long the enslavement lasted. All of the time that one of Jacob's twelve sons was alive, there was no slavery, because it says, "And Joseph and all of his brothers died" (Exod. 1:6), and only afterwards does it say, "And a new king arose over Egypt… and they set over them officers of tribute who afflicted them with their burdens" (Exod. 1:8-11).

Siftei Chachamim, in explaining Rash's comment, notes that Levi was 43 years old when he arrived in Egypt, and died at the age of 137, so he lived in Egypt for 94 years. Since the Hebrews were in Egypt for 210 years, it follows that they were enslaved for a maximum of 116 years (210 less 94).

Similarly, the length of life of Kohath and Amram supply important information concerning the stay of the Hebrews in Egypt, and consequently the meaning of a verse from the Abrahamic covenant. In the words of Rashi:

> From these numbers we may learn that the four hundred years which Scripture gives as the length of the stay of the Children of Israel in Egypt (Gen. 15:13) were not included to imply that they were actually in Egypt for the entire period, but [that four hundred years passed] from the

> birth of Isaac [until they were liberated from Egypt]. [This follows from the fact that] Kohath was one of those who descended to Egypt. Calculate [the sum of] all of his years and the years of Amram and the eighty years of Moses, and you will not find [the sum to be] four hundred years, and many of the years of the sons' lives overlapped the years of their fathers' lives (Rashi on Exod. 6:18).

Alternatively, Targum Yonatan (Exod. 6:18) explains that the length of Kohath's life is mentioned to stress that as a reward for his righteousness, he lived to see Phinehas, the grandson of his own grandson, Aaron the priest. Phinehas is identified with Elijah the prophet, who accompanied the Nation of Israel and watched over them throughout their years of exile.

Abarbanel (Exod. 6:14) claims that G-d specified length of life only for worthy, righteous people, and all of them were in the dynastic branch reaching to Moses, namely Levi, Kohath, and Amram. These men are the heroes of the exodus, and Scripture accentuates this by supplying additional details concerning their lives.

Rashbam proposes a guideline for when Scripture records length of life, which is meant to resolve all such occurrences. In his words (on Exod. 6:16):

> All the years of the generations he counts until Noah, and afterwards from Noah until Abraham, and after Abraham the years of Isaac, and afterwards the years of Jacob, and afterwards the years of Levi his son, and afterwards the years of Kohath, and afterwards the years of Amram, and afterwards the years of Moses, and afterwards Joshua and

the judges and the kings and the Babylonian exile for seventy years and the years of the Second Temple in [the book of] Daniel.

In short, Scripture renders the years of those personages whose length of life enables determination of the historical chronology that appears in *Seder Olam Rabbah*.

ADDITIONAL REASONS FOR INDICATING LENGTH OF LIFE

Without contradicting the explanation of Rashbam, who provides general rules to define when Scripture includes length of life, nor that of Rashi, who explains each case within its own context, it may be suggested that Amram and Kohath represent perfectly righteous people, as Amram was included among the four who died sinless (BT *Shabbat* 55b).

Levi, on the other hand, performed a number of serious sins. Together with Simeon, he was responsible for murdering the inhabitants of Shechem. Commenting on the phrase: "two of the sons of Jacob, Simeon and Levi, Dinah's brothers, each took his sword" (Gen. 34:25), Rashi states: "They were his sons, but nevertheless Simeon and Levi behaved like others who were not his sons, in that they did not seek his counsel."

It was Simeon and Levi who sought to kill Joseph, as Rashi explains:

"And they said to each other… Now let us go and kill him" (Gen. 37:19-20). About whom are we speaking? If you say Reuben or Judah, they did not acquiesce to his being killed. If you say the sons of the handmaids, their hatred [of Joseph] was not complete, as it says: "as a lad he frequented the sons of Bilhah and the sons of Zilpah." Issachar and Zebulun would not have spoken [taken initiative] in the presence of their elder brothers. Perforce, one must say they are Simeon and Levi, whom their father [when blessing them] called "brothers" (Gen. 49:5).

On the other hand, Levi's intentions with regard to Dinah emanated from sincere concern for her predicament. Regarding the words: "the brothers of Dinah" (Gen. 34:25), Rashi comments: "Because they endangered themselves for her [benefit], they are referred to as her brothers [i.e., the fraternal relationship is highlighted]."

In other words, Levi sinned, but he was not evil incarnate, just misdirected. Apparently, he eventually repented in full for his earlier transgressions, and accordingly merited that Moses and Aaron were among his descendants.

Both Levi and Amram lived to the age of 137. Another person who lived to the same age was Ishmael (Gen. 25:17), regarding whom it says: "And Isaac and Ishmael buried him" (Gen. 25:9). Rashi comments on this: "From here it may be inferred that Ishmael repented [of his evil ways] and allowed Isaac to precede him [in the funeral cortege], and this [occurrence] is the 'good old age' which Abraham had been promised [by G-d]."

Perhaps the Torah noted that all of the aforementioned lived to the same age of 137 in order to stress that in the eyes of G-d, one who was a criminal and repented (Ishmael); one who was mediocre and sinned occasionally, sometimes with good intentions, and later sought forgiveness (the tribe of Levi's repentance was manifest at the time of the golden calf, when they did not sin); and one who was pious from birth (Amram)—are all welcomed by the Almighty and acceptable before Him. If G-d allows one to earn his portion in the next world in one moment, surely it is prohibited for a human being, rife with sin, to demand any more of his fellow man.

The Mishnah states with regard to the Passover Haggadah: "It commences with shame and concludes with praise" (BT *Pesachim* 116a).

Why does the Haggadah commence with shame? Perhaps it wishes to elucidate that even after one repents, some aspects of his previous life may be instructive, and even beneficial, during the remainder of his life. This insight leads to a deeper understanding of the teaching of the Sages that the spiritual heights achieved by repentants are higher than those attained by the pious from birth (BT *Berachot* 34b). For example, the period of slavery engrained in Israel a feeling of empathy with the pain of others. By equating Jews of various backgrounds, the Torah wishes to praise those formerly sinful people who bring with them, as newly repentants, the positive elements that they learned and assimilated in their former lives.

THE SIXTH QUESTION: WHY ARE THE SONS OF HEBRON, SON OF KOHATH, NOT LISTED?

Rashbam (Exod. 6:18) explains that the descendants of Levi whose family tree appears in *Va'era* are those who played a role in the continuation of the Pentateuch. The sons of Hebron did not reappear at any stage, and so were not included. *Hadar Zekenim* (Exod. 6:14) adds that for the same reason the sons of Moses and those of Ithamar, son of Aaron, were not mentioned.

The Seventh Question: Why Is Miriam Not Included among the Children of Amram?

Before attempting to answer this question, it would seem that the real question is why it was not dealt with by the classical Biblical exegetes. They did ask why the majority of the tribes were not enumerated, and after responding that the objective of the list was to supply the background of Moses and Aaron, they asked why branches that did not lead to them were included in the family tree, and they then asked why there were different formulations when describing the dynasty, both within the tribes included and between them. At first blush, the most obvious question is: why was the name of Miriam omitted when the children of Amram were presented?

The only commentator that I have found who asks this question is Rabbi Yitzchak ha-Kohen Hoberman (the Zaddik of Raanana), who writes:

> Why was Miriam not mentioned here? Since He wanted to trace Moses and Aaron, He documented the entire tribe of Levi, and in the course of doing so, the tribes of Reuben and Simeon, who have nothing to do with the branch of Moses and Aaron, were included. Certainly Miriam, who was the main reason that Moses and Aaron were even born, as is explained by the Rabbis [should have been included]. If so, why is she not recorded here?[8]

As a first option, one might answer that the Torah is only interested in male offspring. It would not be the first time such a phenomenon

---

8. *Ben le-Oshri Berachah Meshulleshet, Va'era* 6:20.

has been encountered. Also in the portion of *Vayigash* (Gen. 46:8-27), the list of those who descended to Egypt is composed almost entirely of males. Three women are in fact recorded in that portion, but the impression one gets is that they are mentioned not so much for their own merits as for the fact that they were the mother or wife of one of the males on the list. To the extent that the commentators dealt with this subject, it was mainly to justify why the names of even those three women were included.

For example, the Zaddik of Raanana explains that Jochebed's name is mentioned specifically because she is described in verse 20 as the aunt of Amram (the sister of his father, Kohath). According to Torah law (Lev. 18:12, which, of course, was not yet in force), Amram would have been prohibited from marrying her. The Talmud states:

> Why did the kingdom of Saul not endure? Because his background was flawless, as R. Johanan said in the name of R. Simeon b. Jehozadak: One should not appoint somebody as administrator of a community unless he carries a basket of reptiles on his back, so that if he becomes arrogant, one can tell him: Look at your personal history, and you will know who you are [where you came from] (BT *Yoma* 22a).

The Talmud means to say that it is actually important that a leader *should* have a blemish in his family or personal history. On account of such a weakness, he will be extra careful, since he knows that if he slips, the claim that he is an inappropriate choice will be raised and he will be deposed. For that reason, Scripture mentions Jochebed in the genealogy, since she was the "basket of reptiles" in the background of Moses and Aaron, which qualified them to serve in administrative positions.

Alternatively, one may say that the Torah wishes to stress that Moses and Aaron were born of a marriage that would have been forbidden had it taken place after the Torah was given, which would have categorized them, halachically speaking, as bastards. Scripture wishes to demonstrate that in Judaism the determining factors are the personality and behavior of each individual, and not the pedigree. This attitude is formulated by the Mishnah as follows: "A learned bastard takes precedence over an ignorant high priest" (*Horiyot* 3:8).

There exists a difference of opinion between Ramban and *Baal ha-Akedah* (Lev. 18:6) as to whether the limitation of potential sexual partners imposed by Mosaic law should be considered an ethical law, whose justification is accepted by all morally upright people independent of religion, or whether it should be looked upon as a statute to be obeyed merely because it is G-d-given, without a rational explanation. Clearly, some forbidden relationships have a moral basis, such as adultery. Others are Divine decrees, whose rationales are not obvious, such as the prohibition to marry an aunt (since the symmetrical relationship between an uncle and niece is permitted). The dispute between the commentators is with respect to marriage between parents and children, or siblings. The Torah possibly mentions that Amram married his aunt in order to emphasize that he did not commit a moral sin, just as Jacob did not commit an ethical violation by marrying two sisters.

Moving on to Elisheba, wife of Aaron, Rabbenu Bachya (Exod. 6:23) says that she is mentioned because she was the sister of Nahshon, from the tribe of Judah, which was destined to assume royalty. Scripture wishes to indicate that the offspring of Amminadab were blessed with the crown of royalty through Nahshon, as well as the crown of priesthood through Elisheba's marriage to Aaron, i.e., there existed a familial relationship between the progenitors of spiritual and temporal guidance in Israel. Similarly, the mother of Phinehas, one of the daughters of Putiel, is mentioned in verse 25, since Phinehas earned the priesthood on his own merit, and so was treated in many ways like a king, and it is the wont of Scripture to record the names of the mothers of the kings of Israel.

The following quotation from the Talmud cites another reason for including the name of Elisheba:

> And Aaron took Elisheba, the daughter of Amminadab, the sister of Nahshon; since it says the daughter of Amminadab, is it not obvious that she is the sister of Nahshon? Then why does it tell us that she is the sister of Nahshon? From here, it may be inferred that he who takes a wife should inquire about the character of her brothers (BT *Bava Batra* 110a).

In other words, Elisheba is mentioned in order to show that Aaron had an exceptional wife, since he married a woman whose brother, Nahshon, was a man of great faith in the Almighty. He was the first person to jump into the Red Sea, a leap which served as the catalyst for the splitting of its waters (*Mechilta Shemot* 14:22), and he ultimately became the leader and prince of the tribe of Judah (Num. 1:7, 7:12). Nahshon evolved into a symbol of patriotism, daring, and belief in G-d throughout the generations. It is no wonder that all four children of Aaron and Elisheba (according to many commentators) were honorable and virtuous.

Additional reasons have been presented to explain (or justify) the inclusion of each of the three women (Jochebed, Elisheba, and a daughter of Putiel) in the genealogical list. Alshich (Exod. 6:16) says that all three were included for the same reason, namely to rationalize why the children of Moses did not turn out well. The point being made is that the children of Amram, Aaron, and Elazar were all righteous because their mothers were equally righteous. This was not true in the case of Moses' wife Zipporah, who was after all the daughter of an unreformed idol-worshipper and had adopted her father's ways (in accordance with the view of Targum Yonatan[9]).

According to both Rabbenu Bachya and Alshich, women were included in the genealogy in order to reflect on their male descendants. Miriam's name was not mentioned, because including it would not have provided additional insights.

According to the previously cited view of the Zaddik of Raanana, the fact that Jochebed was the aunt of Amram was considered a defect. Counterintuitively, an imperfection in a leader is not considered to be a flaw, but a requirement for leadership that prevents him from assuming dictatorial powers, and enables the public to exercise some degree of control over his reign. Based on this logic, since Miriam was not slated to occupy an administrative post, there was no need to embarrass her by publicizing her questionable pedigree, and that is why her name is not mentioned.

The question that arises is that there exist sources in the Bible, as well as in the Talmud, which indicate that Miriam did in fact assume a position of leadership. In the portion of *Beshallach* (Exod. 15:20-21), Miriam is presented as directing the women in song and dance. Her functioning as a leader is referenced explicitly in the book of Micah, where G-d is quoted as saying: "For I brought you up out of the land of Egypt, and redeemed you

---

9. Exod. 4:24. *Mechilta Yitro* 2 brings a Tannaitic difference of opinion with respect to whether Jethro converted or remained an idolater.

from the house of bondage, and I sent before you Moses, Aaron, and Miriam" (Micah 6:4).

In addition, the Talmud refers to Miriam as one of the three great leaders of the nation in the following dictum:

> Three good leaders arose among the Israelites, namely: Moses, Aaron, and Miriam, and three gifts were conferred [upon Israel] by them: the well [associated with Miriam], the pillar of cloud [associated with Aaron], and the manna [associated with Moses] (BT *Taanit* 9a).

It is therefore reasonable to answer that Miriam became a leader of women, and perhaps of men as well, based on the verse: "And Miriam called out to them [*lahem* in Hebrew, a masculine pronoun, indicating that she called out to both men and women]: Sing to the Lord for He is highly exalted" (Exod. 15:21).

In the past, dialogue with Pharaoh had indicated that he was not inclined to respect his subjects, especially those who were enslaved by him, nor would he relate to the women among them in a gracious, or even dignified, manner. In dealing with Pharaoh, a stern countenance was demanded in order to convey the threat that non-compliance with the request to release the Children of Israel would be met by the imposition of devastating plagues by the G-d of Israel. For such a task, a male, authoritarian figure would be appropriate, while Miriam's leadership qualities would eventually be utilized internally shortly after the crossing of the Red Sea.

It is thus suggested that the intention of the Zaddik of Raanana is not to deny Miriam's leadership qualities, but to point out that her potential in that sphere would not be utilized in the upcoming confrontation with Pharaoh.

Summary

It has been shown that a relatively mundane genealogical list can be the source of interesting moral and ethical insights. A number of the lessons derived from the family tree presented at the beginning of the portion of *Va'era* are listed below:

- Rabbi S.R. Hirsch: Leaders should not be made into gods, but should be highly talented individuals.
- Malbim: Leaders should not be prone to petty jealousies, greed, deceit, or prevarication. Auditing committees should be established in order to suggest alternative policies and to analyze the results of the chosen policies post-factum.
- Ramban: When selecting a leader, one should be considerate of the feelings of those not chosen.
- Alshich: When filling important positions, give all candidates equal opportunities, i.e., do not discriminate on the basis of pedigree (in more general contexts, on the basis of race or religion).
- Seforno: Grandparents and great-grandparents play an important role in educating their offspring.
- *Shlah*: It is imperative to empathize with people who are suffering from physical or mental stress.
- Talmud: He who takes a wife should inquire about the character of her brothers.
- Alshich: A mother's role in turning her children into righteous adults cannot be underestimated.
- Talmud: A leader who has a stain in his background is to be preferred over one who is flawless.
- Author's observation: In the eyes of G-d, a hardened

criminal who repents (Ishmael), an occasional sinner who seeks forgiveness (Simeon), and one who is pious from birth (Amram) are all blessed. Human beings should not demand any more of their fellow man. Also, in Judaism, the determining factors are the personality and behavior of each individual, and not the pedigree.

Bo

In the portion of *Bo*, the Torah proceeds with the story of the exodus from Egypt. After recounting in the previous portion the first seven plagues with which the Egyptians were stricken, the last three are now described. At this point, Pharaoh and his servants are beginning to get the message, and the possibility exists that they will be willing to renounce the servitude of the Hebrews and be rid of them, rather than continue to struggle against G-d. But the G-d of the Hebrews surprisingly intervenes in a manner which seems to conflict with the aspirations of the Children of Israel—who just want to be liberated from slavery—a manner which leads to a prolongation of suffering on the part of the Hebrews. In this vein, the opening verse of the portion of *Bo* states: "And the Lord said to Moses: Come to Pharaoh, for I have hardened his heart, and the heart of his servants, that I might show My signs in his midst" (Exod. 10:1).

Is this behavior on the part of the Almighty surprising? Not really. Already, when Moses was about to return to Egypt from Midian, before he had even appeared before Pharaoh, G-d informed Moses that He would give him the ability to perform miracles, but Pharaoh will not be subdued because G-d will harden his heart, as the verse says: "When you go back into Egypt, see that you perform before Pharaoh all the wonders which I have placed [Rashi: wonders which in the future I will place] in your hand; but I will harden his heart, and he will not let the people go" (Exod. 4:21).

One might be tempted to look at this pronouncement as a one-time occurrence that can perhaps be interpreted differently. However, G-d reiterates this idea after Moses returns to Egypt and immediately before he and Aaron confront Pharaoh, using the following nearly identical language: "And I will harden Pharaoh's heart, and multiply My signs and My wonders in the land of Egypt" (Exod. 7:3).

The Midrash[10] notes that with respect to the first five plagues, the Bible does not mention any involvement in Pharaoh's decision-making on the part of G-d, but does record such behavior regarding three of the last five plagues (the sixth, eighth, and ninth), as well as prior to Pharaoh's pursuit of the Israelites. The relevant verses are enumerated below:

1. After the first plague, blood: "And Pharaoh's heart was hardened, and he did not listen to them, just as the Lord had spoken" (Exod. 7:22).
2. After the second plague, frogs: "But when Pharaoh saw that there was respite, he hardened his heart, and he did not listen to them, just as the Lord had spoken" (Exod. 8:11).
3. After the third plague, lice: "Then the magicians said unto Pharaoh: 'This is the finger of G-d'; and Pharaoh's heart was hardened, and he did not listen to them, just as the Lord had spoken" (Exod. 8:15).
4. After the fourth plague, a mixture of noxious creatures (lions, bears, wolves, and leopards according to Ibn Ezra; wild beasts, snakes, and scorpions according to Rashi; or wolves

---

10. *Tanchuma Va'era* 3.

who attack their prey at night, according to Rashbam): "And Pharaoh hardened his heart this time as well, and he did not let the people go" (Exod. 8:28).

5. After the fifth plague, pestilence: "But the heart of Pharaoh was hard, and he did not let the people go" (Exod. 9:7).

The verses from this point on (with the exception of those following the seventh plague) describe G-d as the cause of Pharaoh's heart being hardened:

6. After the sixth plague, boils: "And the magicians could not stand before Moses because of the boils; for the boils were upon the magicians, and upon all the Egyptians. And the Lord hardened the heart of Pharaoh, and he did not listen to them, as the Lord had spoken to Moses" (Exod. 9:11-12).
7. After the seventh plague, hail: "And when Pharaoh saw that the rain and the hail and the thunders had stopped, he continued to sin, and he and his servants' hearts were hardened. And the heart of Pharaoh was hardened, and he did not let the Children of Israel go, as the Lord had spoken by means of Moses" (Exod. 9:34-35).
8. After the eighth plague, locusts: "But the Lord hardened Pharaoh's heart, and he did not let the Children of Israel go" (Exod. 10:20).
9. After the ninth plague, darkness: "But the Lord hardened Pharaoh's heart, and he would not let them go" (Exod. 10:27).
10. Preceding the pursuit of the Children of Israel: "And the Lord hardened the heart of Pharaoh, king of Egypt, and he pursued after the Children of Israel" (Exod. 14:8).

But even if G-d's behavior is no surprise, and Israel was forewarned that G-d might act that way, that does not mean it is justified. Apparently, the first person to explicitly question this behavior was Ibn Ezra, who asks: "If G-d hardened his heart, what was his crime and what was his sin" (Exod. 7:3).

Was Pharaoh Deserving of Punishment?

Pharaoh was deserving of punishment because he enslaved the Children of Israel, and because he overworked them mercilessly (Exod. 1:13). The following points should be noted:

1. Innate in every person is a basic sense of right and wrong, good and evil. The fact that G-d created man with an intrinsic sense of morality is deduced from the following verse: "Behold, this only have I found, that G-d made man upright, but they have sought out much circumvention [ways to be devious]" (Eccl. 7:29). Rabbi Kook amplified this verse when he described "the natural morality which is implanted in the ingenuous nature of man" (*Orot ha-Kodesh* 3, p. 27). Rabbi Kook possibly based himself on the words of Ibn Ezra, who referred to those laws "which are implanted by the Lord in the hearts of all thinking men" (on Exod. 20:1).
2. Pharaoh transgressed several of the Noahide laws listed in the Talmud, namely incest, murder, and theft, and he certainly should have set up a court system based on a legal code that would have prohibited inhumane slavery. The punishment for a Gentile who disobeys these Noahide laws is the death penalty (BT *Sanhedrin* 56a), which Pharaoh thus deserved.

3. Rabbi Moshe Botchko has explained that not only is one prohibited to sin, but he must also refine his personality to the point that he does not have the urge to sin, since otherwise it would be difficult to restrain oneself. He applies this approach to Gentiles as well, who are required to fulfill the seven Noahide laws. The following elucidation appears in his book, *Hegyonei Moshe* (pp. 94-96):

> We must consider another command: "You should not hate your brother in your heart" (Lev. 19:17). The Midrash notes: "You should not hate your brother: Perhaps this means that you should not curse him, beat him, or slap him. However, the verse says: 'In your heart,' I am referring only to hatred in your heart." It is possible that here lies the answer to our question. For had the Torah only prohibited beating, cursing, and killing, the defendant could excuse himself and explain that I was stimulated to do it by the overpowering force of my hatred, and not by my own free will. But take note at this point that the Torah addresses each person and commands him while still at an early stage—at the emergence of the initial element that could degenerate into a terrible sin. Already at this time, one is commanded to refrain from the first cause—from hatred—before things devolve into a situation where he is, in reality, deprived of his freedom of choice. Even if the Lord had not hardened his heart—and even if he had finally released the Children of Israel as a result of the plagues which struck him—he was deserving of punishment for his wish to act maliciously, for it is evil intention which is at the heart of sin, and the continued degeneration to sin (or abstention from sinning) is no longer subject to his control.

According to Rabbi Botchko, basic morality, which is meant to be intuitive, forbade Pharaoh not only from physically harming the Hebrews, but also from maintaining hostile feelings toward them in his heart—those that eventually led him to enslave, persecute, and torture them.

Was Pharaoh Deprived of His Freedom of Choice?

There are three possible answers to this question:

1. Pharaoh was deprived of his freedom of choice (Rambam).
2. Pharaoh was not deprived of his freedom of choice (Ibn Ezra and *Baal ha-Akedah*).
3. There was a degree of Divine intervention in Pharaoh's personality, not for the purpose of minimizing his freedom of choice, but to strengthen it, or at least to leave it unscathed (Ramban, Saadiah Gaon, Rashi, Yosef Albo, and Seforno).

Rambam: Pharaoh's Freedom of Choice Was Annulled

After explaining that every human being is granted freedom of choice, seemingly inclusive of Pharaoh, King of Egypt, Rambam takes it upon himself, in *Hilchot Teshuvah* (6:1), to explain why, in spite of that principle, Pharaoh was divested of that option. Rambam initiates his treatment by making two points:

1. The Bible describes a number of situations in which G-d's behavior negates the concept of freedom of choice.
2. Sometimes a person is punished for his sins in this world, sometimes in the next, and sometimes in both worlds.

Rambam explains that by repenting (doing *teshuvah*), a person can atone for his sins and be absolved of the designated punishment (*Hilchot Teshuvah* 6:2). Since, in that chapter, Rambam speaks of the freedom of choice with which both Jews and Gentiles have been endowed, it follows that he believes that Gentiles, as well as Jews, can achieve relief from punishment as a result of repentance.

Rambam proceeds to outline his understanding of G-d's actions (*Hilchot Teshuvah* 6:3), which may be summarized as follows:

1. G-d does not necessarily inflict punishment immediately after a person sins. The reason is obvious. If a person were punished at once, his freedom of choice would actually be diminished, for who would sin in such circumstances? Even a mouse recoils from the fear of an electric shock.
2. It is possible for sins to accumulate to the point that the prerogative to repent is denied, and this describes perfectly the situation in which Pharaoh found himself.
3. Rambam asks why G-d sent Moses to urge Pharaoh to repent if He had no intention of allowing him to do so. He answers that G-d did so to inform the Hebrews that sometimes a sin (or an accumulation of sins) is so great that the option of repentance is withdrawn. This may have been one of the principles that G-d wished to convey to future generations when He said: "and that you may tell in the ears of your son, and of your son's son, what I have wrought upon Egypt, and My signs which I have done among them" (Exod. 10:2).

Bo

Baal ha-Akedah's Critique

Baal ha-Akedah does not accept the view of Rambam, since he believes that as long as there is life, there is hope that the wicked will repent from their evil ways. He bases his opinion on Ezek. 18:32, which states that G-d does not desire the death of villains, but that they repent. *Baal ha-Akedah* cites two examples. With regard to King Ahab, who was considered to be the most evil king until his time, it is written, "and Ahab did more to anger the Lord, the G-d of Israel, than all the kings of Israel that preceded him" (1 Kings 16:33).

However, after being chastised by Elijah the prophet for executing Naboth the Jezreelite (on the basis of the false witnesses arranged by Jezebel, 1 Kings 21:10), Ahab attempted to mend his ways, as the Bible states: "And when Ahab heard those words, he tore his clothes, and put sackcloth on his flesh, and he fasted and lay in sackcloth, and walked slowly [as a sign of grief and repentance]" (1 Kings 21:27).

The Lord in fact accepted his repentance, as subsequently stated: "Have you seen that Ahab has humbled himself before Me? Because he humbled himself before Me, I will not bring the evil in his days. In the days of his son I will bring the evil upon his house" (1 Kings 21:29).

The second example is of King Manasseh, who was considered to be the greatest villain not only among the kings of Israel, but among the kings of all of the nations, as is written in Chronicles: "And Manasseh made Judah and the inhabitants of Jerusalem sin, so that they did more evil than the [other] nations, whom the Lord destroyed for [the sake of] the Children of Israel" (2 Chron. 33:9).

Among his sins were the rebuilding of the idolatrous sites which his father, the righteous King Hezekiah, had destroyed; setting up Asherot, altars, and statues for idol-worship inside the holy Temple and its courtyard; passing his sons through fire in the Valley of the Son of Hinnom; and indulging in soothsaying, witchcraft, sorcery, enchantments, and divination (2 Chron. 33:3-7). The Talmud further claims that he killed the prophet Isaiah (BT *Yevamot* 49b).

The Talmud relates the following with regard to King Hezekiah:

> The yoke of Sennacherib shall be destroyed on account of the oil of Hezekiah, which burned in the synagogues and schools. What did he do? He planted a sword by the door of the schoolhouse and proclaimed, "He who will not study the Torah will be pierced with the sword." Search was made from Dan unto Beer Sheba, and no ignoramus was found from Gabbath to Antipris, and no boy or girl, man or woman was found who was not thoroughly versed in the [complicated] laws of cleanliness and uncleanliness (BT *Sanhedrin* 94b).

The Midrash (*Sifrei Va-Etchanan* 32) notes that the educational effort expended by Hezekiah, which reached every man, woman, and child in *Eretz Yisrael* must have certainly been directed at Manasseh, his son, as well. However, all of his father's toil proved to be of no avail until the Lord brought upon him tribulations, at which point he repented, as indicated in the following verses:

> And the Lord spoke to Manasseh and to his people, but they gave no heed. Whereupon the Lord brought upon them the captains of the host of the king of Assyria, who took Manasseh with hooks, and bound him with fetters,

Bo

and carried him to Babylon. And when he was in distress, he sought the Lord his G-d, and humbled himself greatly before the G-d of his fathers. And he prayed to Him; and He acquiesced to him, and heard his supplication, and brought him back to Jerusalem into his kingdom. Then Manasseh knew that the Lord was G-d (2 Chron. 33:10-13).

Baal ha-Akedah emphasizes that if the Almighty accepted the repentance of the most wicked kings, whom Scripture describes as being worse than the foreign kings destroyed for the sake of Israel (including Pharaoh), He certainly would have allowed Pharaoh himself to repent.

Baal ha-Akedah quotes Rambam, who says, after listing twenty-four sins whose transgression excludes their perpetrator from the world to come:

> When was it stated that each of the enumerated has no portion in the world to come? When he died without repenting. But if he repented from his wickedness, and he died as a penitent—then he has a portion in the world to come, for there is no sin that is immune to repentance. Even one who denied the existence of G-d, and repented at his very end, has a portion in the world to come, as it is written: "Peace, peace, to him that is far off and to him that is near, says the Lord, and I will heal him" (Isa. 57:19). All of the villains, evildoers, apostates, and the like, who repent—whether they do so openly or covertly—are accepted, as it says: "Return, you backsliding children" (Jer. 2:14, 3:22). Even if he is still backsliding—for he has repented clandestinely and not in the open—his repentance is accepted (*Hilchot Teshuvah* 3:14).

Baal ha-Akedah continues by stressing that if Jehoiakim, Ahab, Manasseh, and the like did not reach the stage where the gates of repentance were shut, what sin is greater than theirs, and which sinner is so evil that he deserves that the gates of repentance be shuttered before him? He concludes that it is not the Lord's manner to tell the wicked person to increase his wickedness, even if at that point he is in the midst of his rebelliousness. On the contrary, if after all of his impure behavior he has come to purify himself with humility and tears, who would seal the gates of tears and repentance which the Almighty does not close for anyone, and that is His greatest glory.

Perhaps one will ask why the Mishnah (BT *Sanhedrin* 90a) states that three kings do not have a portion in the world to come: Jeroboam, Ahab, and Manasseh. The answer is that in the view of *Baal ha-Akedah*, even though the latter two repented (and were allowed to do so), their repentance was not complete. Since they repented out of fear alone, their penance was not entirely effective (*Tiferet Yisrael* on the Mishnah). According to R. Judah, who disagrees with the first view expressed in the Mishnah, Manasseh was in fact not deprived of his portion in the world to come. The Talmud quotes R. Jochanan, who supports R. Judah, and says: "He who asserts that Manasseh has no portion in the world to come weakens the hands of penitent sinners" (BT *Sanhedrin* 103a).

In short, the difference of opinion between the initial view of the Mishnah and R. Judah is not whether a wicked person can repent. Rather, the question is whether Manasseh's repentance was sufficiently sincere. R. Judah does not argue with respect to Jeroboam because Scripture does not record that he attempted to repent, nor does he differ concerning Ahab, who did repent, and his repentance helped partially, but was insufficient to re-instate his portion in the world to come. However, Manasseh's deep and heart-felt repentance did suffice, but only according to R. Judah, and not according to the first opinion in the Mishnah.

In Defense of Rambam

1. The *Baal ha-Akedah* claimed that everyone has the potential to repent. That is not precise. One can repent only in this world. The Midrash (*Eccl. Rabbah* 1:15) describes two evildoers who were quite friendly in this world. One of them hastened to repent before his demise, and the second did not. In the world to come, he who had repented merited standing next to a group of righteous people, while he who had not was placed next to a group of sinners.
2. As previously noted, Pharaoh had transgressed Noahide commandments which are capital crimes.
3. Everyone is deprived of the opportunity to repent once he dies. What Rambam is saying is that the sins of Pharaoh were so severe that, under normal circumstances, G-d would have punished him with death, and he is thus treated as if he were not among the living. G-d exercises his right to "unjustly" terminate people's earthly existence when doing so is necessary, in His judgment, for the continued, positive functioning of earthly civilization. Certainly, He is also entitled to deprive one of his ability to repent if there is a valid reason to do so, and to settle accounts at a later stage.
4. In short, Rambam is positing three states of existence: routine life, during which time each person (even the most wicked, such as King Manasseh) is given freedom of choice and the right to repent for his transgressions; death, at which point one's fate is sealed with no option to make amends; and clinical death with respect to repentance (such as Pharaoh

experienced), during which the physical functioning of the body remains intact.

5. G-d prefers, and human beings are obligated, to act in accordance with the purest form of justice. However, sometimes the system needs to be tweaked, and it is necessary to deviate from the well-trodden path. Sometimes that involves depriving innocent people of their lives or of certain options (e.g., the option to repent) which are generally available to all living human beings. Independent of which course of action G-d chooses, the final account will be properly adjusted in the world to come.

Why Was Pharaoh Allowed to Remain Alive if He Deserved to Die?

Two answers may be offered to this question:

1. The Torah answers this question quite clearly in the first verses of this portion: "so that I might show these signs of Mine in their midst and so that you may say into the ears of your son, and your son's son, what I have wrought upon Egypt, and My signs [plagues] which I have brought upon them; so that you may know that I am the Lord" (Exod. 10:1-2). In other words, there emerged an opportunity to sanctify G-d's name, but in order to take effect, it was necessary for Pharaoh to remain alive.
2. Rambam points out that there is an apparent contradiction in the Scriptures (*Hilchot Teshuvah* 6:3). On the one hand, Moses tells Pharaoh at G-d's behest: "Let My people go, that they may serve Me" (Exod. 9:13). On the other hand, G-d had

told Pharaoh explicitly that he (Pharaoh) would not free the Jews, when He said: "But as for you and your servants, I know that you will not yet fear the Lord G-d" (Exod. 9:30). Rambam explains that G-d intentionally requested that Pharaoh release the Hebrews, in spite of having deprived him of freedom of choice, in order to show that such an action is also in the realm of G-d's power. G-d even revealed his strategy to Pharaoh himself when He said: "Indeed, for this very reason have I allowed you to stand, to show you My power, and that My name may be declared throughout the earth" (Exod. 9:16).

Based on this logic, Pharaoh should have made a point of releasing the Hebrews in order to disprove G-d's prediction, but he was simply unable to do so. This inability alone was a manifestation of G-d's glory and a stimulus to the spread of His reputation throughout the world. Rabbi Shmuel Tanchum Rubinstein[11] has compared G-d's suppression of Pharaoh's free will to His punishment of causing paralysis of body parts, as in the case of Jeroboam, whose hand had shriveled (1 Kings 13:4), and the inhabitants of Sodom, who lost their eyesight (Gen. 19:10).

IBN EZRA: PHARAOH'S FREEDOM OF CHOICE WAS UNAFFECTED

There exists a view diametrically opposed to that of Rambam, according to which Pharaoh's freedom of choice was preserved in its totality, and G-d did not intervene at all. This is the view of Ibn Ezra, who appends it to the verse: "Oh that their heart would lead

---

11. Footnote in Mosad ha-Rav Kook edition of *Hilchot Teshuvah* 6:3.

them to fear Me and keep all My commandments, that it might be well with them and with their children forever" (Deut. 5:25).

Ibn Ezra points out that the verse says "their heart," and not "My heart," because every person is endowed with freedom of choice, so that in the end his actions are the result of his own decisions. But ultimately, all of a person's capabilities stem from the Almighty, so it is quite reasonable to occasionally attribute one's actions to G-d. That is why, in a number of places, G-d is described as having hardened Pharaoh's heart,[12] but this description in no sense means to relate these actions directly to G-d any more than any other human activities and abilities.

A Question on Ibn Ezra

One may still ask the following question: Even if it is assumed that Pharaoh's behavior at the time of the ten plagues was no more controlled by G-d than his actions on any other occasion (in accordance with Ibn Ezra's view), why does the Bible at this juncture quote G-d as saying: "And I will harden Pharaoh's heart" (Exod. 7:3)? Two answers have been suggested:

1. The text wishes to emphasize the idea that the more one habituates oneself to sin, the easier it becomes to continue doing so, as the Sages say: "One good deed brings about another in its wake, and one sin brings about another sin" (*Ethics of the Fathers* 4:2). In the Talmud, it is taught that: "One is assisted in following the road which he wishes to pursue" (BT *Makkot* 10b), i.e., it becomes easier to proceed in the chosen direction, the further one treads along the given path.

---

12. Exod. 9:12; 9:34-35; 10:20; 10:27.

R. Huna summarized the situation as follows: "Once a man does wrong and repeats it, it becomes permitted for him. It becomes permitted for him? Can you really think so? Rather it becomes for him as something which is permitted" (BT *Kiddushin* 40a).

According to Ibn Ezra, the reason G-d's role is being emphasized in the second set of five plagues is to stress the G-d-made rule of nature, that the more one habituates himself to acting in an evil manner, the harder it is to break the pattern.

2. Shadal (Samuel David Luzzatto, on Exod. 7:3) suggests that G-d's name is mentioned when people act in bizarre and unexpected ways. In such cases, Scripture wishes to remind the reader that G-d has given man freedom of choice, and so he has the potential to act as he pleases. For this reason, G-d, as the ultimate source of all actions, is mentioned with regard to the ten plagues, where Pharaoh's stubbornness is incomprehensible. Shadal quotes two other instances of strange behavior, in reference to which G-d's name is also recorded.

First, at one of the last assemblies of the nation convened by Moses, he states: "and the Lord did not give you a heart to know, and eyes to see, and ears to hear, until this very day" (Deut. 29:3). Moses is referring to man's innate senses of vision and hearing, which does not at all imply unnatural intervention on the part of the Almighty. Yet G-d's name is mentioned because Moses is delineating the extraordinary fact that although G-d had constantly displayed wonderful acts in order to spiritually elevate the Israelites, only towards the end of their forty-year sojourn did these miraculous events make a lasting impression and strengthen their belief in G-d.

Second, Shadal quotes the following verse regarding David's reaction to the curses of Shimei, the son of Gera, when David escaped to Transjordan during Absalom's rebellion: "And the king said: 'What do I have in common with you, sons of Zeruiah? So let him curse, because the Lord has said to him: Curse David; who then shall say: Why have you done so?'" (2 Sam. 16:10). Clearly, G-d never ordered Shimei to curse the king, and His name is mentioned only because Shimei was acting so strangely. The meaning of David's message is: Let the case rest, for G-d has endowed everyone with the freedom to act as he wishes.

COMMENTATORS WHO AFFIRM DIVINE INTERVENTION WITHOUT NEGATING FREEDOM OF CHOICE

A number of Biblical commentators (R. Saadiah Gaon, followed by Rashi, Ramban, R. Yosef Albo, Abarbanel, and Seforno) propose a middle path between Rambam's claim that G-d had cancelled Pharaoh's freedom of choice and Ibn Ezra's claim that there was absolutely no form of Divine intervention. These commentators all agree with Ibn Ezra and *Baal ha-Akedah* that G-d never curtails the freedom of choice of a living human being. Yet they believe that in the present situation G-d intervened, with each commentator defining the essence and extent of the intervention.

SAADIAH GAON

R. Saadiah says that the requisite punishment for Pharaoh's sins was all ten plagues. Had Pharaoh expired as a result of the earlier plagues, he would not have experienced in its entirety the punishment that he deserved (*Emunot ve-De'ot* 4:6). Therefore,

G-d strengthened Pharaoh physically so that he was able to survive the first plagues, and still be alive to suffer the effects of the later plagues. The hardening of Pharaoh's heart did not reduce the pain, nor did it prevent him from repenting. It merely allowed him to remain alive so that he would be able to absorb the next plague, much like a downed boxer who is allowed to continue fighting as long as he is able to stand up by the count of ten.

Baal ha-Akedah[13] agrees with Saadiah Gaon. He explains that in this case, three principles are involved. First, a person may simultaneously transgress a number of sins, and he must be punished for all of them. Second, once the punishment has been decreed, it should not be waived; otherwise, anyone who was convicted could publicly admit his guilt, and the court would have to cancel his punishment. Third, in order for someone to be capable of absorbing the entire punishment, it may be necessary to administer it gradually. On the basis of these three principles, Pharaoh was kept alive until he had received his punishment in full.

Rashi

On the words "And I will harden Pharaoh's heart" (Exod. 7:3), Rashi comments: "Since he has wickedly resisted Me, and it is clear to Me that the heathen nations find no satisfaction in wholeheartedly repenting."

Shadal points out the import of the phrase used by Rashi, "it is clear to Me." Shadal understands Rashi to be saying that G-d would not have deprived Pharaoh of his opportunity to repent. However, since G-d, who knows the future, realized that Pharaoh would not utilize that opportunity sincerely, He took advantage of the situation and used it to bring miraculous plagues, which He knew would make a strong impression on the Children of Israel.

13. *Akedat Yitzchak*, ch. 36.

One may ask concerning Rashi's viewpoint, even if G-d realized that Pharaoh would not reach the level of true repentance, what difference did it make? The main goal was for Israel to be released from the clutches of Pharaoh, and that is what would happen when Pharaoh surrendered as a result of the plagues, even if his submission was not due to the purest motives. Apparently, Rashi himself was aware of this question, and so he added: "It is better that his heart should be hardened, so that I can increase My signs against him and, as a result, you may recognize My strength."

Rashi explains that the pathological stubbornness that G-d implanted in Pharaoh served a positive purpose for the Hebrews, namely to acquaint them with the concept of reward and punishment. *Siftei Chachamim*, in commenting on Rashi, explains that the hardening of Pharaoh's heart was also necessary in order to prevent the Egyptians from being misled. Had G-d not hardened Pharaoh's heart, it would have appeared to the outside world as if Pharaoh had repented, even though his repentance was not whole-hearted. But, as previously indicated, G-d is averse to accepting insincere repentance, and He would thus have continued afflicting Pharaoh. In the eyes of the non-Jews, Pharaoh would have seemingly repented, but would still be suffering; their conclusion would be that the Israelite G-d is an unjust judge, who is cruel and has no pity on His own creations. In order for the world to understand G-d's true nature, it was necessary for them to see that Pharaoh continued to resist G-d's offer.

According to Rashi, freedom of choice was not abrogated, as Seforno states explicitly:

> Had Pharaoh wished to submit to G-d, and return to Him with his whole heart, no preventative measures would have been taken. However, because G-d sees the future,

and He knew that Pharaoh would not fully repent, even though in principle he would have been able to do so, G-d withheld the option from him this time, for the reasons enumerated (on Exod. 7:3).

In summary, a cursory look at Rashi gives the impression that he agrees with Rambam, because he says that the option of repentance was withdrawn from Pharaoh. However, a more thorough investigation indicates that the abrogation was a result of G-d's foreknowledge that Pharaoh would not repent sincerely, and not because it would have been impossible for him to do so had he truly wished to.

Ramban

Ramban brings two answers to the question about G-d hardening Pharaoh's heart. The first is the view of Rambam that his sins were so great that he had lost his chance to repent. His second explanation is as follows:

> Half of the plagues came upon him because of his transgression, for in connection with them it only says: "And Pharaoh's heart was hardened" (Exod. 7:13; 7:22; 8:15); "and Pharaoh hardened his heart" (Exod. 8:28; 9:75). Thus, Pharaoh refused to let the Children of Israel go and honor G-d's request. But when the plagues became too much for him to bear and it was difficult for him to endure them, his heart softened. And he then considered sending them because of the intensity of the plagues, not because he desired to fulfill the wishes of his Creator. At that point, G-d hardened his spirit and made his heart obstinate, so

that His name would be publicized throughout the world (on Exod. 7:3).

According to this view, G-d's intervention was not for the purpose of making it more difficult (or even impossible) for Pharaoh to repent, but to ensure that his repentance, if it did occur, would be based on genuine belief in G-d and not on fear of the pain of the next plague. Ramban says that Pharaoh would have indeed released the Children of Israel had G-d not hardened his heart. But even after G-d hardened his heart, i.e., endowed him with more stamina (so that he could withstand the last five plagues, just as he withstood the first five), Pharaoh could have acquiesced to G-d's request. Had he done so, it would have been considered valid repentance, since this option was still available to him. At this point, Ramban asks himself: "Nevertheless, why harden his heart? Let him free the Israelites already." And to this question, he gives the same answer that Rambam and Rashi had given previously: so that G-d's name would be publicized throughout the world.

Both Ramban and Rashi make it clear that Pharaoh did not reach the required level of repentance. The difference between them is that Rashi says that G-d knew in advance that he wouldn't achieve the necessary level, and hardening his heart indicated the cancellation of his potential to get anywhere near what was needed. Ramban, on the other hand, considered the hardening of the heart to be a prerequisite to ensuring that if he chose to repent, it would be meaningful.

A slight variation to the second approach of Ramban would be to look at the hardening of Pharaoh's heart as a means of returning Pharaoh to the *a priori* situation common to all of humankind. Normally, when a person sins, G-d does not punish him on the spot, i.e., he does not get instant feedback. If he chooses to repent, it occurs after undergoing a prolonged intellectual struggle. Were G-d to punish him immediately, it would be obvious to him that he must repent. Only a fool would refuse, and by doing so prolong his suffering.

Now consider the situation in which Pharaoh found himself. In reaction to every sin that he performed, he was promptly rebuked. Such feedback provided him with an unfair advantage compared to other human beings. The purpose of hardening his heart was not to negate his ability to repent, but to place before him the same challenges and doubts that are encountered by others. G-d does not accept insincere repentance from anyone, just that in the case of Pharaoh it would have been much easier to superficially simulate real repentance, had G-d not instituted the required adjustment.

Summary

Freedom of choice is one of the foundations of the Jewish religion, and is the basis for one of its three fundamental principles, namely reward and punishment. The topic discussed was whether there are cases in which G-d abrogates someone's freedom of will. According to Rambam, this occurs when the totality of a person's sins exceeds a certain limit known only to the Almighty. According to Ibn Ezra, as long as one is alive, this option is available to him, and G-d would never intervene in his life in a way that negates this ability. A number of commentaries who basically agree with Ibn Ezra were quoted. These commentaries do envision G-d's occasional intervention in the private lives of people, but not in a way that deprives them of their freedom of choice. In fact, the intervention may even be necessary to restore true freedom of choice.

Beshallach

The portion of *Beshallach* describes one of the major events of Jewish history—the splitting of the Red Sea, concerning which the Midrash states: "A servant girl saw at the [crossing of the Red] Sea what Isaiah and Ezekiel did not behold" (*Mechilta de-Shirah* 3).

The Nation of Israel reached a summit of spirituality at this period never to be repeated throughout its entire history. But at the same time, some of the less outstanding features of the nation are also displayed, such as their impatience and their tendency to lament when they were unable to achieve immediate satisfaction. Even before facing potential disaster at the Red Sea (but after having seen the ten plagues, and in particular the plague of the firstborn, from which the Israelite firstborn were miraculously spared), they broke out in bitter complaints at the location named Pi ha-Hiroth, as described below:

> 10 And Pharaoh approached, and the Children of Israel lifted up their eyes and, behold, the Egyptians were pursuing them; and they were very scared, and the Children of Israel cried out to the Lord. 11 And they said to Moses: 'Did you bring us to die in the desert because there are not enough graves in Egypt? What did you do to

us by taking us out of Egypt? 12 Is this not what we told you in Egypt, saying: Let us alone and allow us to serve the Egyptians? For it is preferable for us to serve the Egyptians than to die in the desert' (Exod. 14). 13 And Moses said to the people: "Do not fear… " (Exod.14).

Ramban points out that there is a logical inconsistency between what is said in verse 10 and the continuation in verse 11. In verse 10, the Children of Israel beseech G-d for help. In the next verse, they are ungrateful for what G-d has already done for them. Certainly, that is not the best way to coax the Lord to continue helping them. Ramban cites four answers to his question. The third answer quotes Onkelos, who translates the crying out expressed in the phrase "the Children of Israel cried out to the Lord" not as a cry of prayer and supplication, but of dissatisfaction and resentment. According to the interpretation of Onkelos, the Children of Israel had begun to complain already in verse 10, so there is no contradiction between these verses.

This solution indeed answers the query of Ramban, but it does not answer a broader question, namely, what induced the nation that had witnessed so many miracles to ignore all of the wonders that were bestowed upon them until this moment? Ramban's other answers, however, which are listed below, do answer this question.

- First Answer: The nation was composed of different classes of people, and the Bible describes the reaction of each class. One group, referred to in verse 10, was composed of sincere believers who cried out to the Lord in prayer, begging for salvation. A second, religiously inferior group, perhaps the infamous mixed multitude (see Exod. 12:38) that accompanied the Israelites upon their departure from Egypt,

were responsible for the grumbling described in verses 11 and 12. This explanation is based on the Targum ascribed to Yonatan ben Uzziel, which opens the translation of verse 11 with the words: "And the wicked members of the generation said to Moses," indicating that the previous verse is associated with more righteous people. The weakness of this answer is that nowhere does the text mention the transition from the words of the righteous to the words of the wicked.
- Second Answer: The complaints of verses 11-12 were against Moses alone, not against the Almighty. (The third answer, based on Onkelos, was quoted previously.)
- Fourth Answer: Initially, the entire congregation was composed of true believers, as reflected in the prophetic powers of even the simplest people and as indicated by verse 10. But the young nation was still impatient and intellectually immature, so as soon as trouble appeared on the horizon, they were capable of losing their faith in G-d, and that is how verse 11 can be understood.

In conjunction with his first answer, Ramban notes that in verse 10 the nation is referred to as "the Children of Israel" (*bnei Yisrael*), which is the term used to indicate the small number of righteous people, while the lower-class masses are referred to as "the people" (*ha-am*). The Midrash (*Num. Rabbah* 20:23), on which Ramban bases himself, enumerates various instances of misbehavior, where the rebellious group is referred to as *ha-am,* such as in the case of the golden calf, where it appears frequently.[14] Ibn Ezra (on Exod. 32:1) states explicitly that "the people" being referred to is the mixed multitude. Also with regard to the murmurers (Num. 11:1), those who complained about the lack of meat (Num. 11:4), the

---
14. Exod. 32:1, 3, 6, 9, 17, 23, 25, 28, 30, 31, 34, 35.

errant spies (Numbers 14), and the harlotry at Baal Peor (Num. 25:1-4), the sinners are referred to as *ha-am*.

In short, in Ramban's first answer, the disconnect between the end of verse 10 ("and the Children of Israel cried out to the Lord"), which was said by the righteous people, and the beginning of verse 11 ("And they said to Moses: 'Did you bring us to die in the desert because there are not enough graves in Egypt?'"), which is imputed to the wicked people, is indicated by the usage of the term *bnei Yisrael*. This phrase appears twice in verse 10, which apparently is meant to stress that verse 10 was said only by the righteous people, who are termed *bnei Yisrael*, and not verses 11 and 12. Accordingly, when Moses replied to the complainants in verse 13, he addressed them as "the people" (*ha-am*).

The Shortage of Water at Marah – Three Questions

Immediately after the splitting of the Red Sea and the Song of the Sea, the events that transpired at Marah are described in the following verses from Exodus 15:

> 22 And Moses led Israel on their journey from the Red Sea, and they went out into the desert of Shur; and they went three days in the desert, and found no water. 23 And they came to Marah, and they could not drink of the waters of Marah, for they were bitter. Therefore, the name given to it was Marah [bitter in Hebrew]. 24 And the people murmured against Moses, saying: "What shall we drink?" 25 And he cried to the Lord; and the Lord showed

him a tree, and he cast it into the waters, and the waters became sweet. There He made a statute and an ordinance for them, and there He tested them; 26 and He said: "If you will diligently harken to the voice of the Lord your G-d sincerely, and will do that which is right in His eyes, and will obey His commandments, and observe all of His statutes, then I will not strike you with any of the diseases which I have stricken the Egyptians; for I am the Lord your healer." 27 And they came to Elim, and there, there were twelve springs of water and seventy palm-trees; and they encamped there by the waters.

According to the simple interpretation, the Children of Israel complained about the lack of water, a miracle was performed for their benefit, and they were able to slake their thirst. A number of questions may be asked.

1. Were the bitter waters of Marah (v. 23) a punishment? If they were indeed chastisement for past misdeeds, where did the Israelites sin? Three possible locations are: at the seashore (v. 22), during their three-day journey through the desert of Shur (v. 22), or upon their arrival at Marah itself (v. 24). On the other hand, if the bitter waters were not a punishment, why would G-d, after performing so many miracles to benefit the Israelites, torment them unnecessarily, when He could just as easily have arranged for them to encounter a sweet-water well, as He did in the immediate aftermath at Elim (v. 27)? The story seems to indicate a serious lack of planning. In the words of Abarbanel (on Exod. 15):

Beshallach

Why did the Lord initiate a journey in the desert in such a way that it allowed a water shortage to develop for the Israelites, being that water is a great necessity, especially for such a large congregation. How could they go for three days without water, with Marah being at the end, "and He brought them to Marah, and there they found water, but it was bitter." And if He wished to do a miracle for them, it would have been better for Him to supply their needs in that desert from the beginning to the end, rather than that their beginnings should be difficult and bad to the extent that they could not tolerate them, as in the case of the water.

2. The story may be divided into two sections. Verses 22 until the middle of 25 discuss the congregation's lack of water. The second half of verse 25 and verse 26 present some of the principles of Judaism—statutes, ordinances, observing the laws of the Torah, and reward and punishment. What is unclear is why the people's complaint and a list of the principles of Judaism were merged into the same paragraph. The numerous complaints of the nation are recorded in many locations, e.g., in the continuation of this portion, as well as in the portions of *Behaalotcha* and *Chukat* in the book of Numbers. Yet never again were the basic tenets of the religion joined to the description of one or another of their complaints.

3. It is surprising that immediately after the manifest miracles that occurred at the time of the splitting of the Red Sea, the people's behavior degenerated so quickly. It is true that according to the previously cited Ramban (Exod. 14:10), the murmuring was confined to one sect alone—that which was

referred to as "the people" (*ha-am*), but one would still expect even the lowest class to be able to be more restrained.[15]

In order to answer the questions posed, it is necessary to examine the behavior of the nation at each of the three previously mentioned locations, namely the seashore, the desert of Shur, and Marah. If their behavior was flawless, the answer to question 1 will be that they were not being penalized, as they had not sinned; otherwise, one may assume they had sinned. In either case, the relationship between the two sections of the selected verses (question 2) and the precipitous degeneration of their faith (question 3) have to be dealt with.

THE SEA SHORE: UNDERSTANDING THE WORDS *VA-YASSA MOSHE* ("AND MOSES LED ISRAEL")

As a rule, the initiator of the Israelites' journeys was the Almighty, with Moses serving as His earthly representative, the typical verse stating: "And the Children of Israel journeyed." For example, with respect to the trip from the desert of Sin towards Rephidim, the verse states: "And all of the congregation of the Children of Israel journeyed from the wilderness of Sin, according to their journeys, by the commandment of the Lord, and encamped in Rephidim; and there was no water for the people to drink" (Exod. 17:1). In the case of Marah, the Bible reads: *va-yassa Moshe*, "and Moses led" (Exod. 15:22), wording that is strange for two reasons:

---

15. Shalom Noach Berezovsky, *Netivot Shalom* (1995), Exodus, *Beshallach*, "In Marah they were commanded concerning Shabbat."

1. The initiator was Moses and not G-d;
2. The Hebrew word *va-yassa* is in causative form, implying that Moses employed force to get them to move.

POSITIVE INTERPRETATION

As has been noted, the description of the travels of the Children of Israel after traversing the Red Sea begins with the introductory verse: "And Moses led Israel on their journey from the Red Sea" (Exod. 15:22). There exist various opinions as to whether the initiative is related exclusively to Moses. According to one Midrash, the wording is precise.[16] R. Zalman Sorotzkin explains that the Torah, soon to be received on Mount Sinai, had to be accepted of one's own volition, as we are told: "Everything is in the hands of heaven except the fear of heaven" (BT *Berachot* 33b). Since moral character is in the hands of each individual, Moses wished to set an example and display his own enthusiasm to proceed toward the momentous event soon to transpire.[17]

Another Midrashic interpretation[18] assumes that this trip, like all of the others, was enjoined by the Lord, and Moses' name is singled out to stress that the nation behaved in an exemplary fashion, neither questioning where they were going nor how they would subsist, due to the positive influence of Moses. This is recalled by Jeremiah in the famous verse in which he quotes G-d as saying in praise of the Jewish nation: "I still keep the memory of your beneficence when you were young, and your love when you became my bride; how you went after Me in the desert, in an unplanted land" (Jer. 2:2).

---

16. *Mechilta de-Rabbi Yishmael, Beshallach, Va-Yassa,* par. Aleph.
17. *Oznayim la-Torah,* Exod. 15:22.
18. *Mechilta de-Rabbi Yishmael, Beshallach, Va-Yassa,* par. Aleph.

Negative Interpretation

An alternative point of view, cited by Rashi, has the nation behaving in a perverse manner. The mention of Moses' name indicates that he was only able to budge them by force. Pharaoh had bedecked his horses with precious stones that washed up on the shore when his army was drowned, and the Israelites were too busy gathering his jewels to be bothered by spiritual matters.[19]

Kli Yakar (on Exod. 15:22) buttresses Rashi's comments by explaining that Moses feared that the excessive plundering which took place at the sea shore would lead to great wealth, which could have led to terrible sinning, as indeed happened with the golden calf. Great wealth could also lead to haughtiness and laziness, both of which are inimical to Torah study and observance. In addition, by lingering at the shore and accumulating wealth when they knew that Moses was anxious to move in the direction of Mount Sinai, where the Torah was to be given, the Israelites were blatantly displaying their own warped set of values.

Other Midrashic opinions look upon their reluctance to travel as reflective of considerably more serious character defects than mere greed. Upon seeing the corpses of their taskmasters strewn on the seashore, the Israelites allegedly were backtracking to the now defenseless and fertile land with a newly cast icon in the lead, and re-establishing a regimen of idol-worship.[20] Alternatively, they had never abandoned their pagan beliefs[21] and in fact bore Micah's

---

19. *Tanchuma Buber, Beshallach* 16; Rashi, Exod. 15:22.
20. *Mechilta de-Rabbi Yishmael, Beshallach, Va-Yassa,* par. 1; *Exod. Rabbah* 24:2, according to R. Judah.
21. *Mechilta de-Rabbi Yishmael, Beshallach, Va-Yassa,* par. 1, according to R. Judah bar Ilai.

graven image (Judg. 18:30), first sculpted in Egypt, throughout their sojourning.[22]

Moses induced them to proceed in the right direction only by wielding his Divinely charged wand,[23] or perhaps by reminding them that their freedom had been obtained on condition that they eventually serve G-d at Mount Sinai.[24] Once more, a Biblical verse is adduced in support of the proposed approach. Nehemiah, in the early days of the Second Temple, apparently refers to their attempted return in his short recap of the rebellious behavior of the Children of Israel:

> But our fathers dealt proudly and hardened their neck, and did not listen to your commandments, and they refused to hearken, neither were they mindful of the wonders that You did among them; but hardened their neck, and in their rebellion appointed a captain to return to their bondage. But You are a G-d ready to pardon, gracious and full of compassion, slow to anger, and plentiful in mercy, who did not forsake them (Neh. 9:16-17).

CONCLUSION

Two points may be noted. First, a wide range of behavior is ascribed to the Israelites, from righteous belief to classical idol-worship. Second, G-d seems to be remarkably patient with the ostensibly ungrateful multitude, an observation highlighted as well in the

---

22. *Exod. Rabbah* 24:1 according to R. Judah bar Ilai; BT *Sanhedrin* 103b.
23. *Mechilta de-Rabbi Yishmael, Beshallach, Va-Yassa,* par. 1; *Exod. Rabbah* 24:2, according to R. Elazar.
24. *Exod. Rabbah* 24:2 according to R. Judah, based on Exod. 3:12.

verse quoted from the book of Nehemiah. *Midrash Tanchuma*[25] resolves the apparent dissonance by drawing attention to the fact that the same word is used here with respect to the Children of Israel, *va-yassa*, and in the following verse from the book of Psalms: "And He led [*va-yassa*] His people like sheep, and guided them in the wilderness like a flock" (Ps. 78:52). The Midrash continues by saying that just as sheep continually display behavior which is undesirable to their shepherd—here wandering off in different directions and there mutilating the agriculture, so must the performance of the Children of Israel have been a constant irritant to the Almighty. Nevertheless, just as the shepherd patiently gathers his sheep together and treats their infractions with forbearance, so does G-d relate to the Jewish nation. The Midrash clinches this approach by citing a verse from the book of Ezekiel: "And you My sheep, the sheep of My pasture, are men, and I am your G-d" (Ezek. 34:31). The Midrash asks: If they are men, why are they called sheep; if they are sheep, why are they referred to as men? The answer is: The Children of Israel are treated as sheep with regard to punishment (very leniently) and as human beings with regard to reward. The Midrash encourages a benign reaction to good behavior, coupled with relatively light punishment for wrongdoing. The hope is that positive feedback alone, without the trauma and pain associated with severe punishment for their sins, will be sufficient to encourage the Children of Israel to seek out, determine, and eventually implement the proper path to be trodden by each individual.

---

25. *Tanchuma Buber, Beshallach* 15.

BESHALLACH

The Desert of Shur: And They Went Three Days in the Desert

The text states that the Israelites walked in the desert for three days without water. If in fact the entire congregation did not complain of thirst under these conditions, it would seem that they were entitled to a medal.

On the other hand, there is a Talmudic passage that denigrates their activities during the three-day journey to Marah. In tractate *Bava Kamma*, it is stated:

> Those who expound verses metaphorically [*dorshei reshumot*] said: water can only mean Torah, as it says: "Let everyone who is thirsty go to the water" (Isa. 55:1). It thus means that as they went three days without Torah, they immediately became exhausted. The prophets among them thereupon rose and enacted that they should publicly read the law on Shabbat, make a break on Sunday, read again on Monday, make a break again on Tuesday and Wednesday, read again on Thursday, and then make a break on Friday so that they should not be kept for three days without Torah (BT *Bava Kamma* 82a).

On what basis does the Talmud conclude that the three days without water is referring to three days bereft of Torah study? Maharsha explains that it stems from the peculiar structure of the portion under consideration. It starts by mentioning that the Israelites did not find water after a three-day trip, and concludes by stating that G-d gave them statutes and ordinances which He requested that they obey. The clear implication is that what was missing during those three days was an exposure to Torah study and observance, and when they finally did find water, meaning Torah, its taste was bitter, because they had absented themselves for an extended period. What was the solution? It is elucidated in verse 25: "and the Lord showed him a tree." What tree did He show him? He showed him the Torah, which is "a tree of life to those who uphold its contents" (Prov. 3:18), and in so doing clarified that by not abandoning it for three days, "the waters [Torah] became [would remain] sweet." Verse 26 requests that each Jew "diligently hearken [*shamo'a tishma*] to the voice of the Lord." Maharsha understood this redundant language as a means of prescribing the required dosage of Torah reading: Monday, Thursday, and Shabbat.

The Talmud proposes a moral explanation for why the Torah is compared to water:

> R. Hanina b. Ida said: Why are the words of the Torah likened unto water... ? This is to teach you: just as water flows from a higher level to a lower, so too the words of the Torah endure only with one who is modest [by considering himself to be on a low level] (BT *Taanit* 7a).

The previously quoted discourse from the Talmud states that after going three days without Torah, the congregation became exhausted. I would suggest that the text refers to a form of spiritual exhaustion or perhaps confusion. This conjecture is supported by the version of this passage found in the *Mechilta*,[26] where instead of saying that the Children of Israel were exhausted, it says they rebelled. Also, rather than limit the exhaustion or rebellion to Torah study, the Slonimer Rebbe generalizes it to include prayer and Divine service as well.[27]

---

26. *Mechilta de-Rabbi Yishmael, Beshallach, Va-Yassa*, par. 1.
27. *Netivot Shalom, Beshallach, Be-Marah Nitztavu al ha-Shabbat*, Aleph.

Beshallach

The simple question that may be asked on the previously quoted passage from the Talmud is: How can the Israelites be criticized for not studying Torah when the Torah had not yet been given? Targum Yonatan (Exod. 15:22), sensitive to this question, depicts the Israelites during their three-day trip as being bereft of commandments. Although, as previously noted, the Torah was not yet given, there was still plenty that could be dissected and discussed. These included the seven Noahide laws; the law of circumcision—a commandment already given to Abraham (Gen. 17:10) and observed by the Children of Israel in Egypt as a prerequisite to partake of the Pascal lamb (Exod. 12:48); the law of tithes—a precept already obeyed by Isaac[28]; and the law pertaining to the tendon of the thigh (*gid ha-nasheh*), a practice which had been established by Jacob (Gen. 32:33).

Perhaps more than detailed legal analysis, the criticism is of the low intellectual caliber that the nation displayed. After undergoing the most amazing events that man had ever experienced—as the Midrash states,[29] "a servant girl saw at the [crossing of the Red] Sea what Isaiah and Ezekiel did not behold," one would have expected all strata of the nation to be engaged in some level of philosophical dialogue. Yet this is not what occurred. The nation did not seem to be developing the trademark intellectual curiosity and innovation for which it would be known throughout its long history, and some degree of chastisement was necessary in order to steer it in the right direction.

---

28. Rashi on Gen. 26:12, based on Tosefta *Sotah* 10:6.
29. *Mechilta de-Rabbi Yishmael, Shirah* 3.

Marah: And the People Murmured against Moses

Finally, they reached an oasis called Marah and there was indeed a well to be found, but G-d was apparently teasing them. They could not slake their thirst, because the water was bitter. It would seem to be perfectly legitimate to complain under these circumstances regarding the lackluster, even cruel, treatment provided them.

The question to be posed, therefore, is whether the reaction of the Children of Israel was justified, or whether this was the first, but far from the last, time that the nation behaved like a spoiled, ungrateful child.

A number of factors may be observed in support of the innocence of the Children of Israel. First, the people did not express themselves impertinently, as they did in the Wilderness of Sin (Exod. 16:3) and Rephidim (Exod. 17:2). Second, the selected verses (22-26) make no mention of punishment, or even rebuke, as was made when a parallel water shortage occurred at Rephidim (Exod. 17:7). Third, as previously mentioned, in such a situation any normal person would request liquid refreshment, especially if he was responsible for children and the elderly.

Indeed, when Moses enumerates the names of the locations at which the Israelites angered the Almighty, the verse says: "And at Taberah, and at Massah, and at Kibroth ha-Taavah, you angered the Lord" (Deut. 9:22). Moses cites the murmurers at Taberah (Num. 11:3), the complainers regarding the lack of meat at Kibroth ha-Taavah (Num. 11:34), and the inciters to argument described in the present portion (Massah and Meribah [Exod. 17:7], meaning "testing" and "strife"), but he does not refer to the events which occurred at Marah.

R. Chananel: Their Complaint Was Not Justified

Rabbenu Chananel[30] interpreted the phrase in verse 22, "they went three days in the desert," to mean that they went the distance of a three-day journey, but they actually did so in one day. His motivation seems to have been that G-d would never have been so inconsiderate as to expect a mass of people numbering three million, including children and elders, to march for three days without quenching their thirst. Nevertheless, they did complain, and thus, according to Rabbenu Chananel, one may assume that their behavior was not acceptable.

Alternatively, the Talmudic passage previously quoted states that they did not necessarily lack water, since the water referred to was Torah learning. The exhaustion that they experienced was of a spiritual nature, as noted, and in their frustration they complained unnecessarily, rather than expend the required intellectual effort to clarify the issues.

Mechilta

The *Mechilta*,[31] relating the bitterness of the water to their behavior upon arriving at Marah, states: "R. Joshua says: the Israelites should have first consulted with the greatest among them concerning what to drink. Instead, they spoke words of grievance against Moses."

It is not clear whether by "the greatest among them" the Midrash is referring to Moses himself, or to their immediate superiors who would have been in contact with Moses. Either way,

---

30. Quoted by Rabbenu Bachya on Exod. 15:22.
31. *Mechilta de-Rabbi Yishmael, Shirah* 3.

the idea is that instead of making a sincere attempt to solve the problem by making Moses aware of the situation, they used it as an opportunity to malign him. Rashi (Exod. 15:25), basing himself on the same Midrash, states: "They did not consult with Moses in a respectful fashion: 'Request mercy for us, so that we may have water to drink.' Instead they complained."

According to Rashi, their sin was not that they failed to confront Moses, but that when doing so, they spoke in a discourteous fashion. In the same Midrash, R. Elazar compounds their sin by saying that their complaints were directed not at Moses alone, but at the Almighty as well.[32]

According to Rabbenu Chananel, *Mechilta*, and the Talmud, their sin was making an unjustified complaint, and it was independent of, and possibly preceded, the discovery that the water was in fact bitter; i.e., verse 24 ("And the people murmured") might have occurred before verse 23 ("they could not drink of the waters of Marah, for they were bitter").

Netziv: They Sinned, but Only after Finding the Water to Be Bitter

Netziv, in contrast to Rabbenu Chananel, considers the order of the verses to be precise, but nevertheless finds fault with the behavior of the people.

Interestingly, the Bible does not even say that they complained about being thirsty. Only after drinking the water and finding it to be bitter did they grumble. Netziv (Exod. 15:22-24) explains what generated the grumbling. The majority of the Israelites were

---

32. Based on the extra word "saying" in verse 24: And the people murmured against Moses, *saying*: 'What shall we drink?'

still strong in their belief at this stage, having recently witnessed the miracle of the splitting of the Red Sea. In addition, they were not even thirsty. It was only after they drank the water at Marah, which turned out to be bitter, that a minority of the people became worried about the future. What would happen if they really were thirsty? Would the available water be bitter then as well? This faction displayed a lack of gratitude by complaining about a mishap that had not yet even occurred, and perhaps, with a bit of faith, never would occur.

In saying that only a minority of the people complained, Netziv bases himself on the words in verse 24, "the people murmured against Moses." He understands these words to imply that only some of the people protested,[33] as opposed to what happened when the people complained about a lack of bread, where it says that "the whole congregation of the Children of Israel murmured" (Exod. 16:2).

Answering the First Question: Were the Bitter Waters of Marah a Punishment?

It has been shown that some commentaries believe the Children of Israel sinned in at least one of the following three locations: the seashore, the desert of Shur, or Marah. If that is the case, then the bitter waters could have easily been a punishment for their previous behavior.

The punishment was measure for measure (*middah ke-neged middah*). Whether they sinned at the seashore or by complaining about the lack of water at Marah, and even if they had simply failed

---

33. The verse uses the Hebrew word *am*; see Ramban, Exod. 14:10.

to immerse themselves in Torah, which is compared to water, their punishment was commensurate in that they were deprived of water.

On the other hand, Rashbam, Abarbanel, the Zohar, and Midrash Rabbah all hold that the claim of a lack of water was justified after a three-day journey. As noted earlier, these commentators have to answer one question: Why would G-d, after performing so many miracles to benefit the Israelites, torment them unnecessarily when He could just as easily have arranged for them to encounter a sweet-water well, as He in fact did in the immediate aftermath at Elim (verse 27)?

Abarbanel and Rashbam

Both Abarbanel (Exod. 15) and Rashbam (Exod. 15:25) believe that there was a lesson to be learned from the anguish they experienced at Marah. According to both, it was necessary to confront the Israelites with difficulties so that they would entreat the Almighty and be answered by Him. He would satisfy their needs, thereby inculcating in them that G-d is capable of extracting water from a rock and providing bread from heaven. From this event, they would realize that when they find themselves in dire straits, they should seek the Lord through prayer and supplication, and He will respond. The same experience, according to Rashbam, would indicate that just as G-d is capable of sweetening the water, so can He cure their maladies if they obey His law meticulously, for, in His words: "I am the Lord your Healer."

Beshallach

Zohar

The Sages said that the Children of Israel deserved to be redeemed from Egypt because they were particular about four items: they did not engage in incest, they retained their Hebrew names, they adhered to the Hebrew language, and they guarded their secret (namely, that they intended to leave Egypt permanently, with no intention of returning).[34] On the one hand, the women were not suspected of engaging in improper sexual relations; on the other hand, the women diligently accepted upon themselves the task of sexually arousing their husbands, who were thoroughly exhausted from the heavy labor to which they were subjected.[35] In recognition of the fine line that the women were able to draw, the Rabbis stated: "As a reward for the actions of the righteous women of that generation, our forefathers were redeemed from Egypt" (BT *Sotah* 11b).

The Egyptians, who were known to be licentious, and one may assume dishonest as well, spread false rumors to the effect that the younger generation of Jews were actually fathered by Egyptians who had coupled with young Jewish women. There were among the Israelites those who believed these rumors, and this led to quarrels within their families. In order to refute these lies, as well as to indicate to the public at large that the Children of Israel, who were about to receive the Torah, were a pure and modest nation, G-d sought a method of displaying their innocence. The approach taken by G-d was to perform *en masse* the ceremony undergone by a woman suspected of adultery. The central element of that ceremony is the drinking of the "waters of bitterness," which cause swelling of the abdomen of an adulteress who drinks the potion, but

---

34. *Midrash Lekach Tov*, Exodus 12.
35. *Tanchuma, Pekudei* 9.

are harmless to an innocent woman. However, it would have been undesirable to publicize the fact that the women were being tested. It would have engendered satisfaction among the Egyptians whose machinations had necessitated the ceremony, and embarrassed the women, who would have been mortified by even being suspected of such immorality. For that reason, G-d camouflaged the test by having the entire nation, both men and women, drink the bitter waters (*Zohar* 3:142b).

Midrash Rabbah

In connection with the story of the golden calf, G-d said to Moses: "Now let Me alone, so that My wrath may be kindled against them, so that I may consume them; and I will make you into a great nation" (Exod. 32:10). Rashi asks why G-d requested of Moses to cease his lobbying efforts on behalf of Israel. There was nothing to stop, since until this point, there is no indication that Moses had in fact prayed for them. On the contrary, he had heretofore maintained his silence. Rashi's answer is: "Here He opened a door for him [intimated a possible solution], informing him that all depends on him—if he prays for them, He [G-d] will not destroy them" (Exod. 32:10).

In the view of the Midrash (*Exod. Rabbah* 43:3), the proceedings at Marah were inspired by a desire on the part of the Almighty to inculcate in Moses the proper way to intercede on behalf of the Jewish nation.

Verse 25 states: "the Lord showed him a tree." The Midrash notes that the Hebrew word for "showed" should have been *va-yarehu*. Instead, the Torah uses the word *va-yorehu*, which can mean, "He instructed him." G-d instructed Moses regarding the method of transforming a "bitter" decree into a "sweet" one.

This knowledge remained dormant in Moses' memory until the Hebrews were in the desert and, as a result of their rebellious nature, found themselves about to be destroyed by G-d a number of times (Exod. 32:10; Num. 14:12, 16:21, 17:9). At that stage Moses, so to say, reminded G-d that at Marah He had taught him that by praying, a bitter verdict could be sweetened.

Understanding the Netziv

The Netziv (Exod. 15:22-24), as previously noted, held that it was only after they drank the water at Marah that some people sinned. According to his view, one must still relate to the question of why G-d would have arranged a rest stop equipped with bitter water exclusively. Perhaps it was important for Moses, as well as the silent majority, to realize that there existed pockets of immature individuals who would have to be dealt with in the future. In the Midrash, R. Eliezer says unequivocally that the bitter water was an unnatural phenomenon meant specifically to test the mettle of the Children of Israel. This exegesis is based on verse 25, where the Bible states explicitly with regard to Marah: "there He tested them."[36]

Answering the Second Question: Connecting the Second Part: "There He Made a Statute and an Ordinance for Them"

The above phrase, the second half of verse 25, would be logically connected to the previous verses if it were to suggest a means for

---

36. *Mechilta de-Rabbi Yishmael, Shirah* 3.

the Israelites to improve their behavior. This is certainly true if the Israelites had sinned. It also accords with the previously quoted Abarbanel and Rashbam, who believe the incident with the bitter water to have been staged specifically for the purpose of teaching Israel the importance of respecting the law. It is also the approach of Ramban, as is clear from his comments on this phrase:

> He [Moses] instructed them in the ways of the desert, namely to be ready to suffer hunger and thirst and to pray to G-d when they occur, and not to complain. And [he taught them] ordinances to live by, to love one's fellow man, and to follow the counsel of the elders, and to be discreet in their tents when dealing with their women and children, and to deal peacefully with the strangers who come into the camp to sell them merchandise. And [he also imparted] moral instructions, so that they not behave like bands of marauders who do abominable things shamelessly.

A Talmudic Passage from Tractate *Sanhedrin*

The Talmud in tractate *Sanhedrin* states:

> It has been taught: The Israelites were given ten precepts at Marah, seven of which had already been accepted by the children of Noah, to which were added at Marah social laws [jurisprudence], the Sabbath, and honoring one's parents. Social laws, for it is written, "There [at Marah] he made for them a statute and an ordinance" (BT *Sanhedrin* 56b).

On the basis of this Talmudic statement, Rashi comments: "In Marah He gave them a few sections of the Torah to deal with: Shabbat, the red heifer, and the administration of justice" (on Exod. 15:25). See First Overview: The Intellectual Development of the Jewish Nation for an extensive discussion of Rashi's viewpoint.

Ramban wonders, if the intention of the words "statute" and "ordinance" was really to add the laws enumerated in the Talmud, why does the verse limit itself to a two-word description? Why does the Torah not devote a number of lengthy paragraphs to explicate them? These are his words (on Exod. 15:25):

> Why did it not explain here these statutes and ordinances, saying "And the Lord spoke to Moses, command the Children of Israel," as He says in the portions mentioned above, "Speak to all of the congregation of Israel" (Exod. 12:3), and so He does concerning all of the laws given in the Tent of Meeting (Lev. 1:2), the plains of Moab (Num. 35:2), and the desert Passover offering (Num. 9:2)?

In other words, what is needed to properly describe the essence of these laws is an entire section, such as is found regarding the Pascal lamb, which is explained in detail in chapter 12 of the book of Exodus.

Ramban answers that the intention was not to teach those precepts in depth, but to spiritually prepare the nation to receive these laws, in great detail, when the Torah was given on Mount Sinai. He proves his point by noting that Rashi, in citing the Talmudic passage, uses the expression "to deal with," meaning to understand the basic concepts, in the same way that Abraham taught Torah to the "souls that they had made in Haran" (Gen. 12:5). Abraham must have delved into the reasons for the commandments and their beauty, but he certainly did not examine them in detail, nor did he present them in the format that they would eventually assume in the code of Jewish law. Similarly, here at Marah, G-d informed them in a general manner, according to Ramban:

> ... to make them familiar with the commandments and to know if they would accept them with "joyfulness and with goodness of heart" (Deut. 28:47). And this was the test concerning which Scripture says [v. 25] "and there He tested them," and he [Moses] informed them that G-d would yet command them [to fulfill] the precepts of the Torah. This is the intent of the verse [26] "If you will hearken to the voice of the Lord your G-d sincerely... and will obey His commandments"—[it refers to] those which He will command you [in the future] (on Exod. 15:25).

A full discussion of the exact laws that were imparted at Marah, and how they coalesce with the pre-existing seven Noahide laws, as well as with the future Pentateuchal laws, is to be found in FIRST OVERVIEW: THE INTELLECTUAL DEVELOPMENT OF THE JEWISH NATION.

ANSWERING THE THIRD QUESTION: HOW COULD THE ISRAELITES' BEHAVIOR HAVE DEGENERATED SO FAST?

After examining the behavior of the Israelites at the seashore, in the desert, and at Marah, and noting how the events at Marah segued into the transmission of another set of laws to the fledgling nation, it becomes clear that according to most commentators, their deportment was less a reflection of disbelief in G-d than a manifestation that they were still suffering from a slave mentality and had not yet reached the spiritual level which would enable them to receive and adhere to the laws of the Torah.

Although one Midrash accuses the mixed multitude of never having renounced their pagan beliefs, the more accepted interpretation is that the nation was enchanted by the jewelry they found strewn on the seashore. One might compare this to survivors of concentration camps who, being exposed to a plentiful supply of food after years of starvation, were unable to control themselves. Similarly, the freshly released slaves could not tear themselves away from the vast amount of readily available trinkets.

On the three-day trip, the Israelites were faulted for not engaging in intellectual discussions of the laws they had already been given, and for not actively preparing themselves for the additional laws that would be given in the near future. Such behavior is characteristic of the lower classes of any society, who have not benefited from higher education, and is certainly not surprising with respect to a population that had been deprived of all options for self-improvement.

Moving on to the complaints at Marah, it has been noted that their thirst may have been justified, although their manners left something to be desired. Once more, the lack of a wholesome parental and educational background quite naturally leads to such behavior. In fact, the trial of the bitter waters may have been engineered as a means of guidance and preparation for the events that would transpire at the next stage, and it might have also served as a source of edification for both Moses and the Children of Israel as to the efficacy of prayer. Finally, the new ordinances presented at Marah, at least according to Ramban, were meant to serve the same purpose.

Summary

The exodus from Egypt and the miracles that accompanied it were designed to encourage the nation, to revive it, and to restore its optimism and *joie de vivre*. Only after attaining these attributes would the nation be able to take on its future challenges: the conquest and settlement of the land of Canaan and the construction of the Holy Temple.

A number of interpretations have been presented regarding the demeanor of the Children of Israel at the Red Sea, on the three-day trip to Marah, and during their stay at that location. The consensus of the commentators is that the Jews' behavior had not reached the required level, as is reflected by their conduct prior to reaching Marah, as well as their impertinence and impatience upon encountering the lack of potable water. The sweetening of the bitter water was intended to inform them of G-d's capabilities, while the laws transmitted to them were meant to outline the basic principles that serve as prerequisites to the acceptance of the Torah at Mount Sinai. The entire portion thus presents an important stepping-stone in the series of events leading to revelation and the receipt of the Torah.

Yitro

Judaism has its heroes, such as the patriarchs and matriarchs, Moses our teacher, and Queen Esther; as well as its villains, such as Laban, Esau, Pharaoh, and Haman. But there are also figures who can go in either direction, depending on how one interprets the Biblical texts. In this category one may place Noah, Abraham's nephew Lot, and Jethro (*Yitro* in Hebrew).

Jethro is one of five people whose names were chosen as titles of weekly portions, the remaining four being Noah, Korah, Balak, and Phinehas. These people are not major characters in the Torah, and also not necessarily considered to be among the most righteous. The actions of Phinehas, although lauded by Scripture (Num. 25:13), were criticized by the Talmud, which states that the sages of his generation might have excommunicated him had the Almighty not intervened. *Torah Temimah* explains that although the Torah justifies his behavior, the rabbis of later generations felt that it should not serve as a paradigm for others, since most zealots do not act in total sincerity.

The names of more central figures were not used in naming weekly portions, since they appear intermittently throughout the Torah. Actually, various verbal forms describing their actions serve as names of weekly portions; for example, *Lech Lecha* ("Leave your land," said to Abraham), *Toldot* ("These are the generations of Isaac"), *Vayeitzei* ("And Jacob departed"), and *Vayigash* ("And Judah came near"). Certainly, it would have been inappropriate to name any portion after Moses, being that his activities are spread throughout the last four books of the Pentateuch. In fact, the entire Torah is referred to as the Five Books of Moses.

There are six references throughout the Torah to the man reputed to be Jethro—four in Exodus (2:16-21, 4:18, 6:25, 18:1-27), one in Numbers (10:29-32), and one in Deuteronomy (1:9-14), as well as two in the book of Judges (1:16, 4:11). Since many of these sources introduce different names, it is possible to appreciate the Midrashim[37] which state that Jethro actually had seven names (Jether, Jethro, Hobab, Reuel, Heber, Putiel, and Kenite), and also to understand those commentators who do not believe that all of the citations refer to Jethro.

This chapter will be based on two of the references: Exodus 18, which describes the visit of Jethro to the camp of the Israelites, and Numbers 10, which tells of the departure of Jethro from the camp.

THE VISIT OF JETHRO (EXODUS 18)

The longest section in the Torah dealing with Jethro (and that is the only name used here) is found in this portion, which bears his name. Jethro arrives with Moses' wife Zipporah and their children, who had been separated from Moses, and they have an emotional reunion. Jethro brings sacrifices, tenders constructive criticism to Moses concerning how to optimize his daily activities, and returns home to Midian.

---

37. *Mechilta Yitro* 18, par. A; *Lekach Tov, Yitro* 18, *Vayishma Yitro*. See also Rashi on Exod. 4:18, 18:1; Num. 10:29.

The Midrash[38] explains how it happened that Moses sent his wife away. When he returned to Egypt from Midian with his wife and children, Aaron had asked him about his entourage, whereupon Moses explained that they were the members of his family, leading Aaron to tell him: "We are grieving over the former ones [the Hebrews who were already entrapped in Egypt]. Do you want to exacerbate the situation?" Moses immediately asked Zipporah to return to Midian with the children. In the portion of *Yitro*, they are reunited after a separation of over a year (*Exod. Rabbah* 9:12).

THE DEPARTURE OF JETHRO (NUM. 10:29-32)

When Moses informed Jethro that the camp was about to depart from its present location, Jethro decided that the time had come for him to return home, whereupon Moses pleaded with him to stay. The section opens with the following words: "And Moses said unto Hobab, the son of Reuel the Midianite, Moses' father-in-law" (Num. 10:29). The name Hobab appears here for the first time, while Reuel was mentioned in Exod. 2:18 as the priest of Midian who was Zipporah's father. One would thus assume that the words "Moses' father-in-law" in the present verse are referring to Reuel, making Hobab the brother-in-law of Moses. If this conjecture is correct, the present passage is not speaking about Jethro at all, but about his son, and this would explain why it appears in the book of Numbers, far away from the first four references, after Jethro had already been sent home (Exod. 18:27). This is indeed the view of R. Shimon ben Menassiah in the Midrash (*Sifrei* Num. 78) and the first opinion recorded by Ibn Ezra in the book of Numbers (10:29).

---

38. *Mechilta Yitro*, par. A, quoted by Rashi on Exod. 18:2.

However, the majority of commentaries[39] accept the alternative view quoted in the Midrash, namely that it is Hobab who is the father-in-law of Moses, making Reuel the grandfather of Zipporah. If so, why is Reuel identified as the father of Zipporah in the verse: "And when they came to Reuel their father, he said: 'Why did you come home so soon today?'" (Exod. 2:18). The Midrash explains that young children frequently call their grandfather (Reuel) "father."

Why was Jethro given the name Hobab, which means "affection"? Ramban (Num. 10:29) believes that Jethro converted, and accordingly received a new name, based on the Talmudic saying that a person who converts is like a newly born child (BT *Yevamot* 22a). His new name reflected his affection for his new religion.

Four Questions

Based on the above sources, four questions may be asked.

1. Exactly how good (or bad) does the Bible consider Jethro to be?
2. When Jethro arrived at the Israelite camp in the desert, accompanied by Zipporah and her children, was this prior to or following the giving of the Torah?
3. It has been noted that Ibn Ezra in Numbers 10 considers the main character to be the son of Jethro. According to those commentators who disagree and believe that Jethro was the protagonist in both scenarios, did the episode described in Numbers overlap Jethro's visit as related in Exodus, or did it occur at a later stage?

---

39. Rashi, Num. 10:29; Ibn Ezra, Exod. 2:18, 18:1.

4. If the stories in Exodus and Numbers overlap, then it is clear that Jethro left the Israelite camp, since verse 18:27 in Exodus describes his departure. However, if the story in Numbers occurred after that in Exodus, Jethro must have returned to the Israelite camp a second time. The text in Numbers 10 does not clearly indicate whether, after this visit, he chose to stay with the congregation or return home. The question is: what was the outcome of his discussion with Moses?

Answering the First Question: Was Jethro Righteous? (R. Elazar vs. R. Yehoshua)

A key to answering this question may be found in the Midrash based on the following verse: "And Moses sent his father-in-law away" (Exod. 18:27). The Midrash states:

> R. Yehoshua says: He sent him away from the glory of the world. R. Elazar ha-Modai says: He gave him many gifts, for from the reply that he [Moses] gave to him [Jethro] you can learn [that they had a positive relationship], for it says: "Do not leave us" (Num. 10:31). He [Moses] said to him: "You gave us good advice [regarding handling interpersonal problems efficiently] and G-d agreed with your words. Do not leave us." He [Jethro] said to him: "A lantern can only help in a dark area. How can a lantern help where the sun and the moon shine? You are like the sun, and your brother Aaron is like the moon. What benefit can a lantern provide in your presence? Instead, I will go to my land and convert all of my countrymen, and

I will elevate them to the level that they can study Torah and be sheltered under the wings of the Divine Spirit." Perhaps he said so, but did not do so? The verse says: "And the children of the Kenite, Moses' father-in-law, ascended from the city of palm trees" (Judg. 1:16). And it continues: "and they went and dwelt with the people." When the word "people" is used, it refers to intelligent people [implying that the children of Jethro had indeed learned Torah and thus fit in with the intelligentsia].[40]

According to *Or ha-Chaim* (Num. 10:30), R. Yehoshua's view is that Jethro never converted, which was very frustrating to Moses, since Jethro was aware of, and had even experienced, many of the miracles that accompanied the escape of the Israelites from Egypt and their sojourning in the desert. Moses thus sent him away in anger.[41] R. Elazar, on the other hand, felt that he must have converted, since the phrase which he quoted, "Do not leave us," reflects the affection that Moses had for Jethro. Accordingly, when Jethro said: "I will not go, but I will depart to my own land and to my birthplace" (Num. 10:30), the meaning is that I will return to convert those of my kin and countrymen who acquiesce.

According to R. Elazar ha-Modai, Moses preferred that Jethro stay with the nation. The fact that G-d had agreed to Jethro's suggestions was proof that he had much to contribute even when Moses and Aaron occupied leadership positions. His lantern could outshine their light. According to R. Yehoshua, Moses wanted Jethro to remain for much more self-serving reasons. He told

---

40. *Mechilta de-Rabbi Yishmael, Yitro, Masechta de-Amalek*, par. 2.
41. A variant reading of the Midrash (by the Vilna Gaon) is that Moses sent him away with great glory. However, if that is the case, there is very little contrast between the views of R. Yehoshua and R. Elazar.

him: "for you know about our encampments in the wilderness" (Num. 10:31). Moses was afraid that Jethro would reveal the exact location of the Israelites to their enemies, who had been unable to pin them down in the past, since they were concealed by the clouds of glory. Second, Moses was afraid that people would note that Jethro had been privy to the secrets of the faith, and yet had rejected it. This would reflect negatively on the religion as a whole.

THE VIEW OF R. YEHOSHUA

The argument between R. Yehoshua and R. Elazar ha-Modai appears in different contexts. Two Midrashic sources that seem to accept the view of R. Yehoshua are:

1. the previously quoted Midrash,[42] which claims that Jethro conditioned Moses' marriage to Zipporah on their first son becoming an idolatrous priest;
2. the Talmudic passage which identifies Putiel with Jethro, explaining that the name derives from the Hebrew word for fattening (*pittem*), since Jethro fattened calves for idolatrous sacrifices (BT *Sotah* 43a).

Neither of these proofs is absolute, since they refer to Jethro's activities early on, before Moses had a chance to influence him. *Siftei Kohen* (*Shemot*, p. 18) explains that Moses only accepted Jethro's condition for marriage because he realized that Jethro was wavering in his belief, and it was likely that he could be weaned from paganism and convinced of the validity of monotheism, and that, in fact, may be what actually happened.

---

42. *Mechilta de-Rabbi Yishmael, Yitro, Masechta de-Amalek*, par. 1. This Midrash was quoted in the chapter on *Shemot*.

On the other hand, if the Torah chose to call Jethro by the name Putiel, it is possible that he retained his old ways. Based on the verse: "You shall not wrong a stranger, nor shall you oppress him" (Exod. 22:20), the Talmud says that one should not remind a convert of his past evil deeds (BT *Bava Metzia* 58b). If the Talmud in tractate *Sotah* believed that Jethro had become a sincere convert, it would certainly not have referred to him by using a pejorative epithet, especially since a more positive etymology of the name Putiel also existed ("he shed his allegiance to idolatry").[43]

Another source which states that Jethro remained an idolater is found in BT *Bava Batra* 109b. The Talmud refers to the story of Micah, in the book of Judges (18:30), who is said to have hired a priest named Jonathan, the son of Gershom, the son of Manasseh. The Talmud goes on to say that Manasseh is in fact Moses, with the name altered in order to diminish the embarrassment to Moses our teacher. The Scriptural text ascribed his descent to Manasseh (who actually reigned hundreds of years later) because Jonathan acted as wickedly as King Manasseh.[44] The Talmud proceeds to state: "R. Elazar said: One should always associate with good [people]; for behold, from Moses who married the daughter of Jethro, there descended Jonathan." Jonathan's wickedness is being associated with that of his great-grandfather, Jethro.

The View of R. Elazar

Various Midrashic and Talmudic texts support R. Elazar's view and look upon Jethro in a positive manner, giving the impression that he abandoned his paganism and eventually converted. The

---

43. *Mechilta de-Rabbi Yishmael, Yitro, Masechta de-Amalek*, par. 1.
44. Manasseh, son of Hezekiah, was one of the most wicked kings of Judea (2 Kings 21:2).

previously cited Midrash[45] details the seven names of Jethro, making it clear that he was on good terms with both the Children of Israel and their G-d. In addition, the Jerusalem Talmud (*Berachot* 2:8) says that when the Jewish community behaves properly, G-d scouts the nations of the world seeking righteous people, and arranges for them to join the Jewish nation, apparently to benefit that individual and the nation as a whole. Two examples are cited: Rahab and Jethro. Clearly, the import is that these were two highly virtuous individuals who eventually converted. The Babylonian Talmud states explicitly that Rahab converted and became the wife of Joshua (BT *Zevachim* 116b, *Megillah* 14b).

A number of sources make it clear that Jethro's admirable demeanor was not a result of his coming in contact with Moses. The reverse may have been true. Moses might have chosen to associate with Jethro because of his outstanding character. The following legends trace Jethro's righteous behavior to the time of the initial enslavement of the Hebrews, when he served as one of Pharaoh's three advisors.

1. Pharaoh's hostility, stimulated by jealousy, was first expressed when he said: "Behold, the nation of the Children of Israel are too many and too mighty for us; come, let us deal wisely with them, lest they multiply" (Exod. 1:9-10). According to the Midrash (*Yalkut Shimoni*, Exodus 168), Jethro was one of his advisors, and he made every attempt to dissuade Pharaoh from acting maliciously. He pointed out to Pharaoh that the Israelites were G-d's chosen people, and that historically every ruler who attempted to harm them was subjected to G-d's revenge. He reviewed the events described in the book of Genesis—the suffering of Pharaoh and Abimelech after they abducted Sarah

---

45. *Mechilta Yitro* 18, par. A.

and Rebecca, the devastation which resulted when Abimelech expelled Isaac from Gerar, Abraham's military victory against the four mighty kings, and Jacob's successful resistance to the wiles of Laban and Esau. He further reminded Pharaoh how his royal ancestor had appointed Joseph as his viceroy, in gratitude for saving the entire population from death by starvation.

2. Unfortunately, Pharaoh had two advisors, in addition to Jethro, who were not as well disposed toward the Hebrews. The Talmud states: "R. Hiyya bar Abba said in the name of R. Simai: There were three in that plan [to destroy Israel through the decree that every son be cast in the river (Exod. 1:22)]: Balaam, Job, and Jethro. Balaam, who devised it, was slain; Job, who silently acquiesced, was afflicted with suffering; Jethro, who fled [to save his life, since he had spoken, or was about to speak, in defense of the Hebrews[46]], merited that his descendants should sit in the Chamber of Hewn Stone [in the Temple where the *Sanhedrin* met]" (BT *Sotah* 11a).

3. Apparently Jethro was re-instated as Pharaoh's counselor because, at a later stage, the Midrash (*Exod. Rabbah* 1:26) describes the baby Moses, who was raised in the king's palace, as being in the habit of removing Pharaoh's crown and placing it on his own head. Pharaoh's superstitious magicians, aware of a prediction that Pharaoh would eventually be overthrown, accused the baby of being the potential culprit and decreed that he be put to death immediately. At this point, Jethro intervened and pointed out that the infant was far too young to have acted willfully, and was certainly unaware of the implications of his actions. To prove his point, he suggested that there be brought before the child a bowl containing gold nuggets and burning coals, and the king agreed. Of course

---
46. *Iyun Yaakov* on *Sotah* 11a.

Moses, who was mature far beyond his years, actually reached for the gold, at which point his guardian angel, Gabriel, nudged his hand toward the coals. Moses reflexively placed his hand with the coal in his mouth, and that is how he lost the ability to articulate distinctly.

Answering the Second Question: Did Jethro Arrive before or after the Torah Was Given? (Ibn Ezra vs. Ramban)

This question is actually addressed by the Talmud (BT *Zevachim* 116a), which presents the following three-way Tannaitic difference of opinion, based on varying interpretations of the opening verse of the portion of *Yitro*:

> [The verse states:] "Now Jethro, the priest of Midian, heard" (Exod. 18:1). What news did he hear that he came and converted? R. Yehoshua said: He heard of the battle with the Amalekites, since this is immediately preceded by [the verse] "And Joshua defeated Amalek and his people by the sword" (Exod. 17:13). R. Elazar ha-Modai said: He heard of the giving of the Torah and came. For when the Torah was given to Israel its sound travelled from one end of the earth to the other, and all the heathen kings were seized with trembling in their palaces, and they uttered songs of praise, as it says, "The voice of the Lord [heard at Mount Sinai] scares the does and strips the forests bare, and in his Temple all say: 'Glory'" (Ps. 29:9)... R. Eliezer said: He heard about the dividing of the Red Sea, and came, for it is said, "and it came to pass, when all the

kings of the Amorites heard [that the Lord had dried up the waters of the Jordan for the Children of Israel, until they had crossed over]" ... and even Rahab the harlot said to Joshua's messengers, "For we have heard how the Lord dried up the water of the Red Sea" (Josh. 2:10).

The verse quoted by R. Eliezer describes the miraculous fording of the Jordan under the guidance of Joshua. Maharsha explains that if the inhabitants of the entire region heard of the crossing of the Jordan, which was much less spectacular, certainly they would have been aware of the splitting of the Red Sea, which involved the drowning of Pharaoh's entire army. R. Eliezer also notes the parallel usage of the word "heard." In the present portion it says that Jethro heard (without mentioning explicitly what he heard), while in the book of Joshua the same verb is used to say clearly that what the Amorite kings heard was that a body of water was split in order to enable the Israelites to cross.

The view of R. Eliezer is understandable, since the central and most impressive event in *Beshallach* was certainly the splitting of the Red Sea; in addition, he buttresses his stand by examining parallel wording (and using *a fortiori* logic, according to Maharsha). The view of R. Yehoshua is also readily understood, since the portion of *Yitro* follows immediately upon the battle against Amalek, described at the end of *Beshallach*. R. Elazar ha-Modai is the only one who does not base himself on an event in the preceding portion, but an event to be narrated later in *Yitro*.

R. Elazar ha-Modai bases his view on a Midrashic interpretation of Psalm 29. On a literal level, the psalm describes the awe and fear which G-d's power, as manifested in a tropical storm, infuses in nature. The Midrash (see Rashi on Psalm 29) relates the phrase "the voice of the Lord is upon the waters" to the splitting of the Red Sea, and the words "the voice of the Lord is powerful" to the giving of the Torah, when G-d decreased the intensity of his voice to a level that the people could tolerate. The Midrash interprets the verse "the voice of the Lord scares the does and strips the forests bare, and in his Temple all say: 'Glory'" as referring to revelation. At that time, G-d's powerful voice caused the does, which symbolize the titans of the world (the evil monarchs), to tremble, and caused the trees of the forests to shed their bark (i.e., the kings were stripped of their glory), and in the halls of every ruler they praised the Lord and gave Him honor. Jethro was himself considered to be one of the titans of the world, and thus he too heard the voice of the Lord, and it is to that occasion that the words "Jethro, the priest of Midian, heard" refer.

The View of Ibn Ezra

Ibn Ezra (Exod. 18:1) adopts the view of R. Elazar ha-Modai, but does not base his approach on the Midrashic explanation of Psalm 29 alone; rather, he reinforces it by bringing a number of additional proofs. For example, after meeting with Moses, Jethro wonders why the former is constantly surrounded by members of the congregation, whereupon Moses answers: "I inform them of the statutes of G-d, and His laws" (Exod. 18:16). The implication is that the Torah had already been given.

This inference may be refuted by positing that the statutes and laws referred to in the verse are those given at Marah (Abarbanel, Exodus 18). Another possibility is that Jethro arrived before the Torah was given, but his realization that Moses was handling the people's religious and interpersonal problems in an inefficient manner, and that there was a more expedient way of working, only occurred after a considerable amount of time had elapsed. This is exactly the intent of Rashi (Exod. 18:13), who does not take sides in the Tannaitic argument, but posits that even those who believe that Jethro arrived before the Torah was given also hold that his suggestions were made only afterward.

After Ibn Ezra determined that Jethro's arrival in the Sinai desert with the family of Moses took place after the Torah was given, he had to explain why it appears in the text before the description of that event. He gives two reasons. First, it was desirable to attach the story to the previous portion, where it states, "the Lord will continue to war with Amalek from generation to generation" (Exod. 17:16). One might get the impression that Israel wished to conquer the world and had a hostile attitude toward all Gentiles. Therefore, Scripture wishes to show that the attitude toward Jethro was positive, just as Jethro's attitude toward the Hebrews was sympathetic, as indicated by the verse at the beginning of the portion: "And Jethro rejoiced regarding all of the good which the Lord had done to Israel, in that He had delivered them out of the hand of the Egyptians" (Exod. 18:9).

A second reason for the juxtaposition is that the Kenites (Jethro's tribe) lived—at a later period—in the same region as Amalek, and Scripture wished to warn Israel's leaders not to allow them to suffer collateral damage in any future war with Amalek. Saul later took this advice to heart when he said: "Go, depart, go down from among the Amalekites, lest I destroy you with them; for you showed kindness to all the Children of Israel when they came up out of Egypt" (1 Sam. 15:6). The Kenites, on their part, seriously heeded Saul's request, as is seen from the continuation of the verse: "And the Kenites removed themselves from among the Amalekites."

Rashbam (Exod. 18:3) agrees with Ibn Ezra regarding the timing of the events, but proffers a different explanation as to why the story of Jethro appears in Scripture out of chronological sequence, namely: "In order not to interrupt the portions dealing with commandments, he brought forward the story of Jethro." Rashbam wishes to point out that in the portion of *Yitro*, the giving of the Ten Commandments is followed by a stream of laws in the next portion, *Mishpatim*, continuing to the end of Exodus with the description of the structure of the holy Tabernacle (*Mishkan*) and the priestly garments. Placing the Jethro narrative in the middle of this set of commands would be a divergence, so it was made to precede it, even though in reality it occurred after the Torah was given.

The View of Ramban

Ramban, in contrast to Ibn Ezra, accepts the Tannaitic opinion that Jethro arrived before the giving of the Torah. In addition to the obvious reason—based on the order of Scripture, the Torah was not yet given—he claims that if revelation had already occurred, since it was an awe-inspiring event accompanied by thunder, lightning, and the deafening sound of the blast of a *shofar* (Exod. 19:16), how could it be that neither Moses nor Jethro made the slightest reference to it? Although R. Elazar ha-Modai says that first verse in the portion (which says, "Jethro heard of all that G-d had done for Moses and for Israel His people, how the Lord had brought Israel out of Egypt" [Exod. 18:1]) describes the giving of the Torah, the straightforward meaning is that what he heard related directly to the exodus from Egypt. Even R. Yehoshua's attribution of the reference to the battle with Amalek is forced. In the words of Ramban:

Why does it not say that he heard what G-d had done for Moses and for Israel His people by giving the Torah, which is among the great wonders that were done for them, as He said: "For ask about the days past, which were before you, from the day that G-d created man upon the earth, and from one end of heaven to the other, has there been anything as great as this, or has there been heard like it? Did any people ever hear the voice of G-d speaking out of the midst of a fire, as you did, and yet remain alive?" (Deut. 4:32-33). And when Scripture states: "And Moses told his father-in-law all that the Lord had done to Pharaoh and to the Egyptians for Israel's benefit, [and] all the travail which they encountered on the way" (Exod. 18:8), and when Jethro replied, "Now I know that the Lord is greater than all gods" (Exod. 18:11), why didn't Moses tell him about the revelation on Mount Sinai, from which he would know that G-d exists, that His Torah is the truth, and that there is no G-d other than He, as it says: "To you it was shown, that the Lord He is G-d; there is no G-d other than Him. Out of heaven He allowed you to hear His voice" (Deut. 4:34-35).

In summary, Ramban's view is that Jethro arrived with the family of Moses before the Torah was given, so that the first part of the portion of *Yitro* is not out of sequence chronologically, while Ibn Ezra feels that Jethro arrived only after the Torah was given, and he provides reasons for the story appearing out of sequence. Most of the proofs adduced by Ibn Ezra relate to the sacrifices brought by Jethro and the judicial advice that he proffered to Moses. Ramban has alternative explanations for these events. In addition, he agrees that Jethro's stay lasted until after revelation, so some of the occurrences may have taken place later.

Yitro

Answering the Third and Fourth Questions: Did Jethro Visit Twice and Stay the Second Time? (Ramban vs. Ibn Ezra)

The difference of opinion between Ibn Ezra and Ramban is not confined to the timing of the story described in Exodus. The dispute is also whether the texts of Exodus and Numbers relate to the same event or to independent occurrences.

Ibn Ezra

Ibn Ezra (on Exod. 18:1) states quite clearly that the descriptions of Jethro's arrival in Exodus and his departure in Numbers overlap. In his own words: "He [Jethro] answered 'I will not go; but I will depart to my own land, and to my birthplace' (Num. 10:30) and this is [what it states in Exodus], 'And Moses sent his father-in-law away' (Exod. 18:27)."

According to Ibn Ezra, Jethro refused the offer of Moses in Numbers, since the Bible is referring to the same incident concerning which it says explicitly in Exodus that Moses sent him home to Midian (apparently with no vacilation, although the text of Numbers implies otherwise). The degree of affection between Moses and Jethro, in Ibn Ezra's opinion, is not known, although his comment on the verse "And Moses sent his father-in-law away" (Exod. 18:27) is that he sent him off honorably.[47] Apparently, living in close proximity did not work out. If, in fact, Jethro was acceptable and desirable to Moses and the Children of Israel, they were not

---

47. The Vilna Gaon interprets the previously quoted words of R. Joshua in the *Mechilta* in this manner.

successful in conveying that message to him in a clear-cut fashion. Ibn Ezra does not even say whether Jethro actually converted (i.e., whether he adopts the opinion of R. Elazar or R. Yehoshua).

Ramban

Ramban prefers the more straightforward approach—that these two stories are independent events. They appear a great distance from each other, separated by the entire book of Leviticus, and they differ in many details. According to Ramban, they do not even lead to the same conclusion. Although Jethro returns home in Exodus, in the incident described in Numbers, Jethro acquiesces to Moses' entreaties and remains with the Children of Israel. In Ramban's words (on Exod. 18:1):

> It seems to me that what is said here, "And Moses sent his father-in-law away; and he went back to his own land" (Exod. 18:27), was in the first year [of the exodus], and he went off to his land, and later returned to him [Moses]. It is possible that he went there to convert his family, and he returned to Moses while he was still in the Sinai desert, which is close to Midian, as I have mentioned. For when the camp embarked in the month of Iyar [the second month] of the second year, when Moses said to him, "We are journeying… come with us" (Num. 10:29), and he answered, "I will not go; but I will depart to my own land, and to my birthplace" (Num. 10:30), Moses pleaded with him and said to him, "Do not leave us… and you shall be to us instead of eyes. And if you go with us, then whatever good the Lord does to us, the same will we do to [share with] you" (Num. 10:31-32), and he did not answer him.

YITRO

And it would appear that *he accepted Moses' plea* and did as he [Moses] had requested and did not leave them.

Ramban brings a proof text to support his view, but also presents a difficulty with his view. The proof is from a Midrash[48] that says that Jethro was ceded the most fertile part of Jericho, which would indicate that he stayed with the Jewish nation. Also, in the book of Kings (2 Kings 10:15-16), Jehonadab son of Rechab is mentioned, who was of the family of Jethro and helped Jehu murder the priests of Baal. Ramban also cites the descendants of Jehonadab, who lived near Jerusalem and were blessed by Jeremiah (Jer. 35:1-19).

The question which Ramban asks on his own opinion is that in the book of Samuel (1 Sam. 15:6), it says that the Kenites did not dwell among the Israelites, but near the Amalekites, as previously noted. Ramban (Exod. 18:1) answers:

Perhaps when Moses died, Jethro or his sons returned to their land. And it is possible that the Kenites that dwelt with Amalek were of the family of Jethro, but not his children, and he [Saul] showed kindness to the entire family on his [Jethro's] account, just as Joshua did [i.e., dealt kindly] with the family of Rahab (Josh. 6:25).

RASHI'S VIEW

Rashi (on Exod. 18:1) seems to take a view somewhere between that of Ramban and Ibn Ezra. Rashi states that Jethro's name was originally Jether [Hebrew, *Yeter*] but, when he converted, an additional letter was added to his name. On the phrase, "And Moses

---

48. *Sifrei Behaalotcha* 34:1; *Mechilta de-Rabbi Shimon bar Yochai, Yitro* 18:27.

sent his father-in-law away," Rashi says that he sent him to convert his family. Clearly Rashi, like Ramban and in contradistinction to Ibn Ezra, feels that Jethro became unreservedly Jewish. On the other hand, regarding the verse "I will not go; but I will depart to my own land, and to my birthplace" (Num. 10:30), Rashi explains that Jethro owned considerable property in Midian, and also missed the members of his family who dwelt there. The Midrash (*Sifrei Behaalotcha* 79) on which Rashi bases his comment also mentions that Jethro did not want to relinquish his prestigious position as a judge. R. Yosef Bechor Shor (Num. 10:29-30) says that Jethro feared the military confrontations which would be necessary to conquer the land, while Seforno (Num. 10:30) says that he felt that the change of diet and climate would be difficult for a man of his age. Like Ibn Ezra and unlike Ramban, Rashi considers the two texts to be describing the one and only visit of Jethro to the Israelite camp, and therefore it is to be assumed that Jethro in fact declined Moses' entreaties to remain with the camp.

JETHRO CONTRASTED TO OTHER BIBLICAL CHARACTERS

JETHRO'S WEAKNESS

One might ask, what sin did Jethro commit by wishing to go home? The Torah is in favor of spreading the word of G-d. A verse in the next chapter states: "And you shall be unto Me a kingdom of priests and a holy nation" (Exod. 19:6), and Seforno comments: "to understand and to teach the entire human race, that all should call upon the name of the Lord and serve Him in unity." How can one spread the word of G-d? One might suggest that this be done by traversing the world, knocking on doors, and discussing faith in G-d. That is exactly what Jethro intended to do, so why did Moses try to dissuade him (Num. 10:31)? The answer is that such a tactic was not practical then, nor is it today. The State of Israel presently has a population of approximately seven million Jews, while the world population is about seven billion—a ratio of one to a thousand. It is more likely that the messengers would assimilate among the Gentiles than that they would influence the world's inhabitants. The alternative, and this is what the Torah proposes, is to develop an exemplary country that would serve as a model for imitation by the rest of the world.

In modern terms, Jethro could be described as religious (*dati*), but not nationalistic (*leumi*).

Dathan and Abiram

At the beginning of *Beshallach*, instead of directing the Children of Israel to travel through the land of the Philistines, which hugs the Mediterranean Sea, and arrive in the Land of Israel in a few days, G-d directed them to go toward the Red Sea and through the desert, and even to retrace their steps at one point. This maneuver was meant to bewilder Pharaoh and to mislead him into thinking that he could overcome the Hebrews if he pursued them. In the words of the text: "And Pharaoh will say to the Children of Israel: They are entangled in the land" (Exod. 14:3). The question that arises is: How could Pharaoh speak to the Children of Israel after they escaped? Rashi gives the simplest answer by stating that instead of the literal translation "say to the Children of Israel," these words should be translated as: "say of the Children of Israel." Targum Yonatan, on the other hand, adopts a Midrashic approach and explains these words as follows: "And Pharaoh will say to

Dathan and Abiram, of the Children of Israel who had remained in Egypt."

R. Yehuda Nachshoni (*Hagut be-Parshiyot ha-Torah*, p. 268) asks the following question: If Dathan and Abiram did not want to leave Egypt, why were they not among the wicked Israelites who died during the plague of darkness, in accordance with Rashi's comment that only one out of five left Egypt, and four out of five died during the plague of darkness (Rashi on Exod. 13:18). One might add another question: If Dathan and Abiram did not want to leave Egypt, why did they not simply remain there? How is it that their exasperating presence is noted throughout the sojourning, until they died as a result of their involvement with Korah and his congregation? The answer given is that as a result of Moses telling Pharaoh, "We will make a three-day journey into the wilderness, and sacrifice to the Lord our G-d" (Exod. 8:23), the Hebrews were able to borrow vessels from their Egyptian neighbors, who assumed that they would be returning shortly. Moses revealed to his close associates the secret that they were in fact leaving for good. Of course, scoundrels like Dathan and Abiram were not among Moses' most intimate friends, so that they, like the Egyptians, were under the impression that the Hebrews would return after a short excursion.

Dathan and Abiram were eager to be counted among the Children of Israel, and that is exactly what the wicked people who died in the plague of darkness did not want. The two men were only not interested in joining those who planned to bring sacrifices in the desert, because they did not consider themselves to be religious. They thought the Israelites would return after a few days, and it did not bother them (it may have even delighted them) to miss the sacrifices and prayers. However, when they understood that the Israelites were fleeing on a permanent basis, they realized that deep down they wished to join them. But what could they do if they were stranded in Egypt?

Yitro

Dathan and Abiram devised the following strategy. They would tell Pharaoh that they had defected from the Jewish nation and wished to join the Egyptians. To demonstrate their "loyalty" to their new homeland, they proposed that they join the Egyptian army and participate in the pursuit of the Children of Israel. When the army closed in on the Israelites, they offered their services as spies. After all, they told Pharaoh, we understand their language and are familiar with their mores, so we will be able to retrieve exact information for you with regard to their intentions and plans. Pharaoh fell for this hoax, and allowed them to cross the enemy lines as spies. As is well known, they failed to return, remaining in the Israelite camp, and became a severe nuisance to Moses for a number of years until their sordid finish in the Korah affair.

Dathan and Abiram wanted to be part of the Israelite nation, but they could not control their instincts nor bridle their desires, and were perhaps deficient in their faith as well. One could describe them as nationalistic (*leumi*) but not religious (*dati*).

Ruth the Moabite

Ramban considers Jethro to be completely righteous, having undergone conversion, gone to his homeland to convert his household, and returned on a permanent basis with his extended family. R. Yehoshua (in the Midrash) and possibly Ibn Ezra believe that he did not necessarily convert, and eventually returned to his own country and beliefs. Rashi holds the middle ground, considering Jethro to be a righteous person who abandoned idolatry and converted himself as well as others. However, he did not wish to completely assimilate into the Israelite nation, and was thus described as being *dati* but not *leumi*, as opposed to Dathan and Abiram, who were the opposite.

The person who combined both positive elements, religion and nationalism, was Ruth the Moabite.[49] If Jethro was not considered to be the image of perfection, it was not because of an inherent disdain for converts, since Ruth was also a convert. Rather, he was judged by the level of his acceptance, understanding, and performance of his religious duties, and found to be lacking in some areas—areas in which some born-Jews are equally deficient.

Apparently, what attracted Ruth to Judaism was the special personality of her mother-in-law, Naomi. Ruth was intelligent enough to realize that Naomi's impressive character was a result of her religious orthodoxy, her belief in G-d, and her intimate attachment to the Jewish nation. Consequently, even when Naomi tried to dissuade her by saying, "Behold, your sister-in-law is gone back unto her people, and unto her god; return after your sister-in-law" (Ruth 1:15), she realized that in Moab she would not be able to obtain the spiritual charge that she sought. She therefore replied to Naomi: "Do not entreat me to leave you, to return from following you; for where you go, I will go; and where you lodge, I will lodge; your people is my people, and your G-d is my G-d" (Ruth 1:16). The latter phrase summarizes her insight with respect to the basic elements of Judaism.

Ruth instinctively understood the tight coupling of the Torah of Israel with the Land of Israel, and educated her offspring accordingly. On the basis of her perceptiveness, she merited that from her family line the kingdom of Israel was established—by her great-grandson David, who said, when he was coerced to leave Israel: "for they have driven me out this day from cleaving to the inheritance of the Lord, saying: Go, serve other gods" (1 Sam. 26:19). King David, like Ruth, understood that residence in the Diaspora could potentially initiate a process leading to idol-worship.

---

49. *Hagut be-Parshiyot ha-Torah*, p. 288.

Yitro

Summary

There are differences of opinion with regard to each of the four questions that were posed. Ibn Ezra claimed that Jethro arrived after the Torah had been given, stayed briefly, and returned home, as described in Exodus and later in Numbers. Ramban posited that he arrived before the Torah was given, returned home after revelation to convert his family and friends, rejoined the nation at a later stage, and acquiesced to the request of Moses to remain as a permanent member of the Children of Israel.

In terms of Jethro's personality, R. Elazar (whose view was adopted by Ramban) saw him as a righteous convert to Judaism, while R. Yehoshua held that he maintained his pagan beliefs and did not necessarily identify with the Israelite nation. Rashi seems to have taken a view between the two Tannaitic extremes, holding that Jethro did indeed convert, but was perhaps lacking in certain areas.

In the eyes of Rashi, Jethro, Dathan, Abiram, and Ruth were shown to represent permutations of two important aspects of Judaism—religiosity and nationality. Dathan and Abiram were nationalistic, but not religious. Jethro, although religious, was not considered to be a totally righteous individual, and his Judaism did not symbolize the ideal, because it lacked the element of "the nation of Israel dwelling in the Land of Israel," the nationalistic element. The convert who symbolizes the perfect synthesis of these elements is Ruth, and for that reason she serves as a source of inspiration for future generations of the Children of Israel.

Mishpatim

A number of portions in the Pentateuch read like a law book, i.e., they contain a compendium of statutes, mostly civil in nature. *Mishpatim* is the first such portion. Other examples are *Kedoshim* in the book of Leviticus and the three-portion series of *Re'eh*, *Shoftim*, and *Ki Teitzei* in the book of Deuteronomy.

The list of laws in *Mishpatim* actually starts at the end of the previous portion (*Yitro*). The present chapter begins by explaining the difference between the laws detailed in the two portions, proceeds to list the laws introduced in *Mishpatim*, and explains how their sequence reflects the order of the Ten Commandments.

The end of the portion exhibits an abrupt change in content, reverting to narrative prose to describe the ratification of a covenant between G-d and Israel finalizing the commitment to observe the laws of the Torah. Although the style changes, the intimate connection to the preceding legal entries is obvious, since laws cannot be effective in the absence of an obligation to fulfill them. The portion ends with the logical conclusion of the revelatory story—the description of the ascent of Moses on Mt. Sinai for a period of forty days to master the contents of the oral and written law.

Mishpatim

The Conclusion of *Yitro*: G-d-Oriented Laws

After the Ten Commandments were given, the remaining task was to inculcate their message and to accustom the nation to fulfill them. The Torah attempts to accomplish this by continually presenting and reviewing their contents. The first verses that appear after the revelation at Mt. Sinai, at the end of *Yitro*, state: "You have seen that I have talked with you from heaven. You shall not make [idols to worship] with Me—gods of silver or gods of gold you shall not make for yourselves" (Exod. 20:19-20).

Ramban (Exod. 21:1) explains that these verses provide a short synopsis of the first two commandments. He states:

> Warn them again that they should pay attention to what they saw, and they should be punctilious regarding these *mitzvot* that I have commanded them, for "You have seen [that I have talked with you from heaven]," with respect to the [first] commandment, "I am the Lord [your G-d]"; and "You shall not make with Me," with respect to [the second commandment], "You shall not have [other gods]."

Following these laws are a number of verses that discuss the structure of the altar, and then the Torah moves on to the portion of *Mishpatim*. The altar symbolizes the link to G-d that is implemented by observing the laws between man and G-d, that compose the first half of the Ten Commandments. The description of the altar appears before the detailed presentation of the social laws in *Mishpatim* in order to stress that by serving the Lord one stimulates and strengthens the bonds between man and his fellow man, which are regulated by a system of social justice. The close connection between service of G-d and fruitful interpersonal relationships as signified by social law is manifested in the Biblical phrase: "for [sound] judgment [between man and his fellow man] belongs to G-d [is G-dly]" (Deut. 1:17), which, in its simplest interpretation, points to a reciprocal relationship between honest judgment and closeness to the Almighty.

The close connection between the altar, which symbolizes the channel for communication between G-d and Israel, and the laws regulating man's behavior toward his fellow man is not coincidental. Living a moral life and enforcement of social legislation are a direct result of belief in a single, omnipotent Supreme Being. Idol-worship presents a multiplicity of gods bereft of any moral code, as evidenced by the typical behavior and unrelenting internecine conflicts of the gods of Greek mythology.

Just as belief in the unity of G-d leads to a moral lifestyle, moral behavior leads to awareness of the presence of G-d, as the Talmud (BT *Sanhedrin* 7a) states:

> A judge who judges in perfect truth causes the *Shechinah* to dwell in Israel, for it is written: "G-d stands in the congregation of G-d, in the midst of the judges does He judge" (Ps. 82:1). And he who does not judge in perfect truth causes the *Shechinah* to depart from Israel, for it is written: "Because of the oppression of the poor, because of the sighing of the needy, now will I arise [removing the Divine Presence from Israel]" (Ps. 12:6).

Mishpatim

Making an Altar of Uncut Stones

At the end of *Yitro*, the Torah states that the future altar must be constructed of uncut stones: "And if you make Me an altar of stone, you should not build it of hewn stones; for if you lift up your sword upon it, *you have profaned it*" (Exod. 20:22). This command is repeated at the end of the nation's journey, closer to when it was to be implemented, where the Pentateuch states: "And you shall build an altar there to the Lord your G-d, an altar of stones; you shall not lift up an iron tool on them" (Deut. 27:5).

Why was the commandment not to use cut stones announced forty years before it was to be implemented? Perhaps one can answer that the Torah wished to make a statement early on that one should not look at the altar as a means of pacifying G-d independent of one's behavior in accomplishing his diurnal activities. This point is stressed once more upon the recurrence of the command, when the Israelites were required to inscribe on those very stones all of the laws of the Torah, including those between man and his fellow man (Ibn Ezra on Deut. 27:1).

Rashi emphasizes this idea in his comment on the words "you have profaned it," where he states (Exod. 20:22):

> You thus learn that if you raise an iron instrument upon it, then you have profaned it, because the altar was created in order to lengthen man's days [by requesting absolution for one's sins] and iron was created in order to shorten man's days. It is not appropriate that an object that cuts short should be lifted above one that lengthens. In addition, the altar makes peace between Israel and their Father in heaven [when one confesses his sins]. Therefore, there should not

pass over it an object that cuts and destroys. And the following statement follows logically, *a fortiori*: If stones that neither see nor hear nor speak—but because they promote peace, Scripture ordains (Deut. 27:5) that you should not raise an iron tool upon them, then one who makes peace between a man and his wife, between one family and another, between a man and his fellow man, how much more certain is it that he will not experience suffering.

THE FIRST VERSE OF *MISHPATIM*: TRANSITIONING TO CIVIL LEGISLATION

The portion begins with the words "And these are the ordinances" (Exod. 21:1). Rashi[50] notes that the word "and" links the Ten Commandments of the previous portion to the laws presented in the present portion, and he continues by saying: "Just as the former [the Ten Commandments] were from Sinai, so were these from Sinai." In the FIRST OVERVIEW, the following Tannaitic dispute is quoted:

> R. Ishmael said: The general laws were stated at Sinai and the details were given in the Tent of Meeting. R. Akiva said: Both the general laws and the details were given at Sinai, repeated in the Tent of Meeting, and reiterated once more on the plains of Moab (BT *Zevachim* 115b).

According to the view of R. Ishmael, Rashi's comment informs the reader that unlike the rest of the laws of the Torah, which were given to Moses only in outline form at Mt. Sinai, the laws of

---

50. Based on *Mechilta de-Rabbi Yishmael, Mishpatim, Masechta de-Nezikin, parashah* 1.

Mishpatim

Mishpatim were given in detail at Mt. Sinai. However, according to the view of R. Akiva, what new idea is Rashi stating? If every law was spelled out in detail at Sinai, in what way are these particular laws different from the others? R. Eliyahu Mizrachi answers that Rashi should be interpreted as follows:

> Just as the former [the Ten Commandments] were given at Sinai in the presence of all of the Children of Israel and were accompanied by thunder and lightning, so were these, unlike the remaining laws that were taught to Moses in private during the forty days that he spent on Mt. Sinai.[51]

One may now ask—according to R. Mizrachi—why were the laws of the present portion singled out to be given to the accompaniment of thunder and lightning? The Midrash (*Exod. Rabbah* 30:15) provides an answer:

> Just as the Almighty [specially] admonished with respect to the [Ten] Commandments, so did He [specially] admonish with respect to civil law. Why? Because on this [proper judicial decisions] the world rests, as it says: "The king, by virtue of justice, establishes the land" (Prov. 29:4).

Similarly, Ramban states (on Exod. 21:1): "The entire Torah is dependent on justice." These sayings buttress the previously proposed thesis that the purpose of the Torah is to create an environment steeped in peace and brotherly love—a condition that can attain only if there exists sincere and honest enforcement of Pentateuchal legislation.

---

51. The *Or ha-Chaim* feels that R. Mizrachi does not possess the authority to propose such an answer without a source to base himself on.

Rashi's Question Regarding the Juxtaposition of the Portions concerning the Altar and Civil Law

If the portion of *Mishpatim* was transmitted at Sinai on the same occasion as the Ten Commandments, then the paragraph relating to the altar, which appears between them, must have also been given at Sinai. This leads Rashi to pose the following question (on Exod. 21:1): "Why is the section dealing with civil laws placed immediately after the section dealing with the altar?" It has already been mentioned that the law concerning the altar was not applicable for forty years. So why mention it here? Four answers will be presented.

A Simple Answer

One may say that the laws of the altar that appear in the portion of *Yitro* were placed before civil law in the portion of *Mishpatim* to highlight the centrality of the laws between man and G-d as a means of preparation for observing the laws between man and his fellow man. Obeying those laws inculcates the discipline and self-control, as well as the subservience to the dictates of G-d, necessary to excel in interpersonal behavior.

The *Sefat Emet*

Sefat Emet (*Mishpatim* 635) expands on the previous answer by noting that after hearing a number of laws regarding man's duties to G-d at the end of *Yitro* (how to construct an altar), one might have thought that the content of *Mishpatim* is based on pure logic and did not have to be transmitted by the Almighty. Therefore, the Bible reminds the reader that the laws of *Mishpatim* were also given at Sinai, in order to tell the Israelites that even with regard to those laws which are intellectually understandable and reasonable, their compulsory nature stems exclusively from the fact that they were commanded by G-d. Human logic does not create obligation—Divine will does so. The previously quoted verse from Deuteronomy encapsulates this idea when it says: "for [sound] judgment [between man and his fellow man] belongs to G-d" (Deut. 1:17), i.e., also justice must be executed because it is a direct command from the Almighty. The world has witnessed under the regimes of Stalin and Hitler what can happen when one allows laws between man and his fellow man to be legislated by human beings.

For the same reason, it may be noted that the only place where the Torah specifically mentions that the *mitzvot* were given at Sinai is at the end of Leviticus, where the Bible states: "And the Lord spoke unto Moses on Mt. Sinai, saying" (Lev. 25:1).[52] That verse also appears after a series of laws between man and G-d—statutes relating to priests, purity and impurity, and holiday rituals, and it serves as an introduction to a series of laws between man and his fellow man (relating to helping the poor during the Sabbatical year and at other times).

RASHI

Rashi answers his own question as follows: "To tell you that you should seat the *Sanhedrin* [which deals with civil law] near the Temple [other versions: near the altar]," i.e., in one of the chambers of the Temple court called the *lishkat ha-gazit*.[53]

---

52. That segment ends with the concluding verse: "These are the commandments, which the Lord commanded Moses for the Children of Israel on Mt. Sinai" (Lev. 27:34).
53. Eliyahu Mizrachi on verse 21:1.

The Ethics of Exodus

Talmud

The Talmud (BT *Sanhedrin* 7b) relates to the question of the juxtaposition by citing two separate statements which exhort against haughty behavior on the part of judges, both based on the last verse of the portion of *Yitro*: "You should not ascend using steps upon My altar, so that your nakedness be not uncovered on it" (Exod. 20:23). The Talmud states:

> Bar Kappara expounded: From where do we derive that which our Rabbis stated: "Be deliberate in judgment?" (*Ethics of the Fathers* 1:1). From what is written, "You should not ascend using steps upon My altar," which is followed by "And these are the judgments" (Exod. 21:1).

The straightforward explanation of Bar Kappara's insight is that just as one ascends the altar by taking small, measured steps on a ramp, rather than larger steps on a staircase, so must one proceed at an exacting, deliberate pace when making judicial decisions. *Torah Temimah* (Exod. 21:1) sees the words "not ascend" as indicating that one should not ascend figuratively. He should not look upon himself as spiritually superior to others to the point that when it comes to judging civil cases he doesn't feel the need to sift through the minutiae patiently, but allows himself to jump to conclusions without thoroughly examining the evidence, on the assumption that he is infallible.

The Talmud continues:

> R. Elazar said: From where do we derive that a judge should not walk over the heads of the holy people? It is

written: "You should not ascend using steps upon My altar," which is followed by: "And these are the judgments."

Rashi on the Talmud explains that when a judicial decision was explained to litigants, they would sit on the ground, and if the judge would walk among the people, it would appear as if he were trampling on their heads. *Torah Temimah* generalizes the concept as an exhortation to the judges not to act condescendingly toward litigants (referred to by R. Elazar as "holy people") at any time, but to treat each and every one with honor, as a respected member of the congregation. *Kli Yakar* is of the opinion that "holy people" refers to the judges rather than the litigants, i.e., R. Elazar is urging the judges to relate to each other with veneration, affection, and courtesy.

Kli Yakar asks why Rashi would disregard the two Talmudic answers to the question regarding the juxtaposition of the altar and civil law, and instead propose his own answer. He answers that Rashi did not ignore the Talmudic answers. He actually agrees with them, and the answer Rashi himself proposed is the prerequisite that was needed in order for Bar Kappara and R. Elazar to express their views. This explanation will now be elaborated.

The Hebrew word for "upon" (*al*), in the phrase "You should not ascend using steps onto My altar" can mean "upon," but it can also mean "next to." If it means "upon," the verse refers to the altar exclusively. If it means "next to," the verse refers to the *Sanhedrin*, which was situated next to the altar. The inferences of both Bar Kappara and R. Elazar assume that *al* means "next to." But why should it? The answer is only because the next verse is "And these are the judgments," which implies that the previous verses also relate in some way to judicial matters, and that is exactly what Rashi indicates at the beginning of *Mishpatim*.

Kli Yakar notes one additional point. With regard to Bar Kappara's teaching, the word "expounded" is used. That is because what he says is not the simple meaning of the verse, but a Midrashic exegesis. The altar symbolizes the trait of modesty, as indicated at the end of *Yitro* (Exod. 20:21), where the Israelites are commanded to fill the altar with earth. Similarly, a verse in Psalms reads: "[The preferred] sacrifices to G-d are a broken spirit" (Ps. 51:19). Nevertheless, comparing ascending steps to an altar with not acting deliberately in judgment is possible only on the Midrashic level. R. Elazar, on the other hand, relates to the physical act of walking, in keeping with the literal meaning of the verse, merely saying that it should not be done in a disrespectful manner, both on the altar and in court.

Rashi, at the end of *Yitro* (Exod. 20:23), reduces the metaphoric level of R. Elazar's opinion even more than *Kli Yakar*. Even if the given verse refers exclusively to the altar, one may use *a fortiori* logic to say that if one is not supposed to walk in a way that is shameful to the stones of the altar, which actually have no capacity to feel embarrassed, how much more so should one not walk in a manner that degrades people.

The Main Body of *Mishpatim*: Civil Legislation

The end of the portion of *Yitro* presented *mitzvot* between man and G-d, which fortified and deepened the Israelites' commitment to fulfilling the Ten Commandments. Abarbanel (on Exodus 20) describes the continuation of the portion of *Mishpatim* as an expansion and elaboration of the final five commandments, which legislate man's behavior toward his fellow man. These commandments are: "You should not murder. You should not commit adultery. You should not steal. You should not bear false witness against your compatriot. You should not covet" (Exod. 20:13-14).

Abarbanel explains that the prohibition of adultery (the seventh command) should have followed that of stealing, but the order was reversed for two possible reasons:

1. To parallel the second commandment, "You shall have no other gods before Me," since each appears in the second position on their respective tablets. This accords with the Midrash[54] that speaks of three commandments on the second tablet that were purposely placed opposite their corresponding command on the first tablet.
   a. "You shall not murder" was placed opposite "I am the Lord your G-d" to indicate that anyone who spills blood is considered to have diminished the image of G-d, since man was created in His image.
   b. "You shall not commit adultery" was placed opposite "You shall have no other gods before Me" to indicate that anyone who engages in idolatry is like a person who abandons his true partner to pursue an adulterous relationship.
   c. "You shall not bear false witness against your compatriot" was placed opposite "Remember the Sabbath day, to keep it holy" to indicate that he who desecrates the Sabbath is compared to one who testifies falsely by denying G-d's having created the world in six days and resting on the seventh.
2. To focus on two aspects of a married woman. In the words of Abarbanel:

---

54. *Mechilta de-Rabbi Yishmael, Yitro, Masechta de-ba-Chodesh, parashah* 8.

> Because a woman is to some extent part of the man's body—bone of his bones and flesh of his flesh (Gen. 2:23), and on the other hand she is considered his property and his possession,[55] therefore this commandment is placed between "You shall not murder" [indicating the bodily connection] and "You shall not steal" [indicating the monetary connection].

It is possible that Abarbanel thought the proper place for the prohibition of adultery was after the prohibition of theft because he believed that the commandments proceed in order of severity, from the most severe to the least severe. Traditionally, the "stealing" referred to in the Ten Commandments is actually kidnapping (BT *Sanhedrin* 86a). However, even with regard to ordinary theft the Talmud states (BT *Sanhedrin* 108a):

> R. Johanan said: Come and see how great is the power of robbery. Although the generation of the flood transgressed everything [all of the Noahide laws], yet their decree of punishment was sealed only because they stretched out their hands to rob, as it is written, "for the earth is filled with violence because of them, and, behold, I will destroy them with the earth" (Gen. 6:13).

In the view of Abarbanel, if one relates to the natural order of the last five commands (i.e., with stealing preceding adultery), it is possible to understand the ordering of the many commands in the present portion, as will be described.

---

55. Using more modern terminology, one might say that husband and wife share their material wealth.

Mishpatim

You Should Not Murder

Verse	Abarbanel's Commentary
21:2: If you buy a Hebrew servant…	If he does not free him after 6 years, it is as if he murdered him.
21:7: And if a man sells his daughter to be a maidservant…	If the master does not properly release her, it is as if he murdered her.
21:12: One who smites a man to death should surely be put to death.	—
21:15: One who smites his father or his mother should surely be put to death.	If he hits him and causes a wound, a bruise, or a festering sore, he is liable to the death penalty.
21:16: And he that steals a man, and sells him, and he was found in his possession [before selling him], he shall surely be put to death.	He should not steal one of his brothers and sell him… because this is also murdering the elderly father.
21:17: And he that curses his father or his mother shall surely be put to death.	He should not curse them, for that is also like murdering them.
21:18: And if men argue, and one smites another with a stone, or with his fist, and he does not die…	He is called a murderer even if he does not kill him (but he is not liable for the death penalty).
21:19: And if a man smites his slave, or his maidservant, with a rod, and he/she dies under his hand…	—
21:22: And if men strive together, and hurt a pregnant woman causing the fetus to emerge…	This is also included in "You shall not murder."
21:26: And if a man smites the eye of his servant or the eye of his maidservant, and destroys it…	This is also included in "You shall not murder."
21:28: And if an ox gores a man or a woman, so that they die…	This is when the murder can be related (in some manner) to the owner (of the ox).

Abarbanel summarizes the situation as follows:

> All of these laws are considered to be included in "You shall not murder," and none of them were incumbent upon the Children of Noah—other than that they should not kill each other. For that reason it says "And these are the ordinances that you should set before them"—before those who heard the Ten Commandments they should be set, but not before the Children of Noah or the other nations.

In order to validate his theory, Abarbanel included cases that are not subject to the death penalty, but are close (metaphorically) to those that are. Abarbanel apparently accepts the view of Rambam (*Hilchot Melachim* 9:14) that the seventh Noahide law, to establish social laws, meant only enforcing the other six and adjudicating those who transgress them. According to Ramban (Gen. 38:13), on the other hand, who believed that it required the development of an entire system of law, the laws in *Mishpatim* might well have been implicitly included in the seven Noahide laws.

Once more, Abarbanel points out that the prohibition against stealing in the Noahide laws was general in nature and did not even approach the level of detail found in the present portion, which was aimed exclusively at the Israelites, who had been given the Torah. At this stage, similar lists will be displayed for the remaining four of the five ethical commandments that comprise the second tablet: the prohibitions against stealing, adultery, bearing false witness, and coveting.

The second category, according to Abarbanel, connected with the prohibition to steal, contains laws governing financial losses that people cause to each other.

Mishpatim

You Should Not Steal

1. 21:33: And if a man opens a pit, or if a man digs a pit and does not cover it…
2. 21:35: And if one man's ox hurts another's, so that it dies…
3. 21:37: If a man steals an ox, or a sheep, and kills it, or sells it…
4. 22:4: If a man causes a field or vineyard to be eaten [by a beast], and lets his beast loose, and it feeds in another man's field…
5. 22:5: If fire breaks out, and finds thorns, so that the piles of grain, or the standing grain, or the field are consumed…
6. 22:6: If a man gives his neighbor money or vessels to watch, and it is stolen from the man's house…
7. 22:9: If a man gives his neighbor an ass, or an ox, or a sheep, or any beast, to watch, and it dies, is hurt, or is captured…
8. 22:13: And if a man borrows [an animal] from his neighbor, and it is hurt, or dies…

You Should Not Commit Adultery

1. 22:15: And if a man entices a virgin that is not betrothed, and lies with her…
2. 22:16: If her father refuses to give her to him (in marriage), he shall pay money according to the dowry of virgins.
3. 22:17: You shall not allow a sorceress to live. (Abarbanel: A sorceress incites men and young women to have sexual relationships.)
4. 22:18: One who lies with a beast shall surely be put to death.
5. 22:19: One who sacrifices to (idolatrous) gods shall be utterly destroyed. (Abarbanel: Sacrificing to idols is called adultery and prostitution, since they frequently go together.)

You Should Not Bear False Witness

Verse	Abarbanel's Commentary
22:20: You should not deceive nor oppress a stranger.	The Rabbis stated this refers to vexing words, i.e., even though he is a stranger, do not bear false witness by speaking (about/to him) improperly.
22:21: You should not afflict a widow or an orphan.	Even though they seem to have no supporter, do not bear false testimony against them, because their supporter, G-d, is strong.

You Should Not Covet

Verse	Abarbanel's Commentary
22:24: If you lend money to My people, even to the poor among you… you shall not charge him interest.	Included in "You should not covet" is that you should not covet his money to take it as interest.
22:25: If you take your neighbor's garment as collateral, restore it to him by sunset.	Do not covet his clothing.
22:27: Do not revile a judge [or G-d], nor curse a prince of your people.	Do not curse the G-d who gave these laws or the prince that enforces them.
22:28: Do not delay to offer of the fullness of your harvest [to the priest].	Do not delay gifts to the priests, Levites, or poor just because they delay payment of their debts to you.

Mishpatim

After investigating the implications of the last five commandments, which deal with *mitzvot* between man and his fellow man, and listing the laws associated with each commandment, the Torah epitomizes in one short verse the value of behaving in the prescribed manner, which is to attain the mystical status of being holy:

Verse	Abarbanel's Commentary
22:30: And you shall be holy men unto Me.	Fulfilling the G-dly statutes will make you holy unto Me.
22:30: You should not eat flesh [found] in the field that is torn [from beasts].	Eating detested foods can lead to the development of bad traits.

After extrapolating the last five commandments, it is necessary to ensure that they will in fact be implemented. The only way to ascertain that this will be the case is through enforcement. For this purpose, it is necessary to have an honest and efficient court system. Taking the same approach as Abarbanel, it may be noted that this section presents twelve laws dealing with this subject (laws so important that they are repeated in a number of other locations in the Pentateuch).[56]

1. 23:1: You should not spread a false report.
2. 23:1: Do not join with a wicked person to be a false witness. Explanation: For example, by saying as follows: "John Doe owes me 200 dinar, but I have only one witness. If you testify falsely, I will split the money with you" (*Mechilta de-Rabbi Yishmael, Mishpatim, parashah* 20).

---

56. Deut. 1:16-17; 16:18-21; 19:15-20.

3. 23:2: You should not follow a majority to do evil... incline after the majority. (Explanation: For evil, a majority of two is needed. For good, a majority of one suffices [BT *Sanhedrin* 2a].)
4. 23:2: Do not bear witness in a dispute to favor the majority [Rashi: if you disagree], thus perverting justice. (Explanation: Onkelos: Do not favor one side without deliberating. Talmud: Do not differ from those greater than you; therefore, novices express their opinions first [BT *Sanhedrin* 36a].)
5. 23:3: Do not favor a poor man in his case. (Explanation: Do not say, "He's a poor man so I will favor him in his lawsuit" [Rashi on Exod. 23:3].)
6. 23:4: If you meet your enemy's ox or his ass going astray, you should surely return it to him. (Explanation: An uneducated person who accidentally incriminates himself [comparable to a lost ox] may be helped in the formulation of his argument [Abarbanel on Exod. 23:1].)
7. 23:5: If you see the ass of your enemy lying under its burden, should you not help him? Surely you should help him [unload it] (Rashi on Exod. 23:5). (Explanation: An uneducated person who does not know how to present his case [comparable to an ass crouching under its burden] may likewise be helped [Abarbanel on Exod. 23:1].)
8. 23:6: You should not distort the judgment of your poor in his lawsuit. (Explanation: Even if he is poor in *mitzvot*, and his opponent is righteous, be evenhanded [*Mechilta de-Rabbi Yishmael, Mishpatim, parashah* 20].)
9. 23:7: Keep far from a false matter. (Explanation: If a judge is mistaken, he should not try to prove his point to avoid embarrassment. If the judge knows the witnesses are lying, he should not accept their evidence. If a disciple knows his master erred, he should correct him [BT *Shevuot* 31b].)

10. 23:7: Do not slay the guiltless and the righteous, for I will not allow the wicked to escape justice. (Explanation: Do not slay the guiltless—if found guilty, bring him back if evidence of innocence appears. Do not slay… the righteous—if found innocent, do not bring him back if new evidence of guilt arises [BT *Sanhedrin* 33b].)
11. 23:8: And you should not take a bribe, for a bribe blinds those who can see and perverts the words of the righteous. (Explanation: Even [where the intention is] to acquit the innocent or to condemn the guilty, and even if it is just a bribe of words, the Torah postulates, "And you should not take a bribe" [BT *Ketubot* 105a-b].)
12. 23:9: And you should not oppress a stranger, for you know the heart of a stranger, for you were strangers in the land of Egypt. (Explanation: It is forbidden for a judge to discriminate against anyone.)

The Talmud explains why the Torah prohibits bribery:

> Rava stated: What is the reason for [the prohibition against taking] a bribe? Because as soon as a man receives a bribe from another, he becomes so well disposed towards him that he becomes like part of him, and no man sees himself in the wrong. What is [the meaning of] *shohad* [Hebrew for "bribe"]? *She-hu had* ["that he is one," i.e., the giver of the bribe and the recipient are like one entity] (BT *Ketubot* 105b).

The Talmud proceeds to cite a number of examples to show how meticulous the rabbis were in making sure that they would not be prejudiced or subject to bribes:

1. R. Papa said: A man should not act as judge for one whom he loves nor for one whom he hates; for no man can see the guilt of one whom he loves or the merit of one whom he hates.
2. What is to be understood by "a bribe of words"? — As the bribe offered to Samuel. He was once crossing [a river] on a board, when a man came up and offered him his hand. "What," [Samuel] asked him, "is your business here?" "I have a lawsuit," the other replied. "I am disqualified from acting as your judge," he told him.
3. Amemar was once sitting and deciding a law, when a bird flew down upon his head and a man approached and removed it. "What is your business here? [Amemar] asked him. "I have a lawsuit," the other replied. "I am disqualified from acting as your judge," he told him.
4. R. Ishmael son of R. Jose, whose sharecropper was wont to bring him a basket full of fruit [as rent] every Friday but on one occasion brought it to him on a Thursday, asked the latter, "Why the present change?" "I have a lawsuit," the other replied, "and thought that at the same time I might bring [the fruit] to the master." He did not accept it from him [and] said, "I am disqualified to act as your judge." He thereupon appointed a pair of rabbis to try the case for him. As he was arranging the affair, he [found himself] thinking, "If he wished he could plead thus, or if he preferred he might plead thus." "Oh," he exclaimed, "the despair that awaits those who take bribes! If I, who have not taken [the fruit at all], and even if I had taken it, I would only have taken what is my own, am in such [a state of mind], how much more [would that be the state of] those who accept bribes."

Mishpatim

As previously stated, the last set of laws enabled proper implementation of the laws that are based on the second tablet (those prohibiting murder, adultery, stealing, bearing false witness, and coveting). Abarbanel explains the position of the last set differently. He states that after expanding the commandments on the second tablet, the Torah reverts to the first tablet, although the first two commandments do not require elaboration. The first commandment simply acknowledged that G-d gave the tablets, and the second was already included in the seven Noahide laws. Additionally, the Children of Israel had heard them directly from G-d, and perhaps that fact itself implied a higher level of understanding. Finally, it was previously noted that the first two commandments have already been amplified at the end of *Yitro* (Exod. 20:19-20).

The Tannaitic Midrash[57] and the Talmud (BT *Berachot* 33a; *Shevuot* 20b) base the prohibition of making vain oaths on the third commandment, "You shall not take the name of the Lord your G-d in vain" (Exod. 20:7). This prohibition leads naturally to laws pertaining to courts, witnesses, testimonies, and vows, and it is for this reason that when emphasizing the first half of the Decalogue, starting from the third commandment, these laws appear after the last command of the second tablet—not to covet. The only question that might arise is with regard to the last law in the set, which prohibits oppressing strangers. Abarbanel explains that acting in that manner might lead the stranger, in his desperation, to take G-d's name in vain.

Abarbanel proceeds to relate the continuation of the text to the fourth command: "Remember the Sabbath day to keep it holy" (Exod. 20:8). The Sabbatical year is discussed (Exod. 23:10-11),

---

57. *Mechilta de-Rabbi-Yishmael, Yitro, Masechta de-ba-Chodesh, parashah* 7.

which entails working for six years and resting on the seventh, in a parallel fashion to one's weekly routine of working for six days and resting on the seventh. The list of laws concludes with a mention of the Sabbath and holidays (Exod. 23:12-19), which have many common features.

Abarbanel notes that the fifth commandment, "Honor your father and your mother" (Exod. 20:12), is not dealt with here, since a number of the relevant laws were already included in the set of laws associated with the prohibition of murder.

One question that remains with regard to Abarbanel's brilliant explanation of the sequence of laws in *Mishpatim* is why it started with an elaboration of the second set of commandments before dealing with the first set (which parallels the judicial laws). Abarbanel himself answers this question by saying that the latter commandments were located closer to *Mishpatim*, so they were handled first. In addition, the judicial laws may indeed mirror the first set of commandments, but they also supply the means for implementing the civil laws which mirror the second set, and this fact provides a good reason to place them after detailing the laws associated with the last five commandments.

Reviewing the Sequence

Abarbanel (Exod. 23:1) defines three types of commandments in the Torah. The first type he calls testimonies—laws that strengthen one's belief in and respect for the Almighty, and attest to His intervention in the history of the Children of Israel and the concomitant miracles that He performed. The second type is statutes—laws having hidden reasons and purposes. The third type is ordinances—laws that together establish a system of social legislation.

The first five commandments may be considered to be testimonies, while the second five are ordinances. The last verses in *Yitro*, after the description of the revelation at Sinai, deal with laws concerning altars and are also testimonies. *Mishpatim* deals mostly with ordinances, and eventually moves over to testimonies, at which point Sabbath and the holidays are discussed.

Two hypotheses have been presented as to why ordinances were dealt with before testimonies, one based on proximity (Abarbanel) and one based on necessity (laws pertaining to ordinances are implemented by administering oaths). One might also distinguish between the testimonies dealt with at the end of *Yitro*, which are more oriented toward strengthening belief in G-d, respect for Him, and closeness to Him, and those given in *Mishpatim*, which mainly commemorate miraculous historical events.

Statutes are not yet presented at this stage (other than according to the previously cited view that the statute of the red heifer was presented at Marah). They will appear in the later books of the Pentateuch.

Summary

The acceptance of the Torah was not a one-time event, but a gradual process, which started from the time of Adam, when many of the seven Noahide laws were presented to all of mankind, with the remainder being transmitted until the time of Noah. Throughout the generations, more laws were added. The patriarchs observed an increasing number of commandments: Abraham practiced circumcision, Isaac gave tithes, and Jacob abstained from eating the sciatic nerve. Additional laws were given to Amram, Moses' father, in Egypt.[58] In Marah, more laws were given, and some of the Sabbath restrictions were enacted when G-d supplied the Children of Israel with manna. According to R. Ishmael in the Midrash,[59] a set of blessings and curses was presented to the Hebrews before the giving of the Torah, and all agree that a large set of civil laws was presented immediately afterwards (in the portion of *Mishpatim*). During the forty years of wandering in the desert, all of the civil and ritual laws were elaborated upon and analyzed in depth. Studying and observing the law, which represents the essence of Judaism from a behavioral point of view, is seen to have been inculcated using a gradual procedure that eventually segued into full-fledged learning and observance.

---

58. Rambam, *Melachim* 9:1.
59. *Mechilta de-Rabbi Yishmael, Yitro, Masechta de-ba-Chodesh, parashah* 3.

Terumah

The portion of *Terumah* describes the Tabernacle (*Mishkan*) and its vessels. Many commentators saw the Tabernacle as a means of expiation for the grave sin of the golden calf; others believed that it had intrinsic value, but nevertheless felt that its function after the sin differed from its originally intended purpose. The opposing viewpoints are presented in-depth in Second Overview: The Tabernacle Oriented Portions.

The Holy of Holies was one of the most mysterious places in the *Mishkan*, and later in the Temple. Upon entering the premises once a year on Yom Kippur, the high priest took his life in his hands. If he were not worthy, and consequently was unable to withstand the intensity of the holy environment, his body would have to be pulled out by a rope that was tied to his leg before entering. The Ark, which was located inside the Holy of Holies, was even more immersed in mystery, but most exalted of all was the pair of Cherubim, from between which G-d spoke to Moses.

The Ark and Cherubim did not exist in the Second Temple, and there is a Tannaitic dispute concerning what happened to them.[60]

---

60. BT *Yoma* 53b; *Tosafot ha-Rosh* on *Horayot* 12a.

R. Eliezer says that Nebuchadnezzar had them brought to Babylon, together with the precious vessels of the House of the Lord. R. Judah b. Ilai, on the other hand, says that King Josiah concealed them forty years before the destruction of the First Temple in a secret hiding place that had been prepared by King Solomon, who knew prophetically that the Temple would eventually be destroyed. Yehuda Kiel has explained (2 Chron. 35:3) that the Ark was already moved from its proper location to a temporary hiding place when King Manasseh, the grandfather of King Josiah, introduced an idol into the Temple. Later, when Josiah heard the prophesy of Hulda that the Temple would indeed be destroyed, he decided to transfer the Ark and Cherubim to the permanent hiding place that had been designated by King Solomon. The Talmud proceeds to tell of a priest who noted, at some point after the Ark was hidden, that one of the tiles on the Temple floor was elevated a bit higher than those surrounding it, indicating that it had been removed and later replaced, i.e., that the secret alcove was under that tile (BT *Yoma* 54a). When his ax inadvertently slipped, falling on the tile, a fiery blast issued from the floor and consumed the priest.

Three Questions with Regard to the Cherubim concerning their Image, Permissibility, and Purpose

The Torah presents the Cherubim in the following verse: "And the Cherubim shall spread their wings above, screening the Ark-cover with their wings, with their faces one to another; toward the [middle or surface of the] Ark cover shall the faces of the Cherubim be" (Exod. 25:20).

In order to better understand the essence of the Cherubim, it behooves one to answer the following three questions:

1. What form did the Cherubim take?
2. What is the difference between the Cherubim and the golden calf?
3. What role was played by the Cherubim?

First Question – What Form Did the Cherubim Take?

Rashi says that "they had a baby's face" (Exod. 25:18), and Abarbanel describes them as depicting two small children who have no blemish and have not known the taste of sin—one male and one female (Exod. 25:10). Rabbenu Bachya describes one as a grown man and the other as a young child (Exod. 25:18). Apparently, these commentators base themselves on the words in the previously quoted verse "one to another" (literally, "man to his brother"). On the other hand, Rashbam, always the literalist, describes the Cherub as "a large bird having feathers" (Exod. 25:18). He likely bases himself on the words in the same verse, "spread their wings above," while in his opinion "one to another" (or even "man to his brother") is an idiom that can apply to any creature. R. Abraham the son of the Rambam combined both views by stating: "The Cherub from its head to its shoulders had the form of a man, and from its shoulders to the bottom of its body had the form of a bird" (Exod. 25:18).

Second Question – What Is the Difference between the Cherubim and the Golden Calf?

After depicting the form of the Cherubim, one can relate to the question of Abarbanel (Exod. 25:1):

> It would appear that He was transgressing with this [command to make Cherubs, the commandment of] "You shall not make for yourself a graven image, nor any manner of likeness, of anything that is in heaven above, or that is in the earth beneath" (Exod. 20:4). And how could He command them to make what they had been prohibited [from making]?

In explaining Abarbanel, it may be noted that Rambam rules:

> It is forbidden to make figures for purposes of ornamentation, even if they are not for idol-worship, for it says "You shall not make with Me gods of silver or gods of gold" (Exod. 20:20), in other words, figures of gold and silver that are only ornaments, so that those likely to err will not do so, and imagine that they serve idolatrous purposes. But there is no prohibition to make ornamental figures [in general], just [those of] human form (*Hilchot Avodah Zarah* 3:10).

Since it has been shown that many commentators believe the Cherubim to have been of human form, Abarbanel's wonderment is understandable.

Terumah

Two types of answers to this question are proposed:

1. Technical answer: According to the *Tur*, the prohibition relates only to a completed form that includes all of the body parts; a head without a body, or the reverse, is not prohibited (*Yoreh De'ah* 141 at the end). As previously mentioned, according to Rashbam, the Cherubs had the form of birds, while according to Rambam, they had a bird-like body. Therefore, the prohibition did not apply to the Cherubim that were sculpted for the Tabernacle. Of course, it is forbidden to make even a partially human statue if it is designed for idolatrous purposes, and it is to avoid such a transgression that Rabbenu Bachya comments: "And as to the fact that there were two of them and not one, it is in order that one should not think that it represents the form of a god who is worshipped" (Exod. 25:18).

2. Philosophical answer: Rashi provided an answer to this question when he wrote, "[This verse] presents a prohibition regarding the Cherubim which you make to stand with Me [in the Holy of Holies]—that they should not be made of silver, for if you deviate [from My command] to make them of silver [and not of gold], they will be to me as idols" (Exod. 20:20).

Rashi's intention is to explain that although, absent a specific command, the Cherubim would have been included in the prohibition to create sculptures; the principle being demonstrated here is that the same mouth that instituted the blanket prohibition against creating statues (i.e., the mouth, so to say, of the Almighty) has the right to permit them under certain circumstances. What are those circumstances? They occur when one adheres to the guidelines enumerated in the text, namely that they be of gold, that there are two of them, and that they be placed only in the Tabernacle or the

Temple and nowhere else, even if it be a place of worship. If one obeys these rules, not only has he not committed a sin, but he has actually performed a mitzvah. Chizkuni notes that this is not the only case in which the Torah requests the execution of an act that in different circumstances would be prohibited. Other examples are slaughtering sacrificial animals and circumcising on the Sabbath, levirate marriage (i.e., marrying the wife of a deceased brother, which is an incestuous relationship unless the brother died without heirs), and wearing priestly garments (when performing the priestly service) that are made of *shaatnez*, a mixture of wool and linen that is prohibited for normative dress (Deut. 22:11; BT *Yevamot* 4a).

R. Judah ha-Levi uses the same approach to explain the difference between the sin of the golden calf and the command to make Cherubim. He believes that the Israelites constructed the golden calf only because they needed a tangible image of G-d, not because they actually wanted to worship it. However, they were prohibited from making a sculpture of their own volition. Had they waited patiently, they would have been able to fill the void by obeying the commands associated with the *Mishkan*, the altar, and the associated sacrifices. He writes:

> Their sin consisted, then, only in making an image of a forbidden thing, and in attributing Divine approval to a creation of their own hands and of their own volition without a command by G-d.... This sin was not on a par with a lapse from all obedience to Him who had led them out of Egypt, but just a sin against one of His commands, for He had forbidden worshipping [by means of] images, and in spite of this they made one. They should have continued waiting for Moses and not have made a symbol for themselves, and determined a place toward which they

would direct [their prayers] and not have built an altar and brought sacrifices on it.... And indeed this act is strange and shameful in our eyes because in our day worshipping forms has ceased in most nations. However, in that generation such an act was routine, for all the nations worshipped forms.... Those images that G-d permitted, for example the Cherubim, did not seem to them to be a strange thing (*Kuzari* 1:97).[61]

Third Question – What Role Was Played by the Cherubim?

According to Rabbenu Bachya, who bases himself on Rambam, the Cherubim represent the angels who serve as the intermediaries between G-d and Israel. The Cherubim facilitate prophecy and provide the guidance necessary to fulfill the laws of the Torah and to steer the nation in the right direction. In his words:

> In terms of the literal meaning, the Cherubim in the Temple and the *Mishkan* serve as a sign and a testimony to the existence of angels. Just as we are commanded to believe in the existence of G-d, and that is the first principle of the Torah principles, as it says, "I am the Lord your G-d" (Exod. 20:2), so are we commanded to believe in the existence of angels, and that is the second principle, because the angels influence intellectual ability and place speech in the mouths of the prophets at the command of the Almighty. If it were not for that, there would be no prophecy and no instruction, and because of this Scripture

---

61. All *Kuzari* citations are from the Hartwig Hirschfeld translation.

> commands making the Cherubim in order to instruct [us] concerning the existence of angels… because the Cherubim, in my opinion, are an indicator of the existence of angels, and the angels are multitudinous, and therefore we can say, based on this, that the word Cherubim hints at the plural form [i.e., the plurality of the angels as well], and the Almighty, G-d of Israel, is over them, as he says, "You, who are enthroned upon the Cherubim," and if so, the word "Cherubim" stresses two points: plurality and young men (on Exod. 25:18).

In short, the Cherubim symbolize angels, and angels symbolize the constant and continuous connection—from the time of the patriarchs, Moses, and revelation—between the Nation of Israel and G-d.

According to Abarbanel, the purpose of the Cherubim (which have the form of two small, unblemished children, in his view) is to illustrate the importance of education from childhood to contemplate G-d's Torah day and night, and so he says:

> One has the form of a male, and one has the form of a female to hint that with respect to every man and woman of the Children of Israel, it is appropriate that they should persist and spend their days contemplating the Torah of G-d day and night, either by reading it [the Torah] or by fulfilling its commands, because by doing so they will attain their perfection and happiness (on Exodus 25).

Abarbanel, using the Cherubim as a metaphor for the Children of Israel, goes on to explain the verse, phrase by phrase, as follows:

1. "And the Cherubim shall spread their wings above": their wings and thoughts are spread above to serve their Creator by fulfilling the laws between man and G-d.
2. "screening the Ark-cover with their wings": they are attached to and examine closely the Torah that is under the Ark-cover.
3. "with their faces one to another": in brotherly love when dealing with issues between man and his fellow human being.
4. "toward the Ark-cover shall the faces of the Cherubim be": regarding commandments between man and the Almighty, and commandments between man and his fellow man, one should behave according to the dictates of the Torah which is in the Ark, and that should be his direction and orientation.

The final verse pertaining to the Cherubim says: "And there I will meet with you, and I will tell you from above the Ark-cover—from between the two Cherubim that are upon the Ark of the Testimony—about *everything which I command you concerning the Children of Israel*" (Exod. 25:22).

Abarbanel explains the verse as follows:

> By means of the Torah prophecy will occur, for behold in the Ark prophecy will arrive between them [the Cherubim], and therefore from the time that the Ark was hidden, prophecy was concluded and there were no more prophets… and for that reason prophecy did not take place in another nation [that had not received the Torah], and this is the meaning of "everything which I command you concerning the Children of Israel."

There is seen to be a direct link between the Cherubim and prophecy in the Nation of Israel.

MIRACULOUS EVENTS AND THE CHERUBIM

According to some opinions, the Cherubim were not simple statues, but robot-like figures, because they could move their limbs.[62] These miraculous events took place at two locations in three instances.[63] The two locations were either above or adjacent to the Ark,[64] and on the walls of the Temple. In both Temples, images of Cherubim were engraved on the walls; in the First Temple, this was in addition to those that stood next to the Ark. The three instances will be described below.

FIRST INSTANCE OF MIRACULOUS BEHAVIOR BY THE CHERUBIM

The Talmud notes that the direction which the Cherubim faced is described differently in various Biblical locations. In the portion of *Terumah*, it says that the Cherubim were "screening the Ark-cover with their wings, with their faces one to another" (Exod. 25:20). Since the Tabernacle, as well as the Temple, stretched from east to west, the faces of the Cherubim must have faced each other in a northerly-southerly direction. However, in 2 Chronicles, when describing Solomon's Temple, it says: "The wings of these Cherubim were spread over twenty cubits; and they stood on their feet, and their faces were inward" (toward the main sanctuary to the east of the Holy of Holies, where the Cherubim were located). The Talmud (BT *Bava Batra* 99a) addresses this contradiction, and says as follows:

---

62. Ramban, *Bava Batra* 99a.
63. Ritva, *Yoma* 54b.
64. The Cherubim were above the Ark in the Tabernacle and adjacent to it in the First Temple.

Terumah

How did they stand? — R. Johanan and R. Elazar [argue]. One says they faced each other, and the other says their faces were inward [toward the east]. But according to him who says that they faced each other, is it not written, "And their faces were inward?" — [That is] not a question. One [where it says they faced each other] speaks of a time when Israel obeyed the will of the Omnipresent; one speaks of a time when Israel did not obey the will of the Omnipresent [Rashbam: They face each other, comparable to a male and female who are in love, indicating that the Almighty loves Israel. Initially they were constructed facing each other, symbolizing that the Divine Presence rests in Israel and Israel behaves according to G-d's will, and when they don't (do G-d's will) they miraculously turn their faces inwards (toward the east)]. And according to him who says that their faces were inward: Is it not written, "with their faces one to another"? They were slightly turned sideways [Rashbam: A little inward and a little facing each other (at a 45-degree angle). Here he could not answer as before: "One speaks of a time when Israel obeyed the will of the Omnipresent, one speaks of a time when Israel did not obey the will of the Omnipresent." Since the default position of the Cherubim was with their faces inward, it could not possibly indicate that they were usually disobeying G-d's will].

To summarize the Talmudic passage, according to one Tanna, the Cherubim faced each other in order to indicate G-d's love for the Nation of Israel. In other words, the Cherub on the south looked northward, and the one on the north, southward. When the Children of Israel sinned, a miracle occurred and they faced east toward the sanctuary, and so is resolved the contradiction between the verses.

According to the second Tanna, the heads of both Cherubim were permanently set in a diagonal position (with no reference to a miracle). The face of the southern Cherub was directed northeast at an angle of 45 degrees, so that in one direction he saw the second Cherub and in the other direction he peered into the *Mishkan*. The face of the northern Cherub was directed southeast at an angle of 45 degrees, so that in one direction he saw his partner and in the other direction he peered into the *Mishkan*.

Second Instance of Miraculous Behavior by the Cherubim

The second instance occurred when the Children of Israel made their holiday pilgrimage to Jerusalem. The Talmud states:

> R. Kattina said: Whenever Israel ascended [to Jerusalem] for the festival, the curtain was rolled up for them and the Cherubim were shown to them, while their bodies were intertwined with one another [Rashi: stuck one to the other, hugging and embracing each other as a male embraces a female]. And they [the Cherubim] would say to them [the Israelites]: "Look! You are beloved before G-d as the love between man and woman" (BT *Yoma* 54a).

Third Instance of Miraculous Behavior by the Cherubim

The Talmud continues (BT *Yoma* 54b) with a description of the third miraculous occurrence, which took place at the time of the destruction of the Temple:

Resh Lakish said: When the heathens entered the Temple, they saw the Cherubim whose bodies were intertwined with one another. They carried them out [Rashi: They scraped them from the wall] and said: These Israelites, whose blessing is a blessing, and whose curse is a curse, occupy themselves with such things! And immediately they despised them, as it is said: "All that honored her despised her, because they saw her nakedness" (Lam. 1:8).

There is a Talmudic dispute as to whether these miracles happened at the time of the destruction of the First or the Second Temple (or perhaps both). Rashi's comment that the Cherubim were scraped from the wall is necessary according to both opinions. If the miracles occurred at the time of the First Temple's destruction, recall that according to one opinion, the Ark had been hidden in a secret alcove forty years before the destruction, so the Cherubim that were plundered must have been those engraved in the wall. If the reference is to the Second Temple, according to all opinions the stand-alone Cherubim, as well as the Ark, which were found in the First Temple were never retrieved, nor were replacements prepared for the Second Temple, so certainly these are the Cherubim that are being referenced.

The Meaning and Significance of These Miracles

R. Yehoshua Shapira[65] explains that the Cherubim, as male and female respectively, represent the Almighty and the archetype for the congregation of Israel, which is referred to as the Divine

---

65. Yehoshua Shapira, "From between the Two Cherubim – *Parshat Terumah*."

Presence (the *Shechinah*, feminine Hebrew form). When Israel observes the commands of G-d, the prototype and the actual nation are united and intertwined in a loving manner with the Almighty. However, when they do not obey G-d's will, the congregation so to speak separates from its prototype. At such a time, the Almighty and the Divine Presence (which embodies the inherent uniqueness of Israel), who are like a Father and Mother, feel compassion for Israel. A miracle occurs and the Almighty looks eastward toward the congregation and welcomes Israel in spite of its sins. By virtue of His great love, His heart overflows with pity and He urges the nation to repent, as it says, "For I have no pleasure in the death of he who dies, says the Lord G-d; [therefore] return [to G-d] and live" (Ezek. 18:32).

It has been noted that the Talmud says that when the Children of Israel obeyed the Lord, the faces of the Cherubim faced each other. One would expect that in the reverse situation, namely when the Children of Israel disobey the Lord, the Cherubim would face away from each other (they would be back to back), i.e., the Cherub on the north would face north and the one on the south would face south. Yet the Talmud says that their faces were directed inward, the southern Cherub facing northeast and the northern Cherub southeast.

Using the previously described metaphor, R. Shapira answers this question. The Almighty and the figure representing Israel always glance at each other, because the tight bond between them can never be severed. But at the same time, they are the concerned parents who worry about their prodigal son, so they both peer in the direction of the sanctuary, which represents the Children of Israel, who are in need of guidance and direction.

Terumah

R. Shapira continues:

> Beyond this [miracle], at the time of the festivals an even greater spiritual elevation occurs, and miraculously the Cherubim, who face one another, are seen intertwined and embracing in the manner of a male and female who are in love. On the three pilgrimage festivals, the ingathering of Israel is so deep that not only do they converge into the *Shechinah*, but they adhere to the Almighty Himself, as we say in [the prayer called] *Hoshanot*—"embraced and attached to you." This is the elevated situation which reveals itself on the holidays.

The hardest of the instances to comprehend is the justification for the miracle specifically at the time of the destruction. Two explanations attributed to Ri Migash are quoted by Talmudic commentaries.[66] The first reason suggested is to show the Gentiles how much G-d loved the Israelites before they sinned and, according to R. Chaim Shmulevich,[67] to infuse hope in the Children of Israel that they will eventually be able to return to their original level of intimacy. The second explanation is that the embrace was designed to add to Israel's punishment by revealing their nakedness, thus degrading them in the eyes of the Gentiles, as described in the verse from Lamentations.

Another explanation may be offered. Specifically, an embrace that contains elements of love, emotion, and lust represents a concept which cannot be understood by those for whom the Jewish tradition is alien. Such people may realize that the world has both a physical and a spiritual dimension; however, they consider these

---

66. *Shitah Mekubbetzet*, BT *Bava Batra* 99a.
67. BT *Sotah* 54b, quoted by Schottenstein.

two elements to be incompatible. Some religions even prohibit their clergy from intimate sexual relationships, while others ban all alcoholic drinks.

Judaism differs with this approach. Some of the foundational slogans used in describing the religion are the Biblical phrase: "It is not in heaven… neither is it on the other side of the sea" (Deut. 30:12), and the Talmudic phrase: "The Torah was not given to ministering angels" (BT *Kiddushin* 54a).

The implication of these expressions is that Judaism is aware of human impulses and does not wish to repress them. On the contrary, Judaism is in favor of maximizing one's physical enjoyment in this world, as may be understood from the Talmudic maxim: "In the future [world], man will be accountable for everything [edible] that his eye saw and he didn't eat" (JT *Kiddushin* 4:12). The seal of approval given to the most physical possible relationship between a man and a woman is called *kiddushin* (marriage, lit., "sanctification"), and the future groom says to his beloved bride: "Behold you are *sanctified* to me." The Song of Songs exalts the physical connection between a man and a woman, and the Sages present it as a paradigm of the love between G-d and Israel. The message that emanates from the parable and the derived lesson, taken together, is one of sanctification of the physical and material realms, and it is this view that characterizes Judaism. It is thus no wonder that R. Akiva referred to the Song of Songs as *Kodesh Kodashim* ("Holy of Holies"; see Mishnah *Yadayim* 3:5), the same name that is given to the location of the Cherubim in the Temple, since the purpose of both is to demonstrate controlling and guiding, but not repressing, the physical by means of the spiritual.

On holidays, when the nation attempts to attain the highest levels of holiness and spirituality, the Torah requires one to be happy and to eat tasty dishes, in keeping with the rabbinical dictum that "it is not possible to fulfill the requirement to be joyful without [partaking of] meat and wine" (BT *Pesachim* 109a). R. Shneur Zalman of Liadi,[68] the Alter Rebbe, wrote that "Purim and Yom ha-Kippurim [the Day of Atonement] are similar; the meaning of Yom ha-Kippurim is [a day that is] like Purim." Examining his phraseology precisely leads to the conclusion that he considers Purim to be on an even higher level than Yom ha-Kippurim, since he uses Purim as his basis, and Yom ha-Kippurim is only said to be like—i.e., an imitation of, but not identical. This statement may be explained as follows. On the Day of Atonement, one achieves spirituality by means of prayer and fasting. On Purim, one attains spirituality by partaking of a festive meal and being joyful, acts which are more typical of our existence in this world.

In short, Purim is greater than Yom Kippur, because on Yom Kippur the emphasis is on spirituality, and the material aspect—the *mitzvah* to eat on the day before—only strengthens one's ability to fast. On Purim the main focus is on the physical nature of this world, and the spiritual dimension—the *mitzvah* to fast on the day before—fortifies the observant Jew and enables him to cope with the physical world in which he lives. In this vein, the Midrash[69] states: "All of the holidays will be cancelled in the future, with the exception of Purim, for it says, 'and these days of Purim should not pass [out of usage] from among the Jews'" (Esth. 9:28).

SUMMARY

Among the primary vessels found in the Tabernacle were the Ark, the Ark-cover, and the Cherubim. The existence of the Cherubim in the Tabernacle would seem at first to contradict the prohibition

---

68. *Torah Or, Megillat Esther* 95:4.
69. *Shocher Tov*, Prov. 9.

of sculpting and worshipping idols, the very sin for which it was necessary to construct the Tabernacle in the first place. A number of justifications were offered in explanation of why the Cherubim were not considered to be sinful. It was noted that their presence in the Tabernacle actually served to demonstrate central concepts of Jewish practice and thought, such as the existence of prophecy (Rabbenu Bachya), the importance of a well-rounded Torah education for every member of the Jewish nation, and the intimate relationship between the Almighty and the Children of Israel (R. Yehoshua Shapira).

Tetzaveh

After providing detailed instructions regarding the construction of the Tabernacle and the preparation of its associated vessels, the Torah moves on to discuss various aspects of the *kohanim* (priests) who would minister in the Tabernacle. The first half of the portion of *Tetzaveh* deals mainly with the design and composition of the priestly garments, while the second half lists the sacrifices that would be brought at the inauguration ceremony of the *kohanim* and gives a short description of some of the activities that the priests engaged in on a daily basis, namely lighting the candelabrum, the morning and evening sacrifices, and incense offerings. The final section introduces the golden altar.

Two classical questions are asked in connection with *Tetzaveh*.

1. The question of the Zohar:[70] Why is the name of Moses not mentioned in this portion? His name appears in all of the other portions in the books of Exodus, Leviticus, and Numbers, and in most of the portions in Deuteronomy (with the exceptions of *Ekev*, *Re'eh*, *Shoftim*, *Ki Teitzei*, and *Nitzavim*).
2. The question of Ibn Ezra (Exod. 25:22): Why is the golden altar (also referred to as the incense altar or inner altar) described at

---

70. *Pinchas*, pt. 3 (p. 246a).

the end of this portion rather than in *Terumah*, together with the other appurtenances of the Tabernacle, including the copper altar (also referred to as the outside or burnt offering altar, even though other types of sacrifices were offered there as well)?

THE FIRST QUESTION: WHY IS THE NAME OF MOSES ABSENT FROM THIS PORTION?

At first blush, this question is not a question at all. The requirement to publicly read the Torah weekly has been in existence since revelation.[71] However, the Torah was not divided into weekly portions until the Tannaitic period, when the division in Babylon was into 54 weekly portions (whose reading was completed in one year) and the division in the Land of Israel was into 140-175 portions (whose reading was completed in three to three and a half years).[72] Therefore, one cannot even say that the name of Moses did not appear in the portion of *Tetzaveh* at the giving of the Torah, simply because *Tetzaveh* itself did not exist at that time. The maximum that one can say is that in the section of the Torah which discusses the priestly garments, Moses' name does not appear, even though there is no real reason why it should appear. It is a natural extension of the instructions that were meted out

---

71. According to the Talmud (BT *Bava Kamma* 82a), Moses instituted the Torah reading on Monday, Thursday, and the Sabbath; Ezra extended the amount to be read and added a reading on Sabbath afternoon. According to the Jerusalem Talmud (*Megillah* 4:1), Moses only instituted the reading on Sabbath, and Ezra added the readings on Monday, Thursday, and Sabbath afternoon.

72. Not only were there no weekly portions originally, but the words themselves were not separated by spaces (hence the need for final letters). Possibly the only form of separation initially was that between open and closed sections, although the effect of such sectioning differs between Yemenite and non-Yemenite Torah scrolls.

to Moses, starting from the beginning of *Terumah*—the previous portion, where the name of Moses is indeed mentioned. It is interesting to note that the Zohar says a number of times that there are (only) 53 portions (and not 54), and one of the commentators explains that the Zohar united the portions of *Terumah* and *Tetzaveh* so as not to dishonor Moses.[73] More explicitly, because his name is not mentioned in *Tetzaveh*, and in order to assure that there is no portion which does not do so, these two portions were amalgamated into one long portion that does contain his name.[74]

One might ask, if the question is not really meaningful historically, why focus on it at all? I believe that the answers proffered by the sages of various generations illustrate important concepts and frequently supply important insights into Jewish thought, independent of their original intention to answer a possibly extraneous question.

The answers will be divided into three categories:

1. those which reflect negatively on Moses or the Children of Israel;
2. those which reflect positively on Moses;
3. those which impart important lessons in Jewish thought.

Answers Which Reflect Negatively on Moses or the Children of Israel

The Vilna Gaon points out, regarding the first question, that the seventh day of the Jewish month of Adar (Moses' *yahrtzeit*, the

---

73. J.D. Eisenstein, *Otzar Yisrael*, In the entry for "*Parashah*."
74. Although it has been noted that in any case, the name of Moses does not appear in the book of Genesis and in numerous portions in Deuteronomy.

day on which he died; BT *Megillah* 13b) always falls in the week during which the portion of *Tetzaveh* is read from the Torah. Since G-d foresees the future, He knew that *Tetzaveh* would eventually be read on that Sabbath and also that Moses would die during that week, so He arranged for his name to be absent from *Tetzaveh* as a sign of the great loss that the Nation of Israel would sustain.

R. Zalman Sorotzkin notes, with regard to the Vilna Gaon's astute observation, that indeed Moses did die on that day, but according to tradition he was also born on that day (BT *Megillah* 13b), which should be a reason to celebrate. In fact, it was originally Haman who considered the month of Adar to be auspicious for the realization of his wicked plans because of Moses' death, but he neglected to note that it was also the month of his birth, which was sufficient reason to cause his plans to be reversed. This nicety is perhaps being hinted at by the verse in the Megillah that describes Adar as "the month that was turned for them from sorrow to gladness, and from mourning to being a holiday" (Esth. 9:22).

Answer of the Zohar

The Zohar answers its own question as follows:

> Who is greater than Moses? For he said, "If not [if You don't forgive them], erase my name, I pray of You, from Your book which You have written" (Exod. 32:32), and he said it for a purpose, and even though the Almighty acquiesced [and forgave the congregation], still he [Moses] was not spared punishment, and it has been explained that he wasn't mentioned in the portion of *Tetzaveh*, and it [his name] was erased from there.

Tetzaveh

The Zohar bases itself on the following points:

1. G-d had threatened to destroy Israel, as it says: "And now let Me be, and let My wrath reign free against them so that I may consume them" (Exod. 32:10).
2. Moses replied, as previously quoted by the Zohar: "And now, if You will bear their sin [fine, but] if not, erase my name, I pray of You, from Your book which You have written" (Exod. 32:32).
3. Moses' request to have his name erased from G-d's book (the Torah) was only if G-d did not forgive Israel. The implication is that if He did forgive them, Moses would withdraw his request. In other words, Moses' request was conditional.
4. G-d capitulated, so to say, to Moses' threat, i.e., He agreed not to destroy the nation.
5. In spite of the fact that G-d forgave Israel, He still intended to comply with Moses' suggestion that He erase his name from the Torah, even though the condition was not met.
6. Had the Almighty decided to destroy Israel, G-d forbid, He would have fulfilled Moses' request in its totality, i.e., the name of Moses would not appear at all in the text of the Torah.
7. Since in actuality the Almighty decided to spare Israel, He did not implement Moses' request verbatim by removing every mention of the name of Moses from the Pentateuch, but in the most partial manner available—by removing his name from just one portion, *Tetzaveh*.

Questions of Rosh (Rabbenu Asher) on the Zohar

Rosh[75] asks two questions on the answer of the Zohar, the first of which has been hinted at broadly:

1. If Moses conditioned the erasure of his name on the destruction of Israel, G-d forbid, why did the Almighty erase his name at all, even if it was only marginally, when in fact G-d did not destroy Israel, since that was not Moses' original intention?
2. If G-d, in His infinite wisdom, felt that some degree of punishment by the erasure of Moses' name was justified, why was the portion of *Tetzaveh* specifically chosen for this purpose?

Rosh answers his questions, respectively, as follows:

1. "The curse of a wise person, even if conditioned, will materialize." This answer requires clarification. First, by a wise person, Rosh obviously means not only wise, but religiously inspired. Second, the point that Rosh is apparently trying to make is that spiritually elevated people are expected not to lose their temper, not to use threatening language when arguing their point, and to be aware of the power of their words; hence, the implementation of the curse independent of the fulfillment of the condition.
2. "The Almighty said, 'I will ignore the letter of the law for you. I will erase you [your name] from the book which I have written,' in other words from the book [portion] of *Tetzaveh* which I have written before *Ki Tissa*." In answering his second

---

75. *Perush ha-Rosh al ha-Torah*, Exod. 27:20.

question, Rosh attempts to temper the strictness of his first answer by saying that in spite of the justification of a harsh punishment, G-d went out of His way to mitigate the severity of the reprimand. G-d noted that Moses' request was to be erased from the book which "You have [already] written," i.e., Moses' formulation used the past tense. Since Moses' statement appeared in the portion of *Ki Tissa*, his ban related only to what had already been written, namely the previous portions of Exodus. But perhaps his name should have been erased from all of the previous portions? Here again, according to Rosh, G-d gave Moses the benefit of the doubt by noting that he had said "from the book" meaning from a portion of the book, not from the entire existing book. Another explanation is that each weekly portion is called a book, and since the past tense was used, the reference is to the portion that was given or written in the most immediate past. A third explanation is that it was desirable to delay the exhibition of the punishment as much as possible, and the most distant weekly portion from *Ki Tissa* is *Tetzaveh*, which is read almost a year afterwards.

Additional Answers to Rosh's Second Question

A number of additional answers based on details of the original Hebrew of the words "from Your book which You have written" appear in the following table:

Gershon Steinberg (*Parpera'ot le-Parshat ha-Shavua, Tetzaveh*)	*Tetzaveh* is the 20th portion of the Torah: 12 in Genesis, and 8 in Exodus.	מספרך = מספר כ'	מחני נא מספרך
	The Hebrew initials of the words "You have written" indicate the portions in which the name of Moses is absent.	א – אולי עקב, א מחליף ע	מחני נא מספרך אשר כתבת
		ש – שופטים	
		ר – ראה	
		כת – כי תצא	
		ב – ספר בראשית, נצבים	
		ת – תצוה	
Vilna Gaon (*Divrei Eliyahu, Tetzaveh*)	Internal *gematria* is 40+60+1 = 101, number of verses in *Tetzaveh*, showing Moses present in spirit, but not in body.	מ=מם = מ + 40	משה
		ש=שין = ש + 60	
		ה=הא = ה + 1	

Answer of Baal ha-Turim

Baal ha-Turim (also called *Tur*, the son of Rosh) supplies a reason for the absence of the name of Moses based on the content of the portion of *Tetzaveh*. He states:

> This portion discusses the accoutrements of the priesthood—which was originally relegated to Moses, but because he refused to serve as G-d's messenger, it [the priesthood] was taken from him and bestowed on Aaron. Therefore, the name of Moses was not mentioned in this portion, so that he should not feel distressed.[76]

---

76. Exod. 27:20. Not printed in all versions.

Tetzaveh

Tur bases himself on the following passage from the Talmud:

> And the anger of the Lord was kindled against Moses (Exod. 4:14).[77] R. Joshua b. Karchah said: A [serious] consequence is recorded in connection with every time anger is mentioned in the Torah, but no [serious] consequence is recorded in this instance. R. Simeon b. Yochai said: A [serious] consequence is recorded in this instance too, for it says, "Do I not know regarding Aaron your brother the Levite that he is [also] capable of speaking" (Exod. 4:14) [and serving as my messenger]. But was he [Aaron] not a priest [so why is he termed the Levite]? Rather, this is what He meant: I had intended that you would be a priest and he a Levite; now, however, he will be a priest and you a Levite (BT *Zevachim* 102a).

This Talmudic passage indicates that initially the priesthood had been designated for Moses, but because he behaved improperly by continually refusing to carry out the mission with which G-d wished to entrust him, even though he did so out of modesty, G-d decided to revoke His offer. Had Moses not sinned, the contents of *Tetzaveh* would have been relevant to Moses himself. *Tur* says that Moses probably regretted his past behavior, and mentioning his name in this portion would likely have anguished him by prompting him to think of what might have been.

---

77. G-d was angry because, in the previous verse, Moses had told G-d to send his brother Aaron as His messenger to Israel, rather than himself.

Answer of R. Zalman Sorotzkin

R. Zalman Sorotzkin[78] combines the answers of Rosh and *Tur*, and says that Moses erred twice. His first sin was his adamant refusal to be G-d's messenger, when he said, "Please send [Your message] by the hand of whom you are accustomed to send [namely, Aaron]" (Exod. 4:13). His second was in using the expression "erase my name, I pray of You, from Your book" (Exod. 32:32). As previously noted, the priesthood was withheld from him because of the first sin. But until the portion of *Tetzaveh*, when Aaron and his children were commanded to light the candelabrum, the priestly garments were described, and the eight days of the inauguration of the priests were detailed—his punishment was not manifest. Only in this portion, where the spotlight is focused on Aaron and his sons, does the chastisement become perceptible. At this point, G-d also activates the second charge against Moses concerning the erasure of his name from the book—i.e., from the portion of *Tetzaveh*.

According to the view of R. Sorotzkin, both of Rosh's questions have been resolved. The degree of the erasure of Moses' name from the Torah was reduced, since his request was meant to be conditional and not absolute. However, it was not completely forgiven, since he was being censured for a second sin as well, and so the penalty was not entirely abolished (answering the first question). It is clear why the punishment was implemented specifically in *Tetzaveh*, since it was primarily directed at the sin concerning Moses' reluctance to serve as G-d's messenger and priest, and it is the priestly topic that is the central subject of this weekly portion (answering the second question).

---

78. *Oznayim la-Torah*, Exod. 27:20.

Tetzaveh

Answers that Reflect Positively on Moses

R. Avraham Shapira

R. Avraham Shapira[79] objects both logically and ethically to the approach taken heretofore. The so-called sins resulted from Moses' exceeding modesty and outstanding devotion, and such traits should be lauded, not denigrated. Furthermore, both the Biblical text and the Midrash praise him expressly for his behavior. After Moses' supplications for the purpose of saving Israel from G-d's wrath, the Bible states that G-d renewed His covenant with the nation and taught Moses how to pray for mercy in the future by reciting the thirteen G-dly attributes (Exod. 34:6). Additionally, according to the Midrash, Moses received the following reward for his efforts:

> On what basis did Moses merit the pleasant facial expression in this world culled from that which is generally reserved for the righteous in the world to come? Because he performed G-d's will, and sighed for the honor of G-d and Israel all his days [when they were in danger], and he coveted, lusted, and looked forward to there being peace between Israel and their Father in Heaven. How do you know that this is true? For when Israel was in the desert and acted sinfully, and G-d said to Moses, "And now let Me be, and let My wrath reign free against them so that I may consume them" (Exod. 32:10), Moses immediately

---

79. Avraham Shapira. "The Greatness of Moses our Rabbi and His Devotion to Israel," *Sichot Maran ha-Gra Shapira le-Mo'adei Yisrael.*

expressed himself in their favor, as it says: And Moses besought the Lord his G-d, and said: "Lord, why are you angry with your people, that You have brought out of the land of Egypt with great power and with a mighty hand? Why should the Egyptians be able to speak, saying: For an evil purpose did He bring them forth, to slay them in the mountains and sweep them from the face of the earth? Return from Your fierce wrath, and repent of this evil against Your people. Remember Abraham, Isaac, and Israel, Your servants, to whom You swore by Your own name, and said to them: 'I will multiply your seed as the stars of heaven, and all this land that I have spoken of, I will give to your seed, and they shall inherit it forever'" (Exod. 32:11-14). He [Moses] received an immediate reply, for it says: And the Lord repented of the evil that He had intended to bring on His people (*Tanna de-Vei Eliyahu* 4:1).

In consonance with this approach, R. Shapira stated that not only is Moses not absent from this portion, he is present at a far higher level. In other portions, third person phrases such as "G-d spoke to Moses" appear. In *Tetzaveh*, the text allows one to be an implicit observer of the high level of revelatory conversations between Moses and G-d, where such phrases as "You [Moses] will command" (Exod. 27:20) and "You bring near to yourself" (Exod. 28:20) proliferate.

R. Shapira proceeds to say that there were two steps in the preparation of the holy vessels and garments. The first was the transmission of holiness to the object, i.e., its sanctification, and the second was its actual manufacture. With regard to the vessels, sanctification resulted from the involvement of the entire congregation, as well as the artisans Bezalel and Oholiab, and this is indicated by the phrase in *Terumah*: "And they shall make an Ark" (Exod. 25:10), which is in the plural, indicating the participation of the entire congregation. Bezalel and Oholiab are first mentioned (as sanctifiers) in *Ki Tissa* (Exod. 31:1-11). The portion of *Tetzaveh*, on the other hand, is exclusively Moses-oriented. His thoughts, holiness, and inspiration led to the sanctification of the priestly garments, and it was he alone who conducted the inauguration ceremonies and anointed the high priest. Of course the actual building, carving, weaving, and sewing were done by the craftsmen, but that was only the second stage, and it is not dealt with in this portion (but in *Vayakhel* and *Pekudei*).

R. Shapira goes on to say that there is a lesson to be learned specifically from the fact that the name of Moses does not appear, namely that his influence, and indeed the influence of any outstanding rabbi, can be felt even in his absence through the holiness and Torah insights that continue to flourish among his acquaintances and students.

R. Tzadok ha-Kohen

R. Tzadok ha-Kohen of Lublin (*Pri Tzaddik, Tetzaveh*) holds that when Moses said "erase my name, I pray of You, from Your book," he rose to a higher level and almost united with G-d. For that reason he did not have an independent existence as Moses, and so he could not be referred to by his name. R. Tzadok proves his point from the following Talmudic statement:

> If not, erase my name, I pray of You, from Your book which You have written. "Erase my name, I pray of You" (Exod. 32:32): this is the book of the wicked. "From Your

book": this is the book of the righteous. "Which You have written": this is the book of the average [person] (BT *Rosh Hashanah* 16b).

According to this passage, Moses was willing to sacrifice himself in order to save the Israelite nation. After all, if he is not inscribed in the books of wicked, righteous, or average people, then he does not appear in any of the books of the living.

According to R. Tzadok, erasing the name of Moses in *Tetzaveh* flowed directly from his willingness to endanger himself by saying "erase my name, I pray of You, from Your book." Similarly, in the book of Numbers, Moses exhibited empathy for the nation to the point of self-sacrifice when he said: "And if You deal thus with me, kill me, I pray of You, if I have found favor in Your eyes; so that I will not see the evil that has befallen me" (Num. 11:15). In this verse the Hebrew word for "you" is *at*, which is usually feminine. Rashi explains: "Moses' strength grew as weak as that of a woman when the Almighty showed him the punishment that He was going to bring upon them in the future for this [sin]. He [therefore] said to Him, 'If so, kill me first.'"[80]

In short, in the view of R. Tzadok, the absence of the name of Moses from the portion reflects the supreme level of Moses, and is certainly not a punishment for any lack of loyalty to the Nation of Israel and its fate.

The complete Biblical and Midrashic background for the approach of R. Tzadok may be found in Appendix I: BACKGROUND FOR UNDERSTANDING R. TZADOK HA-KOHEN.

---

80. *Siftei Chachamim* explains Rashi to be asking of G-d to make him as weak as a woman (which fits the Hebrew better) to justify the fact that he could not bear to see the destruction of the nation.

Tetzaveh

Philosophical Explanations for the Absence of the Name of Moses

Views have been presented which look upon the absence of the name of Moses as a form of punishment, and others which consider the absence to be a sign of elevated spirituality. A third possibility is that the non-appearance of Moses' name is meant to impart important ideas in the area of Jewish thought, both with regard to the character of Moses himself, as well as with respect to the relationship between the Children of Israel and Moses.

The Character of Moses

Regarding Moses, it has been suggested that erasing his name from the portion read on the anniversary of his death might be considered to be a form of rebuke. The question is: how did Moses himself look upon this form of censure? It is possible that it did not upset him in the least that the entire portion of *Tetzaveh* was to be devoted exclusively to his brother Aaron. Aaron and Moses were meant to work together as a team, as is clear from the following verse: "These are Aaron and Moses, to whom the Lord said: 'Take out the Children of Israel from the land of Egypt according to their tribes'" (Exod. 6:26), on which Rashi comments: "There are some places where [the name of] Aaron precedes Moses [as here] and there are [other] places where [the name of] Moses precedes Aaron. [This was done] to tell you that they were of equal weight." Certainly Moses, who transcribed the words of the Torah, was aware of and in agreement with Rashi's observation.

That Moses and Aaron were favorable to each other is demonstrated in the following verses:

1. Moses gladly concedes to Aaron. "And he [Moses] said: 'Please send [Your message] by the hand of whom you are accustomed to send [namely, Aaron]'" (Exod. 4:13).
2. Aaron gladly welcomes Moses. "And the Lord got angry at Moses, and said: 'I know that Aaron your brother the Levite can speak well. And also, behold, he will come to meet you; and when he sees you, he will be glad in his heart'" (Exod. 4:14).

In short, although the Talmud states that transferring the priesthood to Aaron was a punishment, it is possible that Moses, as the humblest of men (Num. 12:3), was quite satisfied that his name not appear in the portion of *Tetzaveh*, in which his brother is honored and plays the main role. When the Torah was subdivided into weekly portions, it was done in such a way that Moses' name would not be read on the Sabbath of the week during which he died, in order to implement the curse that he had brought upon himself when he asked G-d to erase his name if He doesn't forgive Israel for the sin of the golden calf. However, this curse was for all effects a blessing that manifested Moses' humility, and Moses himself did not relate to it as a curse.

Moses' modesty, devotion, and optimism serve as a source of inspiration to the Nation of Israel. In the words of R. Sorotzkin (on Exod. 27:20):

> There is much humility and modesty reflected in the fact that neither he who received the Torah, nor his students, nor the students of his students required of us to express gratitude for his dedication at the time of Israel's redemption and receipt of the Torah from G-d. Not in vain did the holy Torah testify concerning him: "Now the

man Moses was very meek, more than all the men on the face of the earth" (Num. 12:3). His students, our Sages of blessed memory, went in his ways and upon finding an entire portion of the Torah which does not mention the name of he who received it, they arose and determined to read that portion on the week of the death [and also the birth] of Moses our teacher, who cursed himself with the erasure of his name from the Torah scroll if G-d would not forgive the Nation of Israel for the sin of the [golden] calf, and this curse materialized in this portion. By doing so, they emphasized that this curse is a blessing in our eyes and it serves as an especially salient appreciation of the life of a man of G-d and the most modest of all men, who exposed himself to possible immolation among the heavenly angels in order to receive the Torah. And for this reason he merited for it to be called by his name ["Remember the law of Moses My servant"] (Mal. 3:22). But in spite of that, when G-d threatened to destroy Israel for the sin of the [golden] calf, he "cursed" himself by [requesting] the erasure of his name from G-d's Torah if G-d would not forgive Israel for this sin. Does there exist a greater self-sacrifice for the Nation of Israel than this? G-d proposes to Moses to destroy Israel, who perpetrated a serious sin, and to make Moses into a great nation and to transmit His Torah to him; and Moses, in addition to not agreeing to this proposal (which all worldly kings would have agreed to), requests of G-d to erase his name from His Torah if it is not possible to transfer it to the Jewish nation! Can one say of such a lawgiver that he seeks his own glory?

The Ethics of Exodus

Israel's Relationship to Moses

There is another important lesson to be learned specifically from the erasure of his name. No matter how great Moses was—and the view of R. Tzadok is that from a Torah viewpoint Moses almost merged with the Almighty—it is still prohibited to turn him into a god, thereby diverting attention from the Lord as the true source of Torah, prayer, worship, and veneration.

Regarding this last point, R. Sorotzkin stresses the difference, to his mind, between Judaism and Christianity:

> In this, our Sages of blessed memory wished to emphasize the character of the pure faith of Israel, which did not place the lawgiver, the man of G-d, in the center of religious ritual and service of G-d, as we see in other "faiths," where all of the holidays and festivals revolve around the private life of the lawgiver: the biggest holiday is the birthday of the lawgiver, and after [in importance] comes the day of his demise; and fast days are tied to his suffering and pain. And this makes an impression, for everything was created for his honor, and all "faith" is only in him; and his demands are for his glory, for everyone who grasps the tail of his garment has a share in the world to come, as if he is the owner of the world to come. And after him, the priests of his high places sold atonement for sins and [entry into] the future world to the highest bidder. Not so is the portion of Jacob and his Torah: the lawgiver remains diffident, the nation [except for the learned, who calculated and discovered that he died on the seventh of Adar, and apparently he was also born then, for G-d fills the years of the righteous from their first day to their

last] doesn't know the birthday or day of his death, and *a fortiori*, does not celebrate these important days.

The Second Question: Why Is the Description of the Golden Altar Delayed?

The question of Ibn Ezra (Exod. 25:22) as to why the golden (incense) altar is introduced at a much later stage than the other furnishings of the *Mishkan* may be answered in three different ways. The first answer is that its function is different and perhaps less central than that of the other vessels. The second answer is that on the contrary, its function is more important than that of the others, and so its description merited special and individual treatment. A third answer is that a prerequisite to understanding the essence of the golden altar is an acquaintance with the two subjects that precede it: details of the priestly garments, and the consecration of the priests and the burnt offering altar, along with the accompanying sacrifices.

First Answer: Ibn Ezra Answers His Own Question

Ibn Ezra divides his answer into two sections:

1. "The Ark is in the image of a chair, and behold there is a candelabrum and a set table."
2. "Therefore, it mentions the incense altar only after the burnt offering altar, in order to provide a warning not to bring

upon it a burnt offering and a meal offering and a libation" (Exod. 30:9).

To understand the first section, recall that the Shunamite woman, who provided lodging for the prophet Elisha, stated: "Let us make, I pray of you, a little chamber on the roof; and let us place there for him a bed, and a table, and a chair, and a candelabrum; and it shall be, when he comes to us, he will go there" (2 Kings 4:10).

The room arranged for Elisha is said to be small, so the assumption is that only the most necessary furnishings were placed there, and these were the bed, table, chair, and candelabrum. The latter three items parallel the three mentioned by Ibn Ezra as the basic furnishings of the Tabernacle, and apparently he means to say that the golden altar was not in the same category in terms of importance and necessity.

The *Meshech Chochmah* develops the idea of Ibn Ezra:

> Without an Ark, the tablets are not placed [in the Tabernacle]; and similarly without a [burnt offering] altar, the daily sacrifice is not brought; and similarly without garments the priest is not permitted to do service; and without a candelabrum he is not permitted to light candles; and without the table, showbread is not laid down; but regarding the altar for burning incense, whose main purpose is just for that, is it not established that the incense is burned even if there is no altar?[81]

In short, the *Mishkan* could not function without the furnishings mentioned in *Terumah*, but it could function without the golden altar mentioned at the end of *Tetzaveh*. The *Meshech Chochmah*

---
81. *Meshech Chochmah, Tetzaveh, s.v. ve-asita mizbe'ach miktar ketoret.*

has based himself on the following Talmudic statements: "Rav said: If the altar was damaged, all sacrifices slaughtered there are unfit.... R. Giddal said in Rav's name: If the [golden] altar was removed, the incense was burnt on its [the altar's] site" (BT *Zevachim* 59a). Rambam finalizes the *halachah* in accordance with Rav's views (*Hilchot Pesulei ha-Mukdashim* 3:22; *Hilchot Temidim u-Musafim* 3:22).

The *Meshech Chochmah* points out that had the golden altar been described together with the outer altar, one might have thought that it was the more significant of the two. After all, it was covered in gold, while the outer altar was covered in copper. It stood in the sanctuary, while the copper altar was in the yard. Finally, it was used for burning the incense, concerning which the Midrash states: "Of all the sacrifices which you bring, none is dearer to me than the incense offering" (*Tanchuma: Tetzaveh* 15). In fact, the golden altar was the least critical of the aforementioned furnishings and the only one whose absence did not prevent the routine functioning of the Tabernacle. In order to avoid any possible confusion on this account, its description was distanced from that of the other appurtenances of the Tabernacle.

The halachic difference between the golden altar and the other furnishings has been explained, but what has not been clarified is why such a distinction should exist. Based on the previously cited Midrash, why in fact is the golden altar not the more central and consequently indispensable of the two?

Seforno attempts to answer this question. He states concerning the golden altar:

> This altar was not mentioned with the other vessels in *Terumah* because its purpose was not to ensconce the Almighty in our midst, as was the case with the other vessels,

as it says, "... that I may dwell among them. According to all that I show you, the pattern of the Tabernacle, and the pattern of all its furniture" (Exod. 25:8-9). Nor was its purpose to usher down the appearance of His glory into the house, as was the case with sacrificial work, as it says, "And I will meet there with the Children of Israel" (Exod. 29:43). And so testified Moses when he said, "This is the thing which the Lord commanded that you do, so that the glory of the Lord may appear to you" (Lev. 9:6). But the purpose of this altar was to honor the Almighty after He had willingly accepted the service of his nation by means of the morning and evening sacrifices, and to welcome Him with the gift of incense (on Exod. 30:1).

According to Seforno, the table, candelabrum, and Ark were like a place for G-d to lodge—to become embedded within Israel, and hence the comparison to the small room that the Shunamite prepared for Elisha. People are more able to conceptualize the presence of the Lord by comparing Him to a human king, whom they honor by preparing a luxurious feast, represented by the sacrifices. The direction of inspirational movement, at any rate, was from heaven to earth. The incense altar, on the other hand, was designed to honor the Almighty after He had graciously accepted the nation's sacrifices. The direction of the flow was now from the Tabernacle upward to G-d in heaven.

There is a view that minimizes to an even greater extent the essence of the incense, namely that of Rambam in *The Guide for the Perplexed*. He states that the main purpose of the incense was to diminish the foul odor of the slaughtered animals that were sacrificed on the copper altar: "The smell of the place would undoubtedly have been like the smell of slaughter houses, if nothing had been done to counteract it" (*Guide* 3:45).

Tetzaveh

It is now possible to comprehend the second part of Ibn Ezra's commentary. The description of the golden altar was distanced from that of the copper altar to accentuate that the two altars are not interchangeable. In fact, Rashbam comments quite explicitly on the words "an altar for the burning of incense" (Exod. 30:1) as follows: "And not [for] a burnt offering, peace offering, meal offering, or oblation."

Second Answer: The Gold Altar Is Holier than the Copper Altar

The second answer is the reverse of the first, namely, that the golden (incense) altar was handled separately because it is more spiritual and plays a more central role than the copper altar. The incense altar and the incense (*ketoret*) that was burned on it had special qualities. The Midrash (*Tanchuma: Tetzaveh* 14) even suggests that the Hebrew word for incense is an acronym that alludes to various important Jewish values, as follows:

Meaning	Hebrew	
Holiness	קדושה	ק
Purity	טהרה	ט
Mercy	רחמים	ר
Hope	תקוה	ת

Congregation vs. Individual

Unlike other sacrifices, which are meant to atone for sins, incense is designed to provide directions for living one's life, where one of the guidelines is to experience and radiate *joie de vivre* in order to live up to the directive formulated later by R. Nachman of Breslav: "It is a great mitzvah to be happy at all times" (*Likkutei Moharan* 2:24). The Midrash quoted below says that the *ketoret* is beloved by G-d specifically because it is independent of repentance, and is rather related to establishing a life of joy and spirituality.

> The Almighty said, of all the sacrifices that you bring, none is as beloved to me as the incense offering. All of the sacrifices are to meet the needs of Israel. How is this? The sin offering comes to atone for a sin, as does a guilt offering. The burnt offering comes to atone for sinful thoughts, and peace offerings come to achieve forgiveness, for they come as penance for transgressing positive commandments. But incense comes neither for sin, nor for transgression, not for guilt, but just [to achieve] joy (*Tanchuma Tetzaveh* 15).

The problem with this approach is that, at a later point, the same Midrash contradicts itself and relates the *ketoret* not to the infusion of joy, but to forgiveness of sin. On the Day of Atonement, the high priest would enter the Holy of Holies and place powdered incense on hot coals lying in a censer. The verse then states: "And the cloud of incense will cover the Ark-covering" (Lev. 16:13). The Midrash continues: "What is the meaning of 'will cover'? It is an expression of absolution. But absolution implies sin." The Midrash continues:

> If the cloud of incense formed into a cluster and arose, the nation knew that Israel was forgiven and his [the priest's] service was acceptable, but if the cloud of incense did not cover the Ark, the nation knew that he died, for it says "And the cloud of incense will cover the Ark-covering

Tetzaveh

that is on the testimony, so that he does not die" (Lev. 16:13). One may say that the high priest and all Israel were trembling when the high priest entered the inner sanctum, until he left there in peace. Once he left, there was great joy in Israel that it [his service] was accepted favorably, as it says, "Oil and incense cause the heart to rejoice" (Prov. 27:9). Oil refers to the high priest who was anointed with anointing-oil, and incense—that is Israel, who saw the cloud of incense rising upward and were joyful.

There seems to be a contradiction. On the one hand the incense is said to be disconnected from sin, but on the other hand it is said to indicate forgiveness. The answer is that the incense does not serve as a private sacrifice, but as a communal sacrifice, and as such it represents unity. The merit of the entire congregation is greater than the merit of any individual. The secret of life and death is present in the incense. If he who offers it does so as a private person, he is liable to be burned to death, as in the case of Nadab and Abihu (Lev. 10:2). But if he offers it as a messenger and with the intent of cleansing the public, he can survive and also expedite atonement for all members of the community.

In other words, even though incense effects forgiveness, it is forgiveness for the sins of others. The message is that benevolence and love of one's neighbor pave the way to the achievement of *joie de vivre*, which is the ultimate goal that the Almighty wishes for each individual. Accordingly, the Midrash concludes:

> None of the sacrifices were lauded as much as those of the princes. And why [is that so]? Because they offered the incense as the first of their sacrifices... and therefore the Almighty praises the sacrifice of each one of them

[individually, by saying] "This was the offering of" (Num. 7:12-83). For it is pleasant before Him, and He praises them… Said R. Isaac b. Eliezer: A proof [of this point] is that the Tabernacle was made, as were all its vessels, and the sacrifices were slaughtered and brought and arranged on the altar. And the table and candelabrum were set in order, as was everything else, but the Holy Presence did not descend [at the inauguration of the Tabernacle] until they offered the incense.

Body vs. Soul

In spite of the fact that incense is brought as a communal offering, and not at the initiative of any individual, *Midrash Tadshe* (ascribed to the Tanna Pinchas b. Yair) implies that every individual can have intent to be forgiven through it when it is offered daily in the morning and evening (Exod. 30:7-8), or on the Day of Atonement, when the priest introduces the incense to the Holy of Holies (Lev. 16:12). The Midrash states: "The golden altar is compared to the soul of a person, the copper altar to the body of a person. Just as gold is more precious than copper, so the soul is more precious than the body" (*Midrash Tadshe* 11).

Kli Yakar (Exod. 25:10) fleshes out this idea by noting that the copper altar atones for the body of the sinner by sacrificing the bodies of animals, which decay and disintegrate, while the golden altar atones for the soul and heavenly spirit, which rises to heaven (eventually) like the smoke of the incense. The sinner has allowed his spirit to merge with his bodily urges and to become enslaved to them, rather than ensuring that the soul maintain control. By distancing the descriptions of these two altars and placing the golden altar at the culmination of the description of the Tabernacle and its furnishings, the priestly garments, and the inauguration of the priests and their daily service, the text is indicating the elevated status of the soul that it represents, and the expectation that it will assume responsibility and culpability for each Jew's overall behavior.

Torah and *Derech Eretz*

According to R. Samson Raphael Hirsch as well, the golden altar is on a higher level than the copper altar (Exod. 30:1). Rather than considering the former to represent the soul and the latter the body, he distinguishes between the ideal, which the former represents, and the means to achieve that ideal, which the latter represents. The copper altar is on the outside and, in a sense, part of the architecture of the Tabernacle, while the golden altar is contained within, as part of its contents.

Of course, the means of achieving the ideal are a prerequisite to doing so, and as such their value must not be underestimated. The means include learning the lesson of what has been termed the Universal Stage of human development, i.e., that there is a higher set of values and indeed a higher authority unknown to primeval instinct. Assimilating this concept is sufficient to generate a "sweet savor to the Lord," a phrase repeated regularly when describing the sacrifices brought on the copper or burnt offering altar, but the basic nature of this principle is reflected in the very coarse nature of the physical treatment conferred upon these sacrifices, such as slaughtering, sprinkling of the blood, and burning. The golden altar comes into play after the sweet savor has been generated and as the person moves into the Particularistic Stage (see First Overview). As R. Hirsch has explained in other contexts, the ideal situation involves finding the right balance between Torah and *derech eretz*. According to R. Hirsch:

> The term *derech eretz* is used primarily to refer to ways of earning a living, to the social order that prevails on earth, as well as the mores and considerations of courtesy and propriety arising from social living, and also to things pertinent to good breeding and general education.[82]

R. Hirsch points out that within the sanctuary, the table is positioned opposite the candelabrum. The table, on which the showbread is placed, represents the concept of *derech eretz*, while the candelabrum with its lights represents Torah knowledge, as it says: "For the commandment is a candle, and the Torah is light" (Prov. 6:23). Between these two furnishings are the Ark and the golden altar, forming the following arrangement:

	Ark	
Candelabrum		Table
	Golden Altar	

The Ark transmits the pure spirituality of Torah to the candelabrum and provides instructions for its proper integration with the earthly ways represented by the table. The combination of Torah with *derech eretz* is symbolized by the golden altar, which reflects the finished product back to the Ark.

Third Answer: The Priesthood Is Intimately Related to the Golden Altar

The third set of answers is based on the assumption that a prerequisite to understanding the essence of the golden altar is an

---

82. *The Hirsch Siddur* (Feldheim, 1978), p. 434.

acquaintance with the details of the priestly function, the priestly garments, the consecration of the priests, and the copper altar with the accompanying sacrifices.

Rav Tzadok ha-Kohen

R. Tzadok ha-Kohen (*Pri Tzaddik, Tetzaveh*) relates the golden altar directly to Aaron the priest and his priesthood. For a complete appreciation of the Talmudic passage about to be cited, see Appendix II: Functionaries in Jewish Society in Temple Times.

Three of the furnishings of the Tabernacle were decorated with crowns—the Ark (Exod. 25:11), the table (Exod. 25:24), and the golden altar (Exod. 30:3). With regard to these three crowns, the Talmud states (BT *Yoma* 72b):

> The one of the altar, Aaron merited and received (Num. 18:19). The one of the table, David merited and received (Ps. 18:51). The one of the Ark is still lying, and whosoever wants to take it, may come and take it [Torah learning is not hereditary, and is thus available to everyone]. Perhaps you might think it is less [respected than royalty or priesthood], therefore the text [in which the Torah is metaphorically the speaker] reads: Through me kings reign [Rashi: The kingmaker, here the Torah, is certainly greater than the king that he crowns] (Prov. 8:15).

Rabbenu Yonah points out that by relating the various crowns to specific furnishings in the Tabernacle, the Talmud indicates which of the three is the most respected, namely the Ark—which represents the crown of Torah—since it is the only one that is located inside the Holy of Holies.

Rashi, on the respective Biblical verses, explains the reason for associating the various attributes with each of the furnishings. Clearly, Torah learning is to be associated with the Ark. The table, upon which rested the twelve loaves of showbread, represents wealth, lavishness, and greatness, as becomes a king. The golden altar, upon which the priests brought the morning and evening incense offerings, is rightfully associated with them.

If one wishes to relate the crowns to the leaders of Israel in their travels through the desert, clearly Moses deserved the crown of Torah and Aaron the crown of priesthood. With respect to the verse "And he was a king in Jeshurun [Onkelos: Israel], when the heads of the people gathered" (Deut. 6:5), Ibn Ezra comments:

> It refers to Moses, for the heads of the nation heard the explanation of the Torah from his mouth, and the reason [that he is called a king] is because he was like a king in that the heads of the tribes gathered around him.

In other words, the crown of kingship and the crown of Torah were bestowed upon Moses, and they were represented in the portion of *Terumah* by the Ark and the table. The crown of priesthood relates to Aaron exclusively and is represented by the golden altar in the portion of *Tetzaveh*.

R. Tzadok asks why the crown of priesthood is associated with the golden altar, on which animals were never sacrificed, rather than the copper altar, on which they were regularly brought. Of course, one might answer that according to the Biblical description, only the golden altar was adorned with a golden crown, not the copper altar. But the question is: why doesn't the Torah itself prescribe a crown for the copper altar? R. Tzadok answers that the crown was chosen for the altar that most faithfully reflected the holiness of the priesthood. In his words:

Tetzaveh

The meaning of the holiness of the priesthood indicates that it has the ability to bring people closer to their Father in heaven, since for that reason Aaron is called [in the Zohar[83]] the companion of the queen [*shoshbina dematronita*] (*Pri Tzaddik, Tetzaveh* 11).

The Zohar explains that Moses was compared to the companion of the King (G-d), while Aaron was compared to the companion of the queen (Israel). If the King was upset with the queen, Aaron would appease the King and reinstate the peaceful relationship between them.

In summary, according to R. Tzadok, the golden altar is intimately associated with Aaron's priestly mission, and is therefore appropriately situated in the portion dedicated to the priesthood. APPENDIX III elucidates how, in the view of R. Tzadok, the incense altar emphasized Aaron's mission to bring people closer to each other and reconcile disputants.

THE ISHBITZER REBBE

The Ishbitzer explains that a prerequisite to understanding the purpose of the golden altar and the incense offering that was brought on it, is a deep understanding of the significance of each of the priestly garments. He bases himself on two Talmudic sources.

SOURCE 1: A MISHNAH IN *YOMA*

[For] the third lottery [the following announcement was made by the supervisor of the lotteries]: novices [Rashi: who had never in their lives brought the incense offering] — come and join the lottery (BT *Yoma* 26a).

---

83. Zohar, vol. 3 (*Vayikra*), Metzora.

Explanation: Certain tasks in the Temple were not filled in an orderly fashion in advance, but rather by lottery at the time of execution, and the third such task was to officiate at the daily incense offering, which was brought in the morning and the evening.[84] Since this function was desirable, the right to perform it was raffled among the priests, but only among the novices—those who had never done so in the past. The Talmudic exegesis of the Mishnah states:

> A Tanna taught: Never did a man repeat it. What is the reason? R. Hanina said: because it enriches… Why [does the incense enrich]? … because Scripture says [as part of Jacob's blessing of his son Levi]: They shall put incense before You,[85] and soon after [it says]: Lord, bless his material belongings (Deut. 33:11).

Explanation: Each priest was given one chance to bring the incense offering, and no more, because anyone who brought that offering, even once, would be blessed with wealth, and it would be unfair to allow one person more than one opportunity, when others had not yet had a turn.

In harmony with the Mishnah, the Midrash comments on the verse "Lord, bless his material belongings":

> From here [based on this verse], they said: The majority of the priests are rich. In the name of Abba the preacher they said [the verse]: "I have been young, and now I am old,

---

84. Exod. 30:7-8, and Rashi thereon.
85. Deut. 33:10. Targum Yonatan translates the phrase as follows: "Their brothers the priests will place incense on censers and halt the plague on the day of Your anger," a reference to Num. 17:11.

Tetzaveh

and I have not seen a righteous person forsaken, nor his children seeking bread [because of hunger]" (Ps. 37:25) — this refers to the children of Aaron.[86]

Source 2: A Talmudic Passage:

R. Inyani b. Sasson also said: Why do the sections on sacrifices and the priestly garments appear [in the Torah] one after another? To teach you: just as sacrifices make atonement, so do the priestly garments make atonement (BT *Zevachim* 88b).

Explanation: In the portion of *Tzav* (in the book of Leviticus), the various types of sacrifices are detailed in chapters 6 and 7, and chapter 8 describes how Moses dressed Aaron in the priestly vestments. The purpose of presenting these two sections consecutively is to make a comparison between sacrifices and priestly vestments. Specifically, it was done to indicate that just as the sacrifices that one brings are meant to atone for transgressions—each sacrifice for its designated sin, similarly the priestly garments atone for various sins. This was done in order to ensure that the entire congregation does not suffer as a result of the sins of a few individuals who did not admit to their evil deeds, did not bring sacrifices, and were not convicted in court. The Talmud proceeds to list each of the priestly garments and the sin for which it atones, as follows:

---

86. *Sifrei, Ve-Zot ha-Berachah* 352.

Vestment	Sin
Coat	bloodshed
Pants	lewdness and incest
Mitre (hat)	arrogance—let an article placed high up come and atone for the offense of haughtiness
Belt	improper meditations of the heart—it was fastened near the heart
Breastplate	disobeying civil law
Apron (*ephod*)	idolatry
Robe	slander—let an article that makes noise (it was fringed with bells) atone for the offense of speaking (making noise) improperly
Head Plate	brazenness

The most extreme manifestation of jealousy is murder. With respect to the kidnapping and sale of Joseph, the Bible says: "And they took Joseph's coat, and killed a he-goat, and dipped the coat in the blood" (Gen. 37:31), and the Talmud uses this verse as proof that the priest's coat atones for murder. On the simplest level, one might say that it is appropriate that the coat, which was an accessory to an attempted murder, should atone for future murders. Rashi says that dipping represents atonement. The verse, by mentioning dipping, thus hints that the coat (of the priest) will someday serve as a means of atonement for murder.

The Talmud proceeds to declare that there are two forms of atonement for murder, and two for slander. If the murderer is unknown, the ceremony of decapitating a heifer is performed (Deut. 21:1-9). If the murderer is known, but he had not been pre-warned to desist from the heinous act, then the coat of the high priest accomplishes atonement.

Tetzaveh

With regard to slander, if one does so in public, it is atoned for by the priest's robe. If done secretly, the incense, which is similarly burnt in secret (inside the sanctuary) atones for the sin.

The *Mei Shiloach*

In his commentary on the Torah, *Mei Shiloach* (*Tetzaveh*), the Ishbitzer Rebbe bases his explanation of why the introduction of the golden altar was delayed until the end of the portion of *Tetzaveh* on the previously cited sources. On the one hand, the great joy of the Children of Israel that accompanied the successful completion of the incense offering on the Day of Atonement has been described. On the other hand, the great material awards which accrued to every priest who officiated at the daily incense offering has also been presented. *Mei Shiloach* explains that it was G-d's wish that the nation, as well as the priests, should enjoy these gifts without endangering themselves physically or spiritually. Hence, the self-improvement and atonement symbolized and provided by the priestly vestments were sorely needed. In his words:

> The priest engendered in the heart of every Israelite intense fear [of the Almighty], and after the priest injected fear in the hearts of Israel, there existed the capability of absorbing [and properly experiencing] the joy and love that emanated from the incense.

The meaning of the Rebbe's teaching is that after the Nation of Israel and the priests understood, with the help of the symbolism of the priestly vestments, to what level unbridled hedonism can sink, sufficient fear of the Lord was generated by those garments to provide the people with the will-power and self-control necessary to exult in the joyfulness of filling G-d's commands and the bounty associated with the incense offering, without losing proportion and celebrating in an immoral fashion. Accordingly, it was important to speak of the bringing of incense on the golden altar only after describing the priestly garments.

Summary

In this chapter, two topics were discussed—the absence of the name of Moses from the entire portion, and the placement of the description of the golden altar at the end of the portion, far from the details of all of the other furnishings of the Tabernacle, which are found in the previous portion of *Terumah*.

With regard to the first question, some of the answers view the absence of Moses' name as a punishment for a sin that he, at his elevated level, was guilty of committing. Others look upon the usage of the second person (you) as an even greater compliment than the use of his name.

The answers to the second question all justify the necessity of preceding the description of the golden altar by the details of the priest's apparel and activities.

One explanation that can solve both queries is suggested, and that is the one which stresses the importance of modesty. The Torah emphasizes the extreme modesty of Moses, and that being the case, he might have been perfectly satisfied to share the limelight with Aaron, so that when a portion which discusses priestly garments appeared, he had no qualms about letting it be dedicated exclusively to Aaron, with no mention of his own name. Proceeding with the initiative to stress the importance of this trait, which was one of the two that Rambam indicated should be observed in the extreme rather than by choosing the middle path (*Hilchot De'ot* 2:3), the Torah describes the priestly garments, the purpose of one of which was to highlight the attribute of modesty. Scripture then proceeds to describe the golden altar, on which the incense was brought, an offering that was liable to lead to haughtiness if the priest who brought it was not inculcated properly in the development of a worthy personality from a moral point of view.

In short, the importance of modesty is stressed by the absence of the name of Moses from the portion of *Tetzaveh*, as well as by the description of the priestly garments, and in particular the mitre, which was meant to atone for haughtiness. Finally, the golden altar is introduced, since the incense that was sacrificed on it could indirectly lead to haughtiness, which could be redressed by the mitre.

Ki Tissa

One of the foundational events in the Pentateuch is the story of the golden calf, which immediately leads to the basic question: Did the Children of Israel really sin with respect to the golden calf, and if so, how is this possible so shortly after the miraculous plagues in Egypt, the crossing of the Red Sea, and the revelation on Mt. Sinai? The same question may be asked with regard to Aaron, but in his case the question is even stronger, being that he was, and remained, one of the leaders of the nation; if he was indeed guilty, how could he have retained his position?

On the most elementary level, it is clear that both the nation and Aaron sinned (at least in the eyes of Moses), on the basis of the following verses from Moses' monologue at the beginning of Deuteronomy: "And in Horeb you [the Children of Israel] made the Lord angry, and the Lord was angry with you [and wished] to destroy you" (Deut. 9:8); "And with Aaron the Lord was very angry [and wished] to destroy him" (Deut. 9:20).

In spite of these verses, there exist varied opinions with regard to the questions presented. The different interpretations will be analyzed on two levels: the Tannaitic, Amoraic, and Midrashic literature; and Torah commentaries.

Ki Tissa

The Golden Calf in Tannaitic, Amoraic, and Midrashic Literature

It has been demonstrated that if the text of the Bible is taken literally, one would have to conclude that Israel, under the leadership of Aaron, produced the golden calf of its own initiative, and in doing so, sinned seriously. There exist a number of Midrashic sources that relieve the Children of Israel, at least partially, of the severity of the transgression, and there are more that exonerate Aaron. However, there are other Midrashim that maintain Israel's guilt. Both approaches will now be examined.

Minimizing the Transgression of the Children of Israel

The Midrash devised two mechanisms for minimizing the guilt of the Israelites by placing the blame on either Satan or an evil sorcerer.

Satan Deceived the Nation

The Talmud (BT *Shabbat* 89a) states:

> R. Joshua b. Levi said: Regarding what is written [in the verse] "And the people saw that Moses was delayed" (Exod. 32:1) [Hebrew: *boshesh*, in coming down from the mountain], do not read *boshesh* [delayed] but *ba'u shesh* [the sixth hour had come]. When Moses ascended to heaven, he said to Israel, "At the end of forty days, at the

beginning of the sixth hour [late morning], I will come." At the end of forty days, Satan came and confounded the world. He [Satan] said to them: "Where is your teacher Moses?" They answered him "He has ascended to heaven." He said to them: 'The sixth [hour] has come," but they disregarded him; "he is dead," but they disregarded him. He showed them the image of his bier, and this is what they [were referring to when they] said to Aaron, "as for Moses—the man who brought us up out of the land of Egypt—we do not know what has become of him."

Rashi *in situ* explains their error in greater detail, as follows:

They thought that the day on which he ascended the mountain [7 Sivan[87]] was to be included in this number [Sivan had 30 days, leaving 24 days in Sivan and 16 in Tammuz, returning late morning of 16 Tammuz]. However, he had said to them forty complete days—each day together with its preceding night. But the day of his ascent—its night was not with it, for he ascended on the seventh of Sivan [in the morning]. It follows that the fortieth day really fell on the seventeenth of Tammuz [and not as the people had believed, on the sixteenth]. On the sixteenth, Satan came and confused the world, giving [it] the appearance of darkness and gloom, the appearance of cloudiness and fog and disorder, causing [people] to say, "Surely Moses is dead, for six hours has come and he has

---

87. This is under the assumption that in the year of the exodus, Nisan and Iyar both had 29 days. Starting from 16 Nisan (the first day of the Omer), there were 14 more days in Nisan, 29 in Iyar, and 7 Sivan was the fiftieth day of the Omer.

Ki Tissa

not come." One cannot say that they erred only on account of it being a cloudy day, before noon and after noon [i.e., the people thought it was already afternoon, but it was still morning] for Moses did not come down until the following day [the day after they made the calf], for it says, "And they woke up early the next day, and offered burnt offerings, and brought peace offerings; and the people sat down to eat and to drink, and they stood up to make merry" (Exod. 32:6) [and only afterwards G-d told Moses: "Go down, for your people, whom you brought up out of the land of Egypt, have corrupted themselves" (Exod. 32:7)].

According to this Midrash, the actions of the Israelites did not stem from pure wickedness, but were the result of the malicious deception designed by Satan. Even so, they did not accept his word uncritically, but only after being shown a false vision of Moses' death. On the other hand, Rashi on the Talmud says that Satan is actually the evil inclination, and thus associates a greater degree of guilt with the Israelites themselves by implying that the incitement to sin was generated internally rather than as a reaction to external stimuli. Still, Rashi relates their sin to a mistake in their calculations.

THE GOLDEN CALF EMERGED AS A RESULT OF SORCERY

If the previously cited Midrash focused on "tricks" that Satan played concerning the disposition of Moses, a second Midrash focuses on the golden calf itself, claiming that it came into existence by foul means. Midrash Tanchuma[88] proposes two theories:

---

88. *Tanchuma, Ki Tissa* 19.

First Suggestion

It is well known that when the Israelites left Egypt, they were accompanied by the *erev rav*, the "mixed multitude" (Exod. 12:38). According to Rashi *in situ*, these people were "a mixture of various nations who had become proselytes."[89] They had chosen to join the ranks of the Children of Israel and share their destiny. Nevertheless, the rabbis were perennially suspicious of their loyalty, as will be apparent from some of the commentaries regarding the sin of the golden calf, as well as with respect to other instances of rebellious behavior.[90]

It is, therefore, not totally unexpected that the Midrash would pin the blame for fashioning the calf on the foreign element in their midst, by stating: "There gathered forty thousand who had ascended with Israel, and there were two Egyptian magicians among them... he [Aaron] threw [the gold] into the fire, and the magicians came and worked their magic."

Not only was the mixed multitude condemned for manufacturing the golden calf, they were also accused of being its main worshippers, based on the phrase "this is your god, Israel" (Exod. 32:4). Why does it say "your god," rather than our god? The Midrash[91] deduces that the phrase was uttered by people who did not consider themselves part of the mainstream—namely, the *erev rav*.

Why did the Rabbis look askance at the *erev rav*? Were they prejudiced in their outlook, or at the very least xenophobic?

---

89. It might be more accurate to say who wished to become proselytes, being that the Israelites themselves had yet to undergo a conversion process. See Rashi, Exod. 24:6.
90. For example, Rashi (Num. 11:4) characterizes the "lusters for meat" as being of the mixed multitude. *Midrash Lekach Tov* (Exod. 18:13) claims that the arguments among the people noted by Jethro were caused by the mixed multitude.
91. *Pesikta de-Rav Kahana, Shor o kesev*, par. 9.

Ki Tissa

Certainly such attitudes are not in harmony with the approach of the Torah, which specifically commands one "to love" in three cases—one's neighbor, strangers, and G-d Himself. Furthermore, while love of one's neighbor (Lev. 19:18) and of G-d (Deut. 6:5) are mentioned only once, loving the stranger (Lev. 19:34, Deut. 10:19) is mentioned twice. In fact, a commonly quoted saying in the Jewish religion is that the requirement to treat the stranger kindly and fairly is mentioned on thirty-six occasions in the Torah. In addition, a second Midrash (*Exod. Rabbah* 18:10) states:

> The sincere [people] in Egypt came and celebrated Passover with Israel, and ascended with them, as it says, "And a mixed multitude went up with them," and everyone who wished that Israel not be redeemed died with the firstborn, for it says: "And [He] smote all the firstborn in Egypt, the first-fruits of their strength in the tents of Ham" (Ps. 78:51).[92]

The Midrash clearly states that there were many faultless Egyptians who joined the community, while those who were degenerate perished. Moreover, there is no reason to assume that the ratio of the righteous among the Children of Israel was any higher than it was among the *erev rav*. Midrash Tanchuma[93] states that during the plague of darkness, the wicked among the Israelites died, with one view holding that as few as one out of five thousand survived.

One is now faced with the following question: If both the Israelites and the mixed multitude had undergone a filtering

---

92. Rashash explains that the Hebrew word used for strength (*onim*) is close to the Hebrew word for complainers (*mit'onenim*), indicating that those who opposed the exodus were also slain.
93. *Tanchuma, Beshallach* 1; quoted by Rashi, Exod. 13:18.

process, after which only the virtuous remained, how did such a serious sin transpire at all?

The first thing to note is that the number of actual sinners, out of a group numbering in the millions, was relatively small. The Levites killed three thousand sinners (Exod. 32:28). Statistics were not supplied concerning the other forms of death (by plague [Exod. 32:25] and by drinking the grindings of the golden calf mixed with water [Exod. 32:20]), and the assumption is that the number of victims was not significant enough to be reported. If a larger number died by plague or by drinking the powdered drink, it would certainly have been stated.

But why were there any sinners at all, if they had been completely eliminated? Obviously, some of those who had still been devout during the plague of darkness (among the Israelites) or the plague of the firstborn (among the Egyptians), and were thus spared, changed their minds by the time Moses ascended Mt. Sinai. They may have become disaffected and lost their faith after experiencing hunger (Exod. 16:3), thirst (Exod. 17:1), and especially military battles (Exod. 17:10).

There are a number of explanations for why there might have been a greater amount of treachery among the mixed multitude than among the Israelites. As previously cited in the name of Rashi, the mixed multitude originated from various nations. But the plague of the firstborn only struck the Egyptians, not members of other nations, who survived unscathed. Second, only those who opposed the escape of the Israelites from Egypt were smitten, not those who were idol-worshippers, many of whom may have been awed by the miraculous splitting of the Red Sea, yet were not ready for the religious life demanded of a Jew. Third, after the plague of the firstborn, and until the giving of the Torah, many more non-Israelites may have been absorbed into the mixed multitude. The

Ki Tissa

Midrash (*Exod. Rabbah* 42:6) states that because of Moses' modesty and warmth, he insisted on readily accepting anyone who sought membership in the community. This was against G-d's better judgment, but He acquiesced to Moses' desire, which was only a reflection of his beneficent personality, although G-d did remind Moses at the time of their great sin of His previous warning by calling the miscreants "your people" (Exod. 32:7).

One may make an additional point in support of the mixed multitude. The Midrash[94] brings three opinions with regard to their size. R. Ishmael says they were composed of 1,200,000 people, R. Akiva says 2,400,000, and R. Nathan says 3,600,000. But the previously cited Midrash spoke of only 40,000 members of the mixed multitude who were involved with the golden calf. It follows that just a fraction of the entire *erev rav* was actually guilty. In other words, they were not all villains, and the percentage of sinners may have been smaller than among the Israelites before four-fifths of them died in the plague of darkness.

Second Suggestion

The Midrash[95] brings a second option, which states that the source of the golden calf was not a foreign element, but a born-Israelite by the name of Micah.

Micah is first mentioned in the book of Judges (chapters 17-18) as an evil person. He is said to have stolen 1,100 pieces of silver from his mother. When he admitted his offense and returned the stolen goods, instead of rebuking him, his mother blessed him. She then made a graven image from 200 of the silver pieces and gave it to Micah, who installed it in a house of idol-worship that he

---

94. *Mechilta, Bo, Masechta de-Pascha* 14.
95. *Tanchuma, Ki Tissa* 19.

had constructed. Although he is considered a wicked person, the text indicates that he was raised by a morally challenged mother who was also an idol-worshipper, a not surprising combination. Perhaps his poor background may be looked at as a mitigating factor. Interestingly, he hired an idolatrous priest by the name of "Jonathan son of Gershom son of Manasseh," which in its Hebrew version can be construed as "Jonathan son of Gershom son of Moses." The Midrash[96] and Talmud (JT *Berachot* 9:2) say that in fact Jonathan was the grandson of Moses, which comes to show that even those who have an excellent background can be corrupted. Perhaps the lesson is that a positive background is helpful, but not necessarily decisive in choosing one's path in life.

The Talmud has the following to say about Micah:

> A Tanna taught: Nebat (1 Kings 12:2) [the father of Jeroboam, who rebelled against Rehoboam the son of Solomon and set up the Kingdom of Israel], Micah, and Sheba the son of Bichri [who rebelled against David (2 Samuel 20)] are one and the same. [He was called] Micah, because he was crushed [*ma-ach* in Hebrew] in the building; and what was his real name? Sheba the son of Bichri (BT *Sanhedrin* 101b).

The Tannaim believed in conservation of characters, i.e., when a number of characters act in a similar fashion, just that their names are different, it is conjectured that the Bible may be speaking of the same person, with each name bringing out a different aspect. Rashi explains "crushed in the building" as follows:

---

96. *Avot de-Rabbi Natan* A, 34; *Avot de-Rabbi Natan* B, 37.

Ki Tissa

Crushed in a building in Egypt, where he was placed instead of a brick, as is explained by the legend that Moses said to G-d, You worsened the situation of this nation (Exod. 5:22), for now if they do not have [enough] bricks, they place the children of the Israelites in [the wall of] the building. G-d answered him: They are destroying thorns [children who will grow up to be wicked people], for it is known to Me that if they live, they will be thoroughly wicked people, and if you wish, you may check [whether this is true] and extract one. He went and extracted Micah.

Micah is thus seen to be a good candidate for the villain who fashioned the golden calf, an idea proposed by the Midrash, which continues: "He [Micah] took the tablet upon which Moses had written, 'Arise ox,' when the coffin of Joseph was raised [from the Nile]. He threw it into the furnace among the [golden] rings, and a mooing, wobbling calf emerged."

Once again, to fully appreciate the Midrash, one must be acquainted with another Midrash, which states:

"And Moses took the bones of Joseph with him" (Exod. 13:19). How did Moses know where the bones of Joseph were buried? Serah, daughter of Asher, survived from that generation. She informed Moses where Joseph was buried. The Egyptians had made him a coffin of metal and sunk it in the Nile. Moses came and stood by the Nile. He took a stone and engraved on it: "Arise ox" [Joseph was referred to as an ox in Moses' blessing (Deut. 33:17)], and he cried out, saying: "Joseph, Joseph, the hour when the Almighty is about to redeem his sons has arrived, and the Divine Presence is waiting for you, and the clouds of honor

(Exod. 13:21) are waiting for you. If you reveal yourself, fine. If not, I am freed of your oath [when you made the Children of Israel swear to carry your bones to the Land of Israel (Gen. 50:25)]. Immediately Joseph's coffin rose [to the surface] and floated (*Tanchuma, Beshallach* 2).

The point of the Midrash concerning Micah is that he took a tablet having magical properties and used it for a nefarious purpose. As the Sages said, "On the path that a man wishes to walk, he is led" (BT *Makkot* 10b). Unfortunately, Micah's path also misled many vulnerable people.

Maintaining the Guilt of the Children of Israel

Although the Israelites may have been tricked in supernatural ways, either regarding the disposition of Moses or with respect to the creation of the golden calf, the Rabbis still placed the onus on the people themselves, as may be seen from the numerous citations listed below:

1. With regard to the red heifer (*parah adumah*), the Midrash states:

   To what may this be compared? To the child of a servant who dirtied the king's palace. The king said, let its mother come and clean up the excrement. So said the Almighty, let the heifer come and atone for the deeds of the calf (*Tanchuma Chukat* 8).

Ki Tissa

Of course, it was not the calf that sinned, but those who utilized its molten image as a means of idol-worship. Nevertheless, this ceremony provided a gentle, but clear enough, hint to the congregation to rid themselves of sinful practices.

2. The Talmud states that the horn of a cow may not be used as a shofar "because the accuser may not act as a defender" (BT *Rosh Hashanah* 26a).[97] If the golden calf was, in a manner of speaking, an accuser, obviously Israel was being accused of something. A second Talmudic passage says quite explicitly what it was: "Since the Israelites worshipped the golden calf, they revealed their acceptance of idolatry" (BT *Avodah Zarah* 53b).

3. Another Talmudic passage points out that although they had degenerated to idol-worship, it could have been worse. Upon seeing the completed calf, the Israelites said: "These are your gods, Israel, who brought you out of Egypt" (Exod. 32:4). Had they said, "This is your god," the Talmud says that G-d would have destroyed them on the spot (BT *Sanhedrin* 63a). By using the plural, they at least gave credit to the true G-d, just that they displayed their willingness to worship other divinities as well. In other words, they still believed in G-d, but not in His uniqueness.

4. Before the sin of the golden calf, Scripture states that the "young men" (Exod. 24:5) brought sacrifices. Onkelos translates young men as firstborn. However, eventually the Levites were chosen to replace them in maintaining the Temple service, based on the verse: "And I, behold, have taken the Levites from among the Children of Israel in the place of every firstborn, the first of the womb, among the Children of Israel; and the Levites shall be Mine" (Num. 3:12).

---

97. For the same reason, the high priest changed from his golden clothing into linen clothing when he entered the Holy of Holies on Yom Kippur, since they had sinned using gold.

The Torah does not supply a reason for the substitution, although one might guess that it had something to do with the fact that it was the Levites who helped Moses punish those who worshipped the golden calf, which would imply that they themselves were innocent of wrongdoing, unlike the firstborn. The Midrash[98] identifies a verse in Ezekiel that confirms the accuracy of the previous suggestion:

> And the priests the Levites, the sons of Tzadok, who faithfully functioned in My sanctuary *when the Children of Israel went astray from Me*, they shall come near to Me to minister to Me; and they shall stand before Me to offer to Me the fat and the blood (Ezek. 44:15).

In summary, Midrashic and Talmudic sources that mitigate the extent of the transgression have been presented, but in the final analysis, all of Israel other than the Levites were held responsible for their sinful deeds, each to the extent of his involvement.

WAS AARON GUILTY?

Unlike the consensus regarding the nation, which was that there was a degree of guilt, even if there were extenuating circumstances, with regard to Aaron, almost all of the Midrashic and Talmudic sources exonerate him, although there is some criticism of the tactics that he used to accomplish his purpose. Aaron was such a central and respected figure in Jewish tradition that it would have been difficult to denounce his beliefs or actions.

Specifically, there are two points on which most Midrashim agree, namely that Aaron's faith in G-d was never in doubt, and

---

98. *Midrash Aggadah*, Num. 3:12. See Rashi on this verse.

Ki Tissa

that Aaron did whatever he could to delay the process, hoping all the while that Moses would appear in person and the rebellion would be quelled. In addition, Aaron might have allowed himself to become intimately involved in order to steer the people in the right direction, or perhaps simply to insure that the brunt of the offense should not fall on the shoulders of his beloved congregation. Although there is general agreement that Aaron's intentions were laudable, there is a Talmudic debate concerning whether he should have acted differently under the circumstances. The following points summarize the Midrashic approach:

1. Aaron's faith was untainted. When the populace presented Aaron with their golden rings, the Midrash looks upon him as uttering a verse that would later be incorporated in Psalms: "I lift up my eyes to You, Who are enthroned in the heavens" (Ps. 123:1). Accordingitng to the Midrash, what Aaron was telling G-d was: "You know all [of a man's] thoughts, [and are surely aware that] whatever I am doing is against my will."[99]
2. Aaron used all of his wiles in order to foil the plot. Specifically, he attempted to introduce obstacles at each of three critical stages: the gathering of the gold, the creation of the calf, and finally the act of its worship.

Regarding the collection of the raw material, Aaron said: "Break off the golden rings, which are in the ears of your wives, your sons, and your daughters" (Exod. 32:2). The Midrash explains: "Aaron told them a hard thing [to do], which women would [normally] postpone."[100] In explanation of the Midrash, Rashi on the Biblical verse

---

99. *Tanchuma, Ki Tissa* 19.
100. Ibid.

states: "Aaron said to himself: women and children cherish their ornaments; perhaps the matter will be delayed [because they will hesitate to surrender their jewelry], and in the meantime Moses will arrive."

However, the artifice didn't work, and the gold was produced instantly. Were the women as avid to sin as the men? Rashi believes they were, for he says: "they [the women] didn't wait and they took off their jewelry by themselves [i.e., the men did not have to remove it from them, because they did so willingly and speedily]." The Midrash, in contrast, adamantly insists that the women would not and did not contribute their jewelry in principle; it was the men who gave their gold. The Midrash proves its point from the next verse, which states: "And all the nation broke off the golden rings [that were in their ears]." The Midrash points out that the phrase at the end of the verse is: "that were in their [the men's] ears," even though the original suggestion was to remove those "that are in the ears of your wives." Apparently, the wives refused to cooperate.

As far as the manufacture of the golden calf, the text states that it was Aaron who made it for the Israelites, and built the altar upon which sacrifices to their new god would be brought. According to the Midrash, his only motivation in taking these tasks upon himself was to slow down the process. On the phrase "*And Aaron saw* and built an altar before it [the golden calf]" (Exod. 32:5), the Midrash asks: "What did he see? If **they** build it, this one brings a pebble and this one brings a stone, and their work will be finished at once. If *I* build it, I can be lazy in my workmanship and Moses our teacher will descend and destroy it" (*Lev. Rabbah* 10:3).

Ki Tissa

Regarding the final stage—actually worshipping the golden calf, Rashi maintains that the Biblical text itself indicates that Aaron purposely procrastinated. On the phrase, "Tomorrow is a festival to G-d" (Exod. 32:5), Rashi states: "[Tomorrow], and not today, perhaps Moses will come before they worship it."

3. Aaron made every effort to return the congregation to the right path. Regarding the previously quoted phrase, "Tomorrow is a festival to G-d," the Midrash notes: "It doesn't say, 'Tomorrow is a festival to the golden calf,' but 'Tomorrow is a festival to G-d'" (*Lev. Rabbah* 10:3). In the view of the Midrash, this indicates that Aaron had not abandoned the possibility of stimulating the people to repent. Alternatively, according to Targum Yonatan (Exod. 32:5), Aaron actually said these words in a sad voice, anticipating a bloodbath the next day, which is cynically called a festival, being the day that G-d will exact revenge on His enemies.

4. Aaron participated in most of the activity in order to defray some of the guilt from the Children of Israel. Rather than trying to save his soul and abandoning the sinners, he took an active role, thereby providing the people with the excuse that they were only following their leader, surmising that if he was also involved, there must not be anything wrong with it. Another portion of the previously quoted Midrash states:

What did he see? Aaron said, if *they* build it, the rebellion will be associated with them. Better that the rebellion should be associated with me, and not with the Israelites. R. Abba b. Yudan in the name of R. Abba [says]: This may be compared to a prince who became arrogant and took a sword to stab his father. His pedagogue said to him: Do not tire yourself. Give it to me and I will stab him. The king looked at him and said to him, I know what your intention was. Better that the rebellion should be associated with you, and not with my son. I swear, you will not move from my palace and the leftovers [of the food] from my table you will eat, and twenty-four gifts you will take. Similarly, from my palace you [Aaron] will not move, and the Temple you will not leave, and the remains of my table you will eat, as well as the remainder of the meal offering. Twenty-four gifts you will take. These are the twenty-four priestly gifts that were given to Aaron and his sons. The Almighty said to Aaron, you loved justice, you loved to justify my sons, and you hated to convict them. Therefore G-d, your G-d, has anointed you. I swear that of the entire tribe of Levi, only you were chosen for the high priesthood (*Lev. Rabbah* 10:3).

5. Aaron's amazing devotion to his people, which manifested itself in his willingness to suffer on their account if only it would help them, knew no bounds. In addition to partaking of their sin, so to say, he must have realized what such behavior would do to his reputation, and in particular to his relationship with his beloved brother Moses. But once he had determined that it was the proper thing to do, he proceeded with no regrets and no concern for his personal status. In fact, another Midrash describes how Moses reacted upon seeing Aaron (before actually arriving in the camp):

When Moses started descending from Mount Sinai and saw Israel doing that activity [making the golden calf], he looked at Aaron and he was banging on it with a hammer. He [Aaron] only intended to delay them [Israel] until Moses descended. But Moses thought that he was a partner of theirs, and was disgusted with him. The Almighty said to Moses: I know how good are Aaron's intentions (*Exod. Rabbah* 37:2).

Chiddushei ha-Radal on this Midrash explains that when G-d told Moses, "Bring Aaron your brother and his sons close to you" (Exod. 28:1), the Almighty was referring to the fact that Moses had actually wanted to distance himself from Aaron, based on what he considered to be his inappropriate behavior.

Did Aaron do the right thing? The Talmud (BT *Sanhedrin* 7a) discusses this topic. Although Aaron was an accessory to the congregation's worship of the golden calf, the Talmud explains that he did so for a higher purpose, namely to allow the continued existence of the nation. Whether that was the right decision on his part turns out to be the subject of an argument between Rashi and Tosafot. To obtain a deeper understanding of the various factors involved, see Appendix IV: ARBITRATION IN JEWISH LAW – MOSES VS. AARON.

THE SIN OF THE GOLDEN CALF ACCORDING TO THE CLASSICAL COMMENTATORS

The classical Biblical commentators Rashi, Ramban, and Ibn Ezra in general reach the same conclusion, namely that Israel sinned, but it is not clear whether it was only a small segment of the mixed multitude or a larger group; and Aaron was a true believer in G-d and definitely had no intention of engaging in idol-worship, so that his guilt, if there was any at all, was minor. Of course, there are different nuances associated with each one, which will become evident as they are examined in greater detail.

Rashi's Opinion

The Sin of the Nation

Rashi in *Ki Tissa* cites many Midrashim in connection with the story of the golden calf. One may assume that these Midrashim reflect Rashi's basic approach, unless he brings conflicting Midrashim or stresses that a particular Midrash diverges from the straightforward meaning of the text. Some of the Midrashim referred to by Rashi are listed below.

Recall the first verse of chapter 32:

> And the people saw **that Moses was delayed** in coming down from the mountain, and the people gathered themselves around Aaron, and said to him: "Arise [and] make us *a god who goes before us*; for Moses, the man who brought us up from the land of Egypt, we do not know what has become of him."

1. On the words "that Moses was delayed," Rashi states that Satan misled the Israelites.
2. On the words "a god who goes before us," Rashi brings the Midrash[101] which says: "this [the fact that *elohim*, the word for "god," is in the plural form in Hebrew] teaches that they craved many gods."
3. On the words "he made it into a molten calf" (Exod. 32:4), Rashi cites the Midrash which states that the calf was formed extraordinarily fast by means of sorcery.
4. Rashi on Num. 19:22, basing himself on the Midrash (*Tanchuma Chukat* 8), links the red heifer with the sin of the golden calf.

---
101. *Lekach Tov*, Exod. 32:1

Ki Tissa

5. In the portion of *Bemidbar* (Num. 3:12), Rashi cites the Midrash (BT *Zevachim* 112b) which states that the firstborn were disqualified from serving in the sanctuary as a result of their joining in the worship of the golden calf.
6. On the words "this is your god, Israel" (Exod. 32:4), Rashi cites the Midrash that it was the mixed multitude who initiated the request to make an idol, and actually made it. However, he adds the following significant words: "and afterwards [after making it], they led Israel astray." According to Rashi, the sin may have started with the *erev rav*, but it spread to the entire congregation. In addition, on the words "he made it into a molten calf," Rashi's first explanation is that the calf was conjured by the magicians *among the mixed multitude*.

Based on the above citations, it is seen that Rashi believes that the Children of Israel did indeed sin, having been corrupted by the mixed multitude who initiated the sin, with the Israelites joining later on. Furthermore, even the mixed multitude would not have sinned had Satan not intervened by harping on Moses' supposed tardiness and expediting the manufacture of the golden calf. In the end, the entire congregation sinned and was punished by the transfer of the priesthood from the firstborn to the Levites. The full punishment would have led to the entire nation being wiped out, but instead it was apportioned in installments (Rashi on Exod. 32:34).

Aaron's Sin

The following points outline Rashi's view of Aaron's sin:

1. Rashi (Exod. 32:5) accepts the Midrash that Aaron was willing to take the guilt of Israel upon himself.

2. Aaron attempted to delay by asking the men to remove the women's jewelry. He hoped the women would resist, and was surprised when they didn't.
3. Aaron attempted to delay the entire process by building the altar himself and declaring a holiday only on the next day.
4. Rashi accepts the Midrashic view that when Aaron said, "Tomorrow is a festival to G-d," he was proposing that they worship the real G-d.

Rashi looks upon Aaron as one who was willing to sacrifice himself in order to defend the nation of Israel, to the extent that he was even willing to allow himself to be suspected of idol-worship. Simultaneously, he made every effort to delay the implementation of the scheme being plotted, in the hope that Moses would return in the meantime.

JUDAH HA-LEVI IN THE *KUZARI*

The view of Judah ha-Levi (1075-1140), who lived in the generation after Rashi (1040-1105), differs from that of Rashi in a number of respects. In contrast to Rashi, who relates to only one sin—idolatry—he sees three potential sins. In addition, unlike Rashi, who exempts Aaron from censure entirely, he finds Aaron guilty on at least one count.

Judah ha-Levi believes that the sin of the majority of the congregation was not worshipping the golden calf, which they had no intention of doing, but stemmed from the invention of a palpable intermediary, namely the golden calf, to symbolize the presence of G-d. In the words of the *Kuzari*:

Ki Tissa

Their sin consisted in the manufacture of an image of a forbidden thing, and in attributing divine power to a creation of their own, something chosen by themselves without the guidance of G-d (*Kuzari* 1:97).

The nation should have waited patiently for G-d to issue a command to create such an intermediary, as He eventually did when He required the building of a Tabernacle with its vessels, especially the altars and the Cherubim. As the *Kuzari* states:

> Some decided to do like the other nations, and seek an object in which they could have faith, without, however, prejudicing the supremacy of Him who had brought them out of Egypt.... This sin was not on a par with an entire lapse from all obedience to Him who had led them out of Egypt, as only one of His commands was violated by them. G-d had forbidden images, and in spite of this, they made one. They should have waited and not have assumed power, [and not] have arranged a place of worship, an altar, and sacrifices (*Kuzari* 1:97).

It is impossible for humans to know why a golden calf is prohibited yet Cherubim are permitted; but one who chooses the former, of his own volition,

> ... is like an ignoramus who enters the surgery of a physician famous for the curative power of his medicines. The physician is not at home, but people come for medicines. The fool dispenses them out of the jars, knowing nothing of the contents, nor how much should be given to each person. Thus, he kills with the very medicine that should have cured them (*Kuzari* 1:79).

Based on this parable, Judah ha-Levi says of the Israelites of that generation:

> They resembled the fool of whom we spoke, who entered the surgery of a physician and dealt out death instead of healing to those who came there. At the same time, the people did not intend to give up their allegiance to G-d (*Kuzari* 1:97).

In addition to the lesser sin of the majority, however, there was a small minority, comprised of those who eventually died by the hands of the Levites or otherwise, who actually worshipped the calf as an idol. As the *Kuzari* states: "those who worshipped the calf were punished on the same day, and three thousand out of six hundred thousand were slain."

A third sin was committed by Aaron and those who helped him. Although he did not necessarily commit either of the first two sins, i.e., he didn't wish for the calf to serve as an intermediary and certainly not to be an object of devotion, his actions did allow the sins of the majority and the minority to take place.

Additional Points from *Kuzari* 1:97

1. R. Judah ha-Levi explains why their sin seems so serious to the modern reader: "The whole affair is repulsive to us, because in this age the majority of nations have abandoned the worship of images."
2. In those days, it was quite acceptable to seek a visible form, as the *Kuzari* states: "It appeared less objectionable at that time, because all nations were then idolaters."

3. In addition to idols being normative in those days, *Kuzari* gives a detailed description of how the idea that the calf could be an intermediary developed: "The Israelites had been promised that something visible would descend on them from G-d which they could follow, as they followed the pillars of cloud and fire when they departed from Egypt."
4. In order to allow the modern reader to relate to that generation of Israelites, *Kuzari* suggests a parallel to forms of worship familiar in post-Temple times. Worshipping an idol in ancient times was as common as praying in a house of worship is today: "Had their sin consisted in constructing a house of worship of their own, and making a place of prayer, offering, and veneration, the matter would not have been so grave [in contemporary eyes], because nowadays we also build our houses of worship, hold them in great respect, and seek blessing through their means. We even say that G-d dwells in them, and that they are surrounded by angels. If this were not essential for the gathering of our community, it would be as unknown as it was at the time of the kings, when the people were forbidden to erect places of worship, called heights (*bamot*). The pious kings destroyed them, lest they be venerated beside the house chosen by G-d, in which He was to be worshipped according to His own ordinances. *There was nothing strange in the form of the Cherubim made by His command.*"
5. To justify why Aaron made the golden calf and continued being involved in its worship, Judah ha-Levi explains that he did so in order to weed out the small number of real idol-worshippers. In his words: "For those of higher station who assisted in making it, an excuse might be found in the fact that they wished to clearly separate the disobedient from the pious, in order to slay those who would worship the calf."

6. In spite of Aaron's good intentions, he sinned "in causing what was only a sin of intention to become a sin in deed."

The View of Ibn Ezra

It is likely that there was a certain amount of cross-pollination between Judah ha-Levi (1075-1140) and Ibn Ezra (1092-1164), who knew each other, and some even say that the latter was the son-in-law of the former. Nevertheless, Ibn Ezra reserved the right to express his own opinion, which differed in various respects from that of Judah ha-Levi.

Ibn Ezra (on Exod. 32:1) introduces a new idea by stating that the original intention of the people was to find a replacement for Moses, not for G-d, and this was *not a sin* at all. He argues with his predecessors on several points. Unlike Judah ha-Levi, who criticized Aaron for making it possible for the sins which he enumerates to occur, he holds that Aaron was innocent of any wrongdoing. The only accusation against him is that it happened on his watch. In contrast to Rashi, who accuses the nation as a whole of worshipping idols, either initially or at a later stage, Ibn Ezra absolves them completely. In contradistinction to Judah ha-Levi, who does not mention the mixed multitude at all, and Rashi, who tags them as the instigators, but not as the exclusive sinners, Ibn Ezra limits the sin to them exclusively.

Aaron Was Completely Innocent

Ibn Ezra defends his position quite eloquently by making the following points:

Ki Tissa

1. If actual idol-worship was being proposed, why did Aaron not choose a martyr's death? He states: "Did not many pious people in Israel, whose degree of piety did not reach the sole of Aaron's foot, die after him in defense of the unity of G-d? Behold Daniel's friends were thrown into the burning furnace because they didn't bow down to the idol, so how could Aaron make an idol, whose 'making' is more serious than bowing? Was not Aaron a holy person of G-d and a prophet in Israel, and many laws were given via him and his brother Moses? Can Hur [killed attempting to prevent the worship of the calf] be considered to be better than him?"
2. If actual idol-worship was being proposed, why did Moses not slay him, especially since he told the tribe of Levi to kill anyone who had worshipped the calf, including close relatives (Exod. 32:29)? In the words of Ibn Ezra: "If he engaged in idol-worship, Moses should have killed him before killing those who worshipped the calf. Behold Moses prayed for him, and those who worshipped he killed. And how could he and his descendants atone for the Children of Israel forever? ... and all scholars admit that G-d would not have chosen a messenger whom He knew would in the end worship idols, and [for that reason] not every prophet is a messenger [e.g., the prophet Balaam]."
3. When Aaron died (Num. 20:24), and in three additional locations[102] as well, the reason of his death is recorded as being his behavior at the waters of Meribah. No other reason is mentioned, and therefore Ibn Ezra feels that it is impossible that he in fact engaged in idolatry. He states: "We see that Moses said [in his tribal blessings] before his death 'Your Urim and Tumim were given to Your pious man' (Deut. 33:8). Behold, the story of the calf is not mentioned. Nothing was found to

---
102. Num. 20:12, 27:14; Deut. 32:51.

his detriment other than that which was also found regarding Moses, and that is the case of the waters of Meribah."

4. Aaron was guilty only in the sense that he had ministerial responsibility, since the sin occurred when he was the leader. In the words of Ibn Ezra: "Don't wonder regarding G-d's anger at Aaron (Deut. 9:20), for that is only because he was the reason [being the leader at the time], for he was punished with his brother Moses on the issue of the waters of Meribah, and they did not sin out of wickedness."

The Nation as a Whole Did Not Sin

Ibn Ezra explains:

> Israel did not seek idolatry. They just thought that Moses, who had taken them from the Red Sea, had died after separating [from them]. For they saw that the manna did not descend on Mt. Sinai, and Moses remained there forty days, and no man has the ability to live so long without food… and the word *elohim* implies that glory rests in a physical form, and so they said "an *elohim* that would go before us" … therefore Aaron built an altar before him and announced that they will sacrifice tomorrow to honor G-d, and so they did as he commanded them.

Mainly the Mixed Multitude Sinned

Ibn Ezra states:

> And this is [the meaning of Aaron's words], "You know the people, that they are set on evil" (Exod. 32:22) [literally

Ki Tissa

"*among evil*"], for I did nothing evil to them, for they only asked [for a figure] that would go before them, and in honor of G-d I made it. Just because Israel was mixed with the *erev rav* [did this tragedy occur]. And that is the meaning of "among evil," and he [Aaron] did not say [the people are] "evil".... And behold, all of the worshippers of the calf as an idol... or for whom such was in their mind, were only three thousand. And they are only a half of one-tenth of one-tenth [1/200] of the camp.

Ramban's Opinion

Ramban (1194-1279) lived a number of generations after Rashi, Judah ha-Levi, and Ibn Ezra, and was aware of their views. In comparing his views to those of his predecessors, the following points may be noted:

1. In agreement with Ibn Ezra, he holds that the original intention of the people was to find a replacement for Moses, not for G-d.
2. Unlike Judah ha-Levi and Ibn Ezra, who absolve the nation as a whole of worshipping idols, he accuses many of them of doing so eventually.
3. Like Judah ha-Levi, he does not mention the mixed multitude at all, and accordingly doesn't associate any more guilt with them than with any other element. Ibn Ezra, on the other hand, had completely confined the sin to the *erev rav*, while Rashi had fingered them as the initiators, if not the lone sinners.
4. In contrast to Rashi and Ibn Ezra, but in agreement with Judah ha-Levi, he does not hold that Aaron was completely

innocent of any wrongdoing in this incident. He criticizes Aaron for not sufficiently rebuking the nation and not displaying adequate leadership.

Ramban holds that initially, neither Aaron nor the Children of Israel sinned by making the golden calf. They believed in G-d exclusively, and had no inclination to worship idols. What they sought was a replacement for Moses, who had disappeared, and this request was fair and not in contradiction to *halachah*, so he writes (Exod. 32:1):

> It is known that the Israelites did not think that Moses was a god, nor that he by his own power had made signs and miracles for them. If so, what sense would there be in their saying that since Moses had gone from them, "We will make a god" [Why replace Moses with a god if they realized that Moses himself was not a god]? And also, they said explicitly [that they wanted] "an *elohim* that would go before us" not [a god] that would give them life in this world or the world to come. But they sought another Moses. They said: "Moses, who showed us the way 'from Egypt to here' (Num. 14:19), and the journeys were 'by the word of the Almighty and the hand of Moses' (Num. 9:23), behold he has been lost to us. Make for us another Moses to show us the way by the word of the Almighty and His hand." And this is the reason that they mentioned "Moses, the *man* who brought us up" (Exod. 32:1), not the *god* who brought us up, for they needed "a man of G-d" (Deut. 33:1).

Ramban brings two proofs to his thesis. When Moses asked Aaron to explain himself, Aaron answered: "Do not get angry, my master" (Exod. 32:22), and he proceeded to explain to Moses how he crafted for them a golden calf to be an *elohim* for them. If an idol was intended, how is it that Moses did not get a lot angrier? However, if Aaron was only describing Moses' replacement, one can understand that Moses took it calmly. The second proof is that when Moses saw the calf, he burned it and ground it up, yet the congregation was not upset by his actions. Had the Israelites related to the calf as their god, they would certainly have complained vociferously and violently.

At this point, if there was no transgression, why did Moses command the tribe of Levi: "every man should slay his brother, and every man his companion, and every man his neighbor" (Exod. 32:27)?

Ramban (on Exod. 32:5) answers that it says: "And they woke up early the next day, and offered burnt offerings, and brought peace offerings; and the people sat down to eat and to drink, and they stood up to make merry" (Exod. 32:6).

He notes that it does not say to whom they offered the burnt offerings. That is because Aaron and some of the others had intended the sacrifices to be to G-d. However, by this point, most of the people had in fact become corrupted, so the sacrifices were actually offered to both G-d and the calf. Even though the total number of Israelites who were eventually killed was relatively small (Exod. 32:28, 35), that is because most of the people had only sinned in their minds, and had not actually participated in the worship ceremony (Ramban on Exod. 32:7). At any rate, G-d told Moses to descend Mt. Sinai on the day that the sacrifices were brought (Exod. 32:7), not on the day that the golden calf was constructed. Ramban sees this as proof that, initially, their intentions were perfectly acceptable (Ramban on Exod. 32:6).

With respect to the verse, "And when Moses saw that the people were broken loose, for Aaron had let them loose *for a derision among their enemies*" (Exod. 32:25), Ramban explains that Moses rebuked Aaron not only regarding those who sinned, but also regarding those who didn't. Aaron had not provided them with enough guidance and instruction, which was so vital for them at this primitive stage of their spiritual development. Their behavior showed such confusion and lack of direction, that it would be derided by their enemies in future generations. Alternatively, Ramban cites Onkelos, who translates the last phrase as "a source of evil reports throughout the generations." Ramban explains this to mean that in the future, whenever there would be a desire to worship idols, they would be able to credit the exodus from Egypt to the golden calf. Indeed, Jeroboam, king of the ten tribes, did exactly that, as indicated by the following verse: "Whereupon the king got advice, and made two calves of gold; and he said to them [the Israelites]: You have gone up long enough to Jerusalem; Here are your gods, O Israel, that brought you up out of the land of Egypt" (1 Kings 12:28).

In summary, Aaron's purpose in making the golden calf was merely to have a replacement for Moses, and this was initially also the intention of the Israelites. But when they started bringing sacrifices in the proximity of the golden calf, some of them started worshipping it to varying degrees, and it was necessary to prevent this from continuing. Moses criticized Aaron for not rebuking those who worshipped the calf, and also for not providing more direction and guidance to those who didn't worship the calf. Moses predicted that in the future Israel would be vilified because of the golden calf, as occurred during the reign of Jeroboam. Even though only a minority actually worshipped it, this would not be highlighted, and Aaron would be partially responsible for this state of affairs.

In Ramban's view, Aaron erred by failing to display leadership, and part of the nation sinned by worshipping idols. Although their intentions were initially respectable, the situation degenerated, and Moses had to be summoned in order to restore order. Unlike Rashi and Ibn Ezra, Ramban did not identify the sinners as being exclusively or even mainly members of the mixed multitude.

Summary

After noting that in spite of the enormity of the sin, the number of idol-worshippers—according to all of the commentaries—was proportionally miniscule (Exod. 32:28), it is clear that not many people transgressed. In addition, Rashi, and especially Ibn Ezra, identify the main sinners as being members of the mixed multitude, not typical Israelites. In short, even based on the literal translation of the Biblical verses, most of the nation retained the positive influence of the revelation at Mt. Sinai.

Prof. Nechama Leibowitz, on the other hand, rather than minimizing the sin in quality and quantity, provides the following explanation:

> It is not the one-time hearing [of the voice of G-d] that turns over the man and changes him... but the extended practicing of a life of Torah and *mitzvot* under the constant guidance of G-d's Torah, which encompasses him from all sides, which regulates his days and nights, his weekdays and his holidays, his life at home and on the outside,

his contacts with the members of his family, and his business dealings.... Only that is able to change him and protect him from falling into the dark depths and from retrogression.[103]

In other words, one should not be surprised at the easy lapse of the Children of Israel into sin, because G-dly behavior requires many years of nurturing, and the new nation was still spiritually immature.

---

103. Nechama Leibowitz, *Iyunim Chadashim be-Sefer Shemot* (1987), pp. 399-400.

Vayakhel

The portion of *Ki Tissa* describes the sin of the golden calf—the most serious sin that the Nation of Israel ever committed. The appropriate punishment would have been to destroy the entire nation, but at the request of Moses, G-d agreed not to punish the Children of Israel with one fatal blow, but to do so in installments, as has previously been discussed.

Aaron, who according to most opinions did not succumb to the sin of idol-worship, made every attempt to prevent the nation from sinning, but was helpless against a crowd that numbered in the millions. He formulated what he thought to be a brilliant idea. He told the men: "Break off the golden rings that are in the ears of your wives, your sons, and your daughters" (Exod. 32:2). Rashi explains: "Aaron said to himself: women and children cherish their ornaments. Perhaps the matter will be delayed [because they will hesitate to surrender their jewelry], and in the meantime Moses will arrive."

But in the end, according to Rashi,[104] the women were just as eager as the men, and they removed their own jewelry. Tosafot,[105] on the other hand, holds that the women did not cooperate and

---

104. Rashi on Exod. 32:2, perhaps based on *Exod. Rabbah* 51:8.
105. *Daat Zekenim mi-Baalei Tosafot* 32:25.

did not donate their jewelry toward the manufacture of the calf. In their opinion, the women were superior to the men in terms of their belief, and perhaps this is the basis of the rabbinic saying: "As a reward for the righteous women who lived in that generation, the Israelites were delivered from Egypt" (BT *Sotah* 11b).

This approach was adopted by Rabbenu Bachya (Exod. 35:20-21) in his explanation of the verse: "One man among a thousand I have found; but a woman *among all of these* I have not found" (Eccl. 7:28). On the face of it, the verse is quite derogatory towards women. However, Rabbenu Bachya explains the words "among all of *these*" to mean that there was not even one woman among all those who said: "*These* are your gods, Israel" (Exod. 32:4), i.e., only the men sinned and not the women.

Stories of the devotion of the women to the Nation of Israel and the Land of Israel already appear in the portion of *Shemot*, in the description of the heroic efforts of Jochebed and Miriam in saving the Israelite infants. The portion of *Beshallach* tells of Miriam's leadership after the splitting of the Red Sea. The book of Numbers (27:4) refers to the love exhibited by the daughters of Zelophehad for the Land of Israel. It will be shown that to the various depictions of the righteousness of the women, one may add their behavior at the time of the construction of the Tabernacle.

WOMEN'S DONATIONS TO THE TABERNACLE

In the portion of *Vayakhel*, women are described as being exceedingly generous. Listed below are four references to their participation in the overall effort to collect the means to build the Tabernacle according to G-d's plan, as outlined in the previous portions.

Vayakhel

First Reference

And the men came *on the women* [Hebrew: *al ha-nashim*], every willing-hearted [person] brought earrings [Rashi: bracelets], and nose-rings, and signet rings, and girdles [Ibn Ezra: bracelets], all [of the previously enumerated being] vessels of gold, and every man that brought an offering of gold to the Lord (Exod. 35:22).

Obviously the phrase "the men came on the women" begs for interpretation. Ibn Ezra makes three suggestions. The most straightforward is that "on the women" simply means: with the women. Another explanation is that it means: "after the women," implying that the women were more generous than the men—they arrived first, and the men only joined later, possibly out of embarrassment. Alshich adds to the women's righteousness by pointing out that the original request for contributions was made to the "congregation of the Children of Israel" (Exod. 35:4), which he understands to refer to the men exclusively. The women thus heard of Moses' request only from their husbands, but they were the ones who initiated the process and hurried to make their contributions.

Tzeror ha-Mor notes aspects of the verse that support the latter explanation. Firstly, the items mentioned at the beginning of the verse (e.g., rings, bracelets) are all women's jewelry, which are appropriate for women to donate. Only at the end of the verse are men specifically mentioned as contributing pure gold. The first part of the verse thus refers to what the women gave and the second part to what the men gave; the women's contributions were mentioned first because they were the initiators.

Ibn Ezra has a third interpretation as well, namely that "on the women" means "with the consent of the women." *Toldot*

Yitzchak maintains that this explanation is based on the fact that the words which follow, "every willing-hearted [person] brought," are in the Hebrew masculine form. The implication is that the actual bringing was done by the husbands. This fits in with the assumption that Moses had made the request to the men alone, so it is reasonable that they would have brought the contributions. In addition, it would not be halachically proper for a woman to make a generous donation without her husband's approval. If the husband physically delivered the item, it would be clear that it was mutually agreed upon.

Another interpretation of the words "on the women" is that of Onkelos, who translates it in a completely literal sense by stating that "on" simply means "on." The phrase is thus to be interpreted as follows: "And the men came [when the jewelry was still] on the women."

How is one to interpret this? It can be taken in either a positive or a negative sense. The positive approach is that the women were so eager to donate their jewelry that they didn't even want to take the time necessary to remove it, but rushed off immediately to the collection station. Alternatively they wanted to exhibit maximal participation and to be present when the mitzvah was fulfilled, or perhaps they just wanted to publicly confirm their acquiescence (for without their agreement, it would have been forbidden for their husbands to contribute, even to a holy cause).

The negative approach was taken by R. Chaim of Chernovitz,[106] who based himself on a Talmudic saying that a woman is by nature parsimonious (BT *Berachot* 18b). Therefore her husband does not generally contribute from her belongings to charitable causes, because he loves her, desires her, and does not want to hurt her feelings. He certainly doesn't donate her jewelry, because he does

---

106. *Be'er Mayim Chaim*, Exod. 35:22.

not want to diminish from her attractiveness. Only because of the exhilaration of the men at the opportunity to contribute to the *Mishkan* did they make an exception and decide to donate their wives' jewelry. The translation of the words according to Onkelos, based on the interpretation of R. Chaim of Chernovitz, would thus be: "And the men brought the jewelry that was on the women" [and belonged to them, without speaking to them or asking them whether they agreed]."

R. Tuvia Halevi[107] also interprets the words "the men came on the women" as being critical of the women. In his view, the meaning is that "the men, [whose donations] were superior to [or on a higher level than] that of the women, came." R. Halevi took the approach that women didn't have legal ownership of their possessions. Since property under their control actually belonged to their husbands, they were donating the men's belongings, which was less of a sacrifice than when the husbands donated their own items. In addition, each husband had worked hard to accumulate his wealth, while the wife simply benefited from his labor.

One should not extrapolate from the negative references to women in some of the aforementioned exegeses to the situation today, when things have changed considerably. First, note that most of the commentaries explain the verse in a manner complimentary to women, stress their charitable instinct and devotion, and imply that they excelled in their generosity. Second, if the Talmud said women tend to be stingy, that comment was made in an era when women were not able to become professionals, and were thus totally dependent on their husbands, if they were married at all. They were in an inferior position in terms of replacing items that they had relinquished, and it might well have appeared as if they tended to be miserly in comparison to men, who could easily restore their financial status.

---

107. *Chen Tov*, Exod. 35:22.

Finally, the Midrash lauds the spirit of altruism displayed by both men and women, and explains the word "on" in the phrase "the men came *on* the women" as a means of stressing the density of the crowd which resulted from the eagerness of the entire nation to donate with alacrity. In the words of the Midrash:[108]

> All Israel rejoiced in the construction of the *Mishkan*, and they brought every donation with joy and alacrity. See what it says: "And the men came on the women." They were pushing each other, and men and women approached in disorder. In two days they brought all of the [necessary] donations, as it says, "And they brought him more donations morning after morning" (Exod. 36:3). And it says, "For the goods that they had were sufficient to complete all of the work, and [even] too much" (Exod. 36:7).

The Midrash explains the words "on the women" to mean "mixed in" with the women. Although normally people do not squeeze together, out of courtesy and modesty, in this case the congregation was so excited at the prospect of fulfilling the *mitzvah* to participate in the construction of the Tabernacle, that they unintentionally bumped into each other in order to speedily deliver their donations. The Midrash then derives from the repetition of the word "morning," in the second verse cited, that the entire procedure took only two days, with everyone bringing their donation on the first day. After a fast inventory was taken to see what was still needed, on the second day further donations were made to fill all of the shortages.

---

108. *Num. Rabbah* 12:16; *Tanchuma, Pekudei* 11.

Vayakhel

Second Reference

> And all the women that were wise-hearted spun with their hands, and brought [to the collection point] that which they had spun—the blue, and the purple, the scarlet, and the fine linen (Exod. 35:25).

From this verse it is clear that not only did women donate materials, but they also donated their time and were actively involved in the preparations to set up the *Mishkan*.

Rashbam explains the words "wise-hearted" as "a wise woman." Saadiah Gaon adds: "Every woman who was skilled with her hands brought woven material." These comments emphasize three points in connection with the status of women in that society:

1. The Torah appreciated their intelligence.
2. The women acquired professions that were applicable and appropriate for those days.
3. Israelite society of that period did not hesitate to utilize the women's expertise, and integrated them in the on-going work—whether to help prepare items needed for the Tabernacle or for any other work. If they had mastered a skill, it was desirable for them to use it and thereby contribute to the community.

Third Reference

> And all the women whose heart endowed them with wisdom, spun the goat hair (Exod. 35:26).

Note that the heart is considered the source of wisdom. The previous verse spoke of weaving threads of blue, purple, scarlet, and linen. The present verse speaks of weaving fabric out of goat hair. The Talmud explains what this verse adds to what was presented in the previous verse:

> Our Rabbis taught: The lower curtains (Exod. 26:1) [in the Tabernacle were made] of blue [wool], purple [wool], crimson thread, and fine linen, and the upper ones (Exod. 26:7) were of goat [hair]. And greater wisdom [skill] is mentioned in connection with the upper than in connection with the lower. For concerning the lower ones it is written, "and all the women that were wise-hearted spun with their hands," while in reference to the upper ones it is written, "and all the women whose heart endowed them with wisdom." And it was taught in R. Nehemiah's name: It was washed [while still] on the goats and spun on the goats (BT *Shabbat* 99a).

The Talmud is pointing out that weaving goat hair requires greater adeptness, which was to be found among some exceptional women. The Midrash explains that goat hair is both thin and rigid.[109]

What is gained by weaving goat hair while still attached to the goat? Seforno explains the benefit: "in order that the fabric have an extra shine, for many detached [items] will be diminished a bit in their quality when they are uprooted from their place of growth" (Exod. 35:26).

Meshech Chochmah (Exod. 35:25) gives another reason, namely that live animals cannot become *tamei* (religiously impure), and there was thus less chance that the product would arrive in the *Mishkan* in an impure state.

---

109. *Midrash ha-Gadol* 35:26.

Rashi summarizes the Talmudic explanation succinctly by stating: "This required exceptional skill, for they spun it while it was [still] on the backs of the goats" (on Exod. 35:26).

Fourth Reference

Every man and woman whose heart volunteered them to bring [contributions of materials or skilled labor] for all the work that the Lord had commanded to be made by the hand of Moses—the Children of Israel [thus] brought a freewill offering to the Lord (Exod. 35:29).

This is a summary verse parallel to the first reference cited, which begins: "And the men came on the women." The present verse once more stresses the participation of the women in contributing material for the Tabernacle and its contents. It implies that the actual design and construction was performed by Moses. However, in the next chapter, Moses appoints Bezalel and Oholiab to execute the work. Apparently, "by the hand of Moses" means "under the guidance of Moses."

How the Women Were Rewarded for Their Generosity

It has been seen that four of the verses at the end of chapter 35 relate to the unique contribution of the women to the construction of the Tabernacle in the desert. Most of the Midrashim and commentators see the emphasis on the role that the women played as a means of expressing gratitude to the women of that generation. Did the women, at least at a Midrashic level, receive a special reward for their exemplary behavior, which served as an ideal for the men? On the one hand, one is commanded not to be like the servant who serves his master only to receive a reward (*Ethics of the Fathers* 1:3). On the other hand, one of the major axioms of the Jewish faith is the principle of reward and punishment, and the Almighty, who is thoroughly righteous, certainly rewards those who observe his law, even if only in the world to come. In fact, there are Midrashim which state that various rewards were bestowed upon the righteous women for their physical efforts and spiritual leadership at the time of the construction of the Tabernacle.

LENGTH OF LIFE

At the end of the forty-year journey in the desert, Moses took a census, concerning which the Bible states:

> But among these there was not a *man* of those who had been counted by Moses and Aaron the priest, who numbered the Children of Israel in the wilderness of Sinai. For the Lord had said of them: "They shall die in the wilderness." And no *man* of them was left, save Caleb the son of Jephunneh, and Joshua the son of Nun (Num. 26:64-65).

Rashi notes that both verses use the word "man" rather than a more inclusive form or an additional word to imply that women were also included in the decree. Therefore, Rashi states:

> But the decree [resulting from the action] of the spies did not include the women, because they cherished the land. The men said, "Let us appoint a leader, and let us return

to Egypt" (Num. 14:4), and the women [the daughters of Zelophehad] said, "Give us a possession" (Num. 27:4).

A proof of Rashi's viewpoint is to be found in the censes themselves, namely that which took place upon their arrival in Egypt, and that which was taken in the portion of *Pinchas*. There was a gap of 250 years between the two (slavery in Egypt for 210 years, and another 40 years in the desert), yet the names of two specific women are (almost) mentioned in both locations—Jochebed, and Serah daughter of Asher.

Regarding Serah, in the portion of *Vayigash* in the book of Genesis, it is written: "And the sons of Asher: Imnah, and Ishvah, and Ishvi, and Beriah, and Serah their sister" (Gen. 46:17). Meanwhile in the portion of *Pinchas*, it states: "And the name of the daughter of Asher was Serah" (Num. 26:46).

Regarding Jochebed, her name does not appear in writing in the portion of *Vayigash*, but Rashi, basing himself on the Talmud, counts her as one of those referred to in the Biblical phrase: "all the souls of the house of Jacob, that came to Egypt, were seventy" (Gen. 46:17). In fact, Targum Yonatan writes her name explicitly in his translation/interpretation of that verse. In the portion of *Pinchas*, her name is included in the text of the Bible itself in the verse: "And the name of Amram's wife was Jochebed, the daughter of Levi, who was *born* to Levi in Egypt" (Num. 26:59). Rashi comments: "Her birth was in Egypt, but her conception was not in Egypt. When they traversed the [city] wall she [her mother] gave birth to her, and she completed the count of seventy." Jochebed was thus exactly 250 years old at the time of the later census, while Serah was even older, having been born before the exile to Egypt. The additional information provided by Rashi is that not only these two women, but many others survived the journey through the desert, since they were not included in the decree imposed on the male population who were over twenty at the time of the spies' evil report.

R. David Adani provides another explanation for the survival of the women who left Egypt:

> And the men came *on [after] the women*: this teaches that the women preceded the men, therefore the women of that generation merited more than the men, so that these [the women] entered the land, and these did not enter.[110]

R. Adani does not accept Rashi's view that the longevity of the women was a result of their not participating in the rebellion incited by the spies, since nowhere does the Torah declare that that was in fact the case. On the other hand, in the present portion, the considerable contribution of the women is emphasized, and it is therefore more logical to connect their survival to their enthusiastic participation in the donation of materials needed for the construction of the *Mishkan* and the manufacture of its contents.

THE HOLIDAY OF THE NEW MOON

The women received an additional reward in light of their generous contributions to the Tabernacle. On the words "And the men came on the women," Tosafot comments:

> To take their jewelry away from them, as it says, "earrings and nose-rings" (Exod. 35:22), and nonetheless the women were joyful and careful regarding heavenly work, as it says, "And all the women whose heart lifted them up"

---
110. *Midrash ha-Gadol*, Exod. 35:22.

Vayakhel

(Exod. 35:26). Therefore, the women were rewarded by not having to work on the New Moon, for in the instance of the golden calf their jewelry was forcibly removed from them, as may be understood from what it says, "And all the golden rings that were in the ears of the people were broken off" (Exod. 32:3). And in the making of the *Mishkan* they rejoiced in the giving, therefore He gave them the New Moon as a holiday, and it seems to me that this is the New Moon of Nisan when the *Mishkan* was set up, and based on the precedent of that New Moon, all of the New Moons during the year are observed.[111]

The linkage between the women's behavior in the story of the golden calf and their contributions to the Tabernacle sheds new light on the previously analyzed phrase: "And the men came *on the women*" (Exod. 35:22). Note the following points:

1. Basing himself on the explanation of Ibn Ezra that "on the women" means "with the women," R. Avraham Menachem Rapoport[112] explains that the women accompanied their husbands because they had lost their confidence in them, after they had previously used their gold to make the golden calf, so they joined them this time to keep an eye on them. In other words, the women were the righteous initiators, but because of the law that a woman cannot make a large donation without her husband's consent (cited previously in the name of *Toldot Yitzchak*), the women could not donate on their own. And since they did not want to rely on their husbands, they went with them.

---

111. *Daat Zekenim mi-Baalei Tosafot*, Exod. 35:22.
112. *Minchah Belulah, Parshat Vayakhel*.

2. One of the previously presented exegeses was that "on the women" means that the donations of the men were superior to those of the women (R. Tuvia Halevi). The Gerrer Rebbe[113] says that specifically because the men had sinned with the golden calf and were now returning to the right path, they were on a higher level, because one who repents is considered to be on a higher level than one who never sinned.

3. R. Bunem Sofer,[114] based on the same points, arrives at the opposite conclusion. He concludes that "on the women" means that the donations of the women were superior to those of the men. Since the men sinned with the golden calf, their contribution to the *Mishkan* was not meaningful, since they indiscriminately donated to everything—sometimes to idol-worship and sometimes to G-d's Temple. Furthermore, their donation had an ulterior motive—to cleanse themselves of the sin of the golden calf.

   The women, on the other hand, who had not sinned with the golden calf,[115] donated their jewelry with no ulterior motives. One might conjecture that the women had not contributed to the golden calf because they didn't want to relinquish their jewelry, and not because they detested idolatry. Now, however, when they readily and speedily contributed to the Tabernacle, it was clear that the reason they didn't give up their gold for the calf was because of genuine fear of G-d, and that is why their present contribution was superior to that of the men.

4. It has been previously noted that the words "every willing-hearted [person] brought" are in the masculine form in Hebrew. *Kli Yakar* (Exod. 35:22) explains that since in

---

113. *Sefat Emet, Vayakhel* 35:22 (5635).
114. *Shaarei Simcha, Vayakhel* 35:22.
115. Accepting the view of the *Midrash Tanchuma, Ki Tissa* 19.

essence the contributions of the men were meant to atone for the golden calf, the women, who were innocent, did not need atonement. Nevertheless, because of their yearning for holiness, they too contributed. However, they didn't want to donate their gold jewelry, lest it appear that they too were attempting to seek forgiveness (for a sin that they did not commit). For that reason, they gave their jewelry to their husbands, but did not want to personally be present when it was delivered. *Kli Yakar* even suggests that he would be willing to accept the explanation of Onkelos that the men took the jewelry by force when it was still on the women. However, he stresses that their refusal was not because they didn't want to contribute in principle, but because they preferred to be totally dissociated from any connection to the golden calf. And that is why, with regard to the woven fabrics, the women did not hesitate to come forward on their own.

Tosafot's Source

The source of Tosafot's claim that the women were rewarded by making the New Moon into a holiday is found in *Pirkei de-Rabbi Eliezer*, which tells how Aaron tried to delay the creation of the golden calf by telling the women to donate their jewelry.[116] The Midrash[117] portrays the reaction of the women to Aaron's suggestion:

> The women heard, and they did not accept upon themselves to give their nose-rings to their husbands, but said to them:

---

116. As quoted in Rashi, Exod. 32:2.
117. *Pirkei de-Rabbi Eliezer* 44.

You want to make a detestation and an abomination that does not have the power to save [anything]. They didn't hearken to them, and the Almighty rewarded the women in this world and the next. And what reward did he give them in this world and the next? That they observe [as a holiday] New Moons, for it says, "Who satisfies your old age with good things; so that your youth is renewed like the eagle [which retains its vitality in old age]" (Ps. 103:5).

Rabbenu Bachya (Exod. 35:20-21) expands the last sentence of the Midrash as follows:

G-d gave the women their reward in this world and the next.... In this world that they observe New Moons more than men, and in the next world that they will be renewed as New Moons, for it says, "Who satisfies your old age with good things, so that your youth is renewed like the eagle."

Tosafot modifies the Midrash in two ways:

1. While the original Midrash relates the reward to the women's behavior at the time of the golden calf without mentioning their generosity with respect to the *Mishkan*, Tosafot makes their exuberance in connection with the latter occurrence the main cause of their reward, while the first is mentioned only as an aside. It is possible that Tosafot sought a link between their good deed and its reward. If their behavior was in connection with the *Mishkan*, it is understandable that its reward would have taken place on the day of its erection, *Rosh Chodesh Nisan* (the first of the month, which is the day of the New Moon). The

Vayakhel

extension of the holiday to every New Moon follows naturally. On the other hand, if the good deed was with respect to the golden calf, how is that related to transforming the New Moon into a special holiday?

2. The Midrash says that the women refused to allow their jewelry to be used in making the golden calf, and hence the men could only use gold that they had access to, while Tosafot says that the men removed the women's jewelry by force. The Midrash ameliorates the wickedness of the men in the sense that even if they had no respect for G-d, at least they respected their wives' opinions and physical being. In addition, the Midrash maintains the possibility that the men had learned from the incident of the golden calf and had mended their ways, since it only singles out the women's positive behavior with respect to the golden calf. Tosafot paints a more dire picture of the behavior of the men, who were so desperate to make an idol that they compelled their wives to relinquish their gold, and did not even attempt to repent in the aftermath of the great heresy by generously donating to the *Mishkan*, while the women's behavior is commended.

The Connection between *Rosh Chodesh* and the Women's Generosity

It was noted that according to the Midrash the women were rewarded for not participating in making the golden calf, while according to Tosafot the reward was mainly for their generous contributions to the Tabernacle, which took place just before the New Moon. Other than the chronological juxtaposition, the question is whether there is an intrinsic connection between their good deed and its reward.

First Answer

In answering the question, reference will be made to a second Midrash which tells of the altruism of the women in Egypt. In describing the construction of the copper basin used for ceremonial ablutions, the Bible states: "And he made the laver of copper, and its base of copper, from the mirrors of the women who assembled, who assembled at the door of the Tent of Meeting" (Exod. 38:8). Rashi, basing himself on Midrash Tanchuma,[118] comments as follows:

> The Israelite women possessed mirrors [of copper], which they looked into when they dressed up, and even these they did not hesitate to bring as a contribution to the Tabernacle, but Moses was disgusted by them, since they were made to pander to their evil inclination. The Almighty said to him: "Accept [them], for these are dearer to Me than everything [all the other contributions], for by means of them the women raised multitudes in Egypt!" When their husbands were tired as a result of the crushing labor, they used to go over [to them], bringing them food and drink, and feeding them, and they would take the mirrors, and each gazed at herself with her husband in the mirror, saying endearingly to him: "I am more comely than you," and through this [behavior] they stimulated their husbands' desire and submitted to them [sexually], became pregnant, and gave birth there, as it says, "I awakened you [your love and desire] under the

---

118. Tanchuma, *Pekudei* 9.

apple tree [where they worked]" (Songs 8:5). This is what it refers to when it says "The women who assembled [who raised an assembly—a multitude of children]." And the basin was made of them [the mirrors], for it [the basin] is used to promote peace between a man and his wife, by giving to drink from the water in it to she whose husband was jealous of her [suspected her of having an affair] and [who nevertheless] concealed herself [with a strange man. Drinking the bitter water provided her with an opportunity to prove her innocence].[119] And there is a proof that they [the basin and its base] were actually made from these mirrors, for it says: "And the copper of the offering was seventy talents and two thousand and four hundred shekels. And they made from it the sockets for the door of the Tent of Meeting, and the copper altar, and its copper grating, and all the vessels of the altar" (Exod. 38:29-30), but the basin and its base are not mentioned there [among the articles made from that offering]; hence you may learn that the copper of the basin was not from the copper of the offering [but rather from the women's mirrors]. That is how R. Tanchuma explained it (Rashi on Exod. 38:8).

R. Yissocher Frand[120] explains that from the Midrash, one may deduce that as a result of the travail they had endured in Egypt, the men lost hope and became depressed, and consequently separated from their wives because they did not want to bring children into such a sordid reality. The women, who were not oppressed, were able to see the bigger picture, and realized that in the long run

---

119. The procedure is described in Num. 5:11-31.
120. Yissocher Frand, *Rabbi Frand on the Parashah* (2001), pp. 137-140.

there was hope, and it was only necessary to endure the hard times which would eventually terminate. They therefore encouraged their husbands to return to them.

A second instance when the men became dejected was at the initiation of the construction of the Tabernacle. Before the sin of the golden calf, the intention had been that the Divine Presence would rest within the nation, that it would permeate the entire camp until the point of saturation. When the nation sinned, they were no longer worthy of hosting the Divine Presence at that level of immanence. From that point onward, the encampment was divided into three—the priestly, levirate, and Israelite sections, while the Divine Presence was enclosed within its own area—the Divine camp.[121]

Until the *Mishkan* was built, the men were optimistic that the evil decree would be annulled, and the original plan would materialize. When construction began, they understood that the pre-existing situation would not return and that the consequences of the sin of the golden calf would not be erased, and this realization once more engendered among them a feeling of desperation. Under these circumstances, the men found it hard to contribute to the *Mishkan*, which they viewed as the symbol of their failings.

Once again, the women were able to overcome the unfortunate predicament. They told the men not to cry over past events that cannot be changed; one must look forward and proceed in such a way that the future will be as bright as possible.

In Egypt, the women's optimism saved Israel from physical decimation. In the desert at the time of the building of the Tabernacle, their faith and confidence spared the nation from spiritual atrophy, and injected hope that they could once more intimately approach the Almighty.

---

121 Rashi, Num. 5:2.

Vayakhel

On the basis of the Midrash, one can say that *Rosh Chodesh* signifies the renewal of the moon. Even in the darkest state, one knows that the moon will appear anew and return to its original luminance. In that aspect, it is an emblem of faith and hope for the Jewish nation, which may also pass cyclically from absolute darkness to brilliant light. These tidings were brought to the men of Israel by their wives through the "mirrors of the multitudes" and the construction of the Tabernacle, and accordingly they were rewarded by a celebration of the natural phenomenon which symbolizes the message that they brought to the Jewish nation.

Second Answer

The following Midrash[122] finds the building of the Tabernacle to be an expiatory undertaking by noting a number of parallels between the portion of the golden calf and the portion of *Vayakhel*:

> And He commanded Moses to instruct them as regards the making of the Tabernacle and all of its vessels, to atone for the golden calf. Allow "And let them *make* Me a sanctuary" (Exod. 25:8) to come and atone for "Arise [and] *make* us a god" (Exod. 32:1). Let the assembly convened by Moses our teacher, as it says, "And Moses *assembled* all the congregation of the Children of Israel" (Exod. 35:1), come and atone for the assembly of Aaron, for it says, "and the people *assembled* themselves around Aaron" (Exod. 32:1). Let the saying by Moses our teacher, as it says, "and he [Moses] *said* to them" (Exod. 35:1), come and atone for the saying of Aaron, for it says, "and [they] *said* to him: 'Arise [and] make us a god'" (Exod. 32:1). Let "*These* are

---

122. *Pesikta Zutrata*, Exod. 34.

the words" (Exod. 35:1) come and atone for "*this* is your god, Israel" (Exod. 32:4).

A number of opinions have been presented regarding the degree to which the women participated in the sin of the golden calf, ranging from Rashi (Exod. 32:2), who said they eagerly removed their jewelry and donated it to the cause, to Rabbenu Bachya (Exod. 35:20-21), who exempted the women from all guilt, as well as a number of intermediary viewpoints.

Specifically, according to those views that the women participated—either because they actually believed in idols, or even though they didn't and their jewelry was taken from them against their will—they still might have felt some degree of guilt. What is important is that regarding their contribution to the Tabernacle—and it was shown that the Midrash considered it to be a form of atonement for the sin of the golden calf—their steadfastness and generosity indicated repentance at the highest level. It is well known from the stories of Adam,[123] Joseph,[124] and David (2 Samuel 12)—not to mention its central function on the holiest day of the year, Yom Kippur—how important the role of repentance is in the Jewish religion. As a result of their magnanimous behavior, the women reached at the very least the fourth stage of repentance, *kabbalah le-atid* (accepting not to commit the sin again).[125]

Repentance is important because it symbolizes renewal; no matter how much a person sinned, he has an opportunity to start afresh and cleanse his record. The most clear-cut representation of renewal is the moon, and the refraining of women from working on *Rosh Chodesh* emphasizes their significant contribution to this subject.

---

123. Abba Engelberg, *The Ethics of Genesis* (2014), p. 26.
124. Ibid., p. 175.
125. Ibid., pp. 264-269.

Summary

From the interpretations offered for the various Midrashim, it may be understood that the women of the Pentateuchal era superseded the men in two areas: optimism (they did not lose hope in the future of the nation) and generosity (in donations to the Tabernacle). What is the significance of this finding today?

It is unlikely that these good attributes are limited to women. The first attribute is the innate optimism of the women, versus the susceptibility of the men to depression. But modern statistics show that the chances of a woman suffering from depression are twice as great as those of a man.[126]

Regarding generosity, both in terms of financial matters as well as interpersonal relations, it is difficult to accept that the Sages believed that this trait is more common among women than men. It will suffice to cite a few quotes from the Talmud, for example: "A woman looks with a more grudging eye upon guests than a man" (BT *Bava Metzia* 87a), "women are prone to jealousy" (*Gen. Rabbah* 45:6), and "women are rapacious, and each may be suspected of uncovering her neighbor's cooking pot in order to know what she is cooking" (Mishnah *Taharot* 7:9).

To characterize an entire group on the basis of specific traits borders on sexism. One must assume that such sayings in the Talmud reflect the opinion of that Tanna or Amora, and this is demonstrated by the fact that frequently a Tanna describes a group as possessing a specific trait, while a second Tanna describes them as being deficient with respect to the very same trait.

Scientists have concluded that the factors which contribute to depression are: living in abusive conditions, solitude, and long-

---

126. MayoClinic.com.

term pressure in the workplace. The conditions of the Hebrew slaves will now be examined. The Sages said concerning the Egyptians: They imposed men's work on women and women's work on men (BT *Sotah* 11b). One may conclude that men were required to perform tasks normally relegated to women, such as sewing, and women were forced to do men's work, such as drawing water. But did this release the men from heavy labor that could only be performed by men? Apparently it did not, for a previously cited Rashi spoke of "husbands [who] were tired as a result of the crushing labor" (Exod. 38:8). In addition, one cannot ignore the literal meaning of the following verses:

> You shall not continue giving the people straw to make bricks, as you did yesterday and the day before. They will go and gather straw for themselves. And the amount of bricks, which they made yesterday and the day before, you shall require of them; you shall not diminish from it, for they are slacking; therefore they cry, saying: Let us go and sacrifice to our G-d. Let heavier work be placed upon the men, and make them do it, and let them not speak lying words (Exod. 5:7-9).

One may thus assume that women's work was demanded of the men, as well as work that only they could perform, and as a result of being overworked, they experienced a state of despair and depression—a condition that naturally leads to deficiencies in the areas of faith and positive attributes. One can then understand how the women in Egypt, who in spite of being required to carry a heavier than normal, but still manageable, work load, were in a better state of mind. In order for their behavior in those days to influence both themselves and their husbands in the future, they were granted the right to celebrate the holiday of hope and optimism, *Rosh Chodesh*, the New Moon, that begins each month of the Hebrew calendar.

Pekudei

This portion opens with the words: "These are the amounts of [the materials used for] the Tabernacle, the Tabernacle of the Testimony" (Exod. 38:21). The Midrash explains:

> The Almighty said: Let the gold of the *Mishkan* come and atone for the gold of the calf. The Almighty said to Israel, when you made the calf you angered me [saying] "*these* are your gods, [Israel, who brought you out of Egypt]" (Exod. 32:4); now that you have made the Tabernacle with [the words] "*these* [are the amounts of the Tabernacle]," I am reconciled with you (*Exod. Rabbah* 31:8).

One may ask: Is it reasonable that forgiveness for idolatry, the most serious sin in the Jewish lexicon, can be attained by using a particular code word—"these" in the present instance?

Or ha-Chaim (Exod. 38:21) answers that the Midrash does not mean that the word "these" is the cause of G-d's pardoning the nation, but the opposite. It means to say that for every sinful action that the Israelites performed while making the calf, where the word "these" was used, a parallel atoning activity was performed in making the Tabernacle. The word "these" is used to show that the Israelites acted in a way that indeed led to forgiveness, but the word "these" is not in itself the reason that the sin was pardoned.

Achieving the Highest Level of Repentance

The stages of repentance are:

1. confession (*viddui*),
2. regret (*charatah*),
3. abandoning the sin (*azivat ha-chet*),
4. acceptance for the future [not to commit the sin] (*kabbalah le-atid*),
5. complete repentance (*teshuvah gemurah*).

Rambam defines the last stage as follows:

> What is complete repentance? It refers to one who has an opportunity to commit a sin and nevertheless refrains from doing so because he is penitent, and not because he is afraid of being unable to transgress or too weak to do so. For example, if one had illicit relations with a woman, and soon finds himself alone with her again, and he still loves her and is physically capable of having relations, and is in the same region where he previously sinned, and yet he controls himself, then he has accomplished complete repentance (*Teshuvah* 2:1).

Or ha-Chaim explains that the correction for a sin should be done in a way that is as close as possible to the way in which it was originally performed. This method will certainly bring the sinner as near as possible to achieving complete repentance (even if he did not find himself in the exact same position as he was when he sinned originally). In the present case, *Or ha-Chaim* noted a number of parallels between the sin and the attempts at correction, for example:

Action	Making the Golden Calf	Building the Tabernacle
Making an altar and bringing sacrifices	He built an altar before it… and offered burnt offerings, and brought peace offerings (Exod. 32:5-6).	And he made the altar of burnt offering (Exod. 38:1).
Removing jewelry	And all the people broke off the golden rings that were in their ears (Exod. 32:3).	Every willing-hearted [person] brought earrings, and nose-rings, and signet rings, and bracelets, all vessels of gold (Exod. 35:22).
Contributing more than was needed	He said to them: "Break off the golden rings." They immediately broke them off, and the entire nation continued giving him until he said to them "Enough" (*Exod. Rabbah* 51:8).	For the material they had was sufficient for all the work to make it, and too much (Exod. 36:7).

In light of the successful attempts of the Children of Israel to achieve complete repentance, *Or ha-Chaim* explains the words in the opening verse, "the Tabernacle of the testimony," on the basis of the Midrash which states: "It [the Tabernacle] is a testimony to the entire world that there is forgiveness for Israel" (*Exod. Rabbah* 32:34).

Pekudei

The efforts of the people to fulfill a command in parallel to each sin that they had committed, and to thereby neutralize it, accomplished its goal, and a large part of the guilt stemming from the golden calf was cleansed. As noted previously, G-d allayed the punishment, but at the same time said: "on the day of reckoning, I will visit their sin upon them" (Exod. 32:34), which Rashi understood to mean that: "No punishment ever befalls Israel in which there is not partial compensation for the sin of the golden calf."

The Importance of Unity

R. Gedalia Schorr[127] answers the question concerning the mechanics of the absolution of the Children of Israel by taking a different approach. In his opinion, what is important are not the parallels between the case of the golden calf and that of the *Mishkan*, but the necessity to work together in order to set up the *Mishkan*. In his opinion, the overriding characteristic in understanding the story of the golden calf is the degree of unity that prevailed in the nation.

The Level of Unity at the Time of the Giving of the Torah

R. Schorr explains that before the Torah was given, the Children of Israel achieved an exemplary level of unity, as indicated by the verse "and Israel encamped there before the mountain" (Exod. 19:2), upon which Rashi comments, based on the Midrash: "as one man with one mind."[128] This comment relies on the fact that

---

127. Gedalia Schorr, *Or Gedalyahu, Vayakhel-Pekudei*.
128. *Mechilta, Yitro, parashah Aleph*.

the Hebrew word used for encamped is in the singular form, even though the camp was composed of many individuals. Apparently, they were so united that they could be referred to in the singular.

According to the Zohar, the Hebrew word for Israel is an acronym that can be expanded to the following sentence: There are 600,000 letters in the Torah. The Hebrew expansion is shown below:

English	Hebrew Word	Hebrew Letter
There exist	יש	י
sixty	ששים	ש
myriads (10,000s)	רבוא	ר
letters	אותיות	א
in the Torah	לתורה	ל

R. Schorr explains that in the fifty days from Passover to the Festival of Weeks (*Shavuot*), the 600,000 souls of the Israelites united and achieved a maximum attachment to the Lord, to the point that they were "as one man with one mind," and only then were they worthy of receiving the Torah, whose 600,000 letters are also united for one purpose. Although there are some inaccuracies in connection with these numbers,[129] what is being stressed is the importance of unity, which was enabled by the spiritual high engendered by the miracles that the people jointly experienced at the time of the exodus, both in Egypt and while escaping via the Red Sea. The 600,000 letters were each associated with one of the

---

129. The actual number of letters in the Torah is 305,000. Also, the number 600,000 refers to the number of males between the ages of 20 and 60. Under the assumption that women, children, and older men also have souls, the real number is at least two million.

600,000 souls, and each of the two sets of 600,000 coalesced into a single unit, leading to a close-knit relationship among the people, and between them and the Torah.

This is how R. Schorr describes the unity that existed at the time the Torah was given:

> For at Mt. Sinai the Children of Israel were in the situation that all of them saw clearly the unity of the Creator, and they were attached to the root of unity, and as it says, "You were shown, in order to know, that the Lord—He is G-d; there is none other than Him" (Deut. 4:35), and the unity was from above to below, for from the unity they saw how all the details of creation came into existence, and how they all coalesced into one. The belief in one G-d annulled the selfishness of each individual, for on the one hand, the entire nation was directed toward the one G-d above, and on the other hand, all are equal in their nothingness vis-à-vis that Supreme Being, and where there is no personal pretension, love and brotherhood prevail.

Now one can understand the verse from the Passover Haggadah: "Had he brought us to Mt. Sinai and not given us the Torah, it would have been enough for us." The level of unity was so exceedingly great that it was worthwhile to achieve it even if, G-d forbid, Israel had not actually received the Torah there. From then to this very day the nation seeks to recreate the level of unity that existed on that occasion.

R. Chaim Sabato[130] believes that the equivalence between the unity of G-d and Israel is reflected in a Talmudic passage (BT *Berachot* 6a), which says that just as the *tefillin* of a Jew contain the

---

130, *Vayakhel ke-Tikkun la-Egel*, www.yb.org.il.

verse, "Hear, O Israel: the Lord our G-d, the Lord is One" (Deut. 6:4), which proclaims the unity of G-d (and the two Hebrew letters ע and ד, which spell the Hebrew word for "witness," are enlarged to emphasize that the Nation of Israel testifies to this unity from the time of revelation on Mt. Sinai), similarly the *tefillin* which, in a manner of speaking, G-d wears, contain the verse, "And who is like Your people Israel, one nation on earth" (1 Chron. 17:1), where once more the word "one" stresses the attribute of unity within the Nation of Israel.

The Loss of Unity

When the Children of Israel sinned by making the golden calf, the spell which held them together was broken, and they separated, thereby losing the level of unity that existed at the time of revelation. Instead, they attempted to attach themselves to the many non-unified powers that exist in creation, and this is the intention of the Talmud when it states, regarding those who bowed to the golden calf, that they "craved many gods" (BT *Sanhedrin* 63a). The word "these" in the verse "These are your gods, Israel, who brought you out of Egypt" (Exod. 32:4) points to a multitude of powers.

R. Schorr explains the phenomenon as follows:

> The basis of these things is clear, for the anchor of the Children of Israel is in unity, and when they sin, then separation occurs, for sin is the waste material that prevents unity, and to the extent that the Children of Israel are attracted to their anchor and believe in the one G-d, the souls of the Nation of Israel below unite.

Pekudei

Lest one ask that, regarding the sin of the golden calf, it also says, "and the people assembled themselves around Aaron" (Exod. 32:1), R. Schorr explains:

> Although this gathering appears to represent unity, it is anchored in separation, as it says, "all the workers of iniquity shall be scattered" (Ps. 92:10), for they have no connection to unity... but it [unity] is only in an imaginary world, and eventually separation emanates from it.

When people distance themselves from the true G-d, every individual does it for his own personal reasons, and even when many people do it simultaneously, each is interested in satisfying his own drives. In the end, there will be a confrontation between the desires of those involved, and the unity will disintegrate.

Repairing the Separation

After sinning with the golden calf and losing the high degree of unity among them, a possible remedy was to invite the people to join each other in accomplishing a shared goal, as was stated in the Midrash[131] cited previously in the portion of *Vayakhel*:

> Let the assembly convened by Moses our teacher, as it says, "And Moses *assembled* all the congregation of the Children of Israel" (Exod. 35:1), come and atone for the assembly of Aaron, for it says, "and the people assembled themselves around Aaron" (Exod. 32:1)·

---

131. *Pesikta Zutrata*, Exod. 34.

The joint plan is the building of the Tabernacle. In order to stress that although each person contributes a different item or activity, it all flows toward the same common project, the Torah repeats the refrain "as G-d commanded Moses"[132] after the description of each one of the vessels.

That the project united the Children of Israel in accomplishing a joint goal is emphasized by the first words of the portion: "These are the amounts of the Tabernacle," which initiate a process of atonement for the sin of the golden calf. R. Schorr explains the Midrash on those words as follows:

> With these ideas, one can explain the words of the Midrash,[133] which said they sinned with "these" and they sought forgiveness with "these" … the intention is that "these" indicates a multiplicity of details and powers, and that was the sin connected with "these." And the remedy for this was: "These are the amounts of the Tabernacle," that with regard to each detail of the Tabernacle, the Children of Israel intended to return it [to the overall picture] and enter it into the all-inclusive.

Weakness of Attempts to Repair the Separation

Uniting in order to accomplish a joint task in a natural fashion was not able to achieve the level of spiritual elevation that had resulted from the supernatural experiences that had emanated directly from the Almighty. For this reason, after Rashi notes that at Mt. Sinai

---

132. For example, Exod. 39:1,5,7,21,26,29,31,43; 40:19,21,23,25,27,29,32.
133. *Exod. Rabbah* 31:8.

the Children of Israel were "as one man with one mind," he adds: "but all their other encampments were [made] with complaints and dissension."[134]

R. Schorr explains the difference between the original unity that existed at the time of revelation and the artificial unity that Israel toiled to achieve in the aftermath of the golden calf:

> This unity after the sin was not on the same level as at Mt. Sinai, for at Mt. Sinai the Children of Israel were in the situation that they clearly saw the unity of the Creator, and they were attached to the root of unity... and the unity was from above to below, for from the unity they were able to see how all details of the creation came into being, and how they all unite into one [unit]. However, after the sin, when they came to [a state of] separation, the work [of unification] was from below to above, to tie together all of the details and the powers manifested in creation and to unite them until the point that they arrive at the root of unity, and for that reason it says regarding every detail of the *Mishkan*, "as G-d commanded Moses," for after the Children of Israel sinned and came to [a state of] separation... it was necessary that they investigate every detail, for everything is part of the one.

The Connection of Faith in G-d to Laws between Man and His Fellow Man

In order to understand the equivalence between the unity of G-d and that of the Nation of Israel, it is necessary to look into the

---

134. Exod. 19:2, based on the *Mechilta*.

definition of paganism (which is divided into *avodat kochavim*—belief in stars, constellations, and planets; and *avodat elilim*—worshipping trees, stones, icons, and statues). Paganism allows for more than one supernatural force in the world. The result is that those gods do not transmit a code of behavior to human beings, for each god can contradict the opinion of his counterpart. In addition, they do not serve as role models, because they themselves are embroiled in arguments with each other and do not behave in a moral fashion. They actually exhibit the traits of hedonism and selfishness, with no consideration for others.

For example, in Greek mythology, one reads of Zeus, the father of the gods, who married his sister Hera (incest). They had two sons, Ares and Hephaestus. Ares became the god of war, bloodlust, and violence. Hephaestus was born weak and ugly, and his mother Hera (who was also his aunt) wanted to dispose of him and accordingly threw him off of Mt. Olympus. He survived miraculously and eventually married the adulterous Aphrodite, goddess of beauty and love, who also had a sexual relationship with his brother Ares. Such are the pagan gods.

On the other hand, the Torah and its commandments can endure and flourish only if the belief in the oneness and uniqueness of G-d is sufficiently strong for Israel to loyally adhere to His code of behavior, and not to that of any other god. The code that G-d wants Israel to fulfill is one that engenders love among mankind, as Rambam says: "the entire Torah was given to make peace in the world" (*Hilchot Chanukah* 4:14).

On a more individual level, Hillel summarized the message of the Torah as: "What is hateful to you, do not do to your neighbor" (BT *Shabbat* 31a). In other words, the main goal of the Torah, and indeed its essence, is to institute harmonious relations among fellow humans.

Pekudei

Rambam also referred to every person when he wrote in *The Guide for the Perplexed* that belief in G-d of necessity leads to a moral lifestyle, and these are his words:

> Our Sages declare it, wherever opportunity is given, that the idea of G-d necessarily implies justice; that *He will reward the most pious for all their pure and upright actions, although no direct commandment was given them through a prophet; and that He will punish all the evil deeds of men, although they have not been prohibited by a prophet*, if common sense warns against them, as e.g. injustice and violence (3:17).

Rambam, accordingly, believes that there exist absolute moral truths, independent of any written statutes, which are intended to serve as a basis for human behavior. It should be noted that one of the seven Noahide laws is the prohibition against idol-worship. As indicated, the logic is clear. Idol-worship and morality are inimical to each other.

The Midrash[135] states that those who built the tower of Babel were not punished as severely as the antediluvian generation, because even though the former group rebelled against the Lord, at least they were united and worked together harmoniously. One might look upon this as contradicting the claim that morality and monotheism must co-exist. However, one should realize that the story of the tower of Babel occurred soon after the great flood, when the most severe scoundrels were removed from the scene, and the only survivors were Noah's family. So even if some of their descendants eventually degenerated and lost their faith in G-d, by inertia their ethical lifestyle was maintained. No doubt that as time passed, moral breaches would (and did) become commonplace.

---

135. *Gen. Rabbah* 38:6. Cited by Rashi, Gen. 11:9.

Sabbath as an Antidote to the Transgression of the Golden Calf

After noting the equivalence of pristine faith in the Almighty and the unity of the nation, i.e., commands regulating man's behavior toward his fellow man (in particular, love of one's fellow man and of one's spouse), the purpose of the Sabbath may be better understood, namely to return the members of the faith, if just a little, to the level of unity that prevailed immediately prior to revelation. On the Sabbath, Jews gather as a community for the purpose of prayer and social interaction, and the family unit becomes stronger and better integrated.

Because unity serves as a prerequisite for the Divine Presence to repose within the nation, before the command to build the Tabernacle, the Pentateuch devotes a small section at the beginning of *Vayakhel* to present once more some laws concerning the Sabbath.[136]

According to R. Schorr, the word *Shabbat* is derived from the Hebrew word *shav*, meaning *return*, "for everything returns to its roots on the Sabbath, and when everything gets attached to its source and root, then automatically unity prevails." R. Schorr continues:

> When the Children of Israel sinned with the calf and a state of dispersal commenced, the relevance to them of building a Tabernacle was lost, for they had to be in a state of unity to build the Tabernacle and for the Divine Presence to rest in the world, and they had to be in [a state of] unity in order

---

136. Exod. 35:1-3, having previously commanded observance in the Ten Commandments (Exod. 20:8-12), with repetitions in Exod. 23:12, 31:12-18, 34:21.

to unite the entire creation and elevate it to its root so that it be worthy enough for the Divine Presence to rest in the world, and for this purpose Moses commanded them the portion of the Sabbath, because Sabbath contains the secret of oneness, and through the strength of the Sabbath they unite so that they will be worthy of building a Tabernacle in his name.... Moses our teacher, through the command concerning the portion of the Sabbath, raised the Children of Israel to [the level of] being one congregation, so that unity would be relevant to them, and from this unity they would be able to build the Tabernacle.

The Third Temple

On the verse, "Awake my glory, awake the harp and the lyre"(Ps. 57:9), the Midrash[137] interprets homiletically:

Awake from the [destruction of the] First Temple, which will be rebuilt in the future by Ezra. Awake from the [destruction of the] Second Temple, which will be rebuilt by You as a completed structure. This is [the meaning of] what is written: "The Lord builds up Jerusalem. He will gather together the dispersed of Israel" (Ps. 147:2).

How will the miracle of G-d constructing the Temple be accomplished? According to Rashi,[138] it will be built and perfected in heaven, and simply float down to the Temple Mount, as described in the verse: "the place [Temple], O Lord, which *You have made* for Your dwelling, the sanctuary, O Lord, which *Your hands have established*" (Exod. 15:17).

---

137. *Midrash Tehillim* (Buber) 22:9.
138. BT *Sukkah* 41a, s.v. *ee nammei*.

According to *Or Gedalyahu*, the joint construction of the Tabernacle by the Children of Israel was in itself a necessary means of purification and improvement, so that one may ask how the required preparation will be accomplished if the Temple materializes without human involvement. Two answers will be proposed, which will then be combined into one comprehensive solution.

First, although in theory participating in a joint project should lay the basis for peace and harmony among the Israelites, as well as strengthen belief in the unity of the Creator and observance of His law, this approach apparently did not succeed with the first two Temples, as indicated by the following Talmudic passage:

> Why was the first Sanctuary destroyed? Because of three [evil] things which prevailed there: idolatry and immorality and bloodshed.... But the second Sanctuary [when, throughout its existence,] they were occupying themselves with Torah, [observance of] precepts, and beneficence, why was it destroyed? Because there prevailed hatred without cause—to teach you that groundless hatred is considered to be equivalent to [all the] three sins [of] idolatry, immorality, and bloodshed (BT *Yoma* 9b).

In other words, the joint effort to build the first two Temples was not sufficient to elevate the nation to the required level, and therefore there will be no great loss if such action is not needed in building the Third Temple. Instead, what is required is independent attempts on the part of the nation to engender unity and brotherhood.

A second answer is that although in general the Third Temple is to be presented to mankind by G-d, there are parts of it that are concealed in the ground and will have to be uncovered and installed by the Israelites, namely the Ark and the gates (see Appendix VI: WHAT HAPPENED TO THE HOLY ARK?), so a certain amount of cooperation is still called for.

Combining both answers, one might say that since assembling the *Mishkan* and both Temples did not lead to the desired result, G-d wished for man to devote more energy on his own to achieving peace and brotherhood, and reaching a high level of spirituality in fulfilling his G-dly obligations. After sufficient progress, the final stage will occur when the nation joins hands in finding and installing the long-buried items, the Temple's gates and the Ark. These items were not chosen randomly. Rather, they possess symbolic significance. Installing the entrance symbolizes the construction of the entire Temple, the physical manifestation of G-d's presence on earth, while the Ark represents His spiritual presence.

SUMMARY

According to the Midrash, the purpose of the Tabernacle was to atone, as much as possible, for the sin of the golden calf. The views of two commentaries were examined, *Or ha-Chaim* and *Or Gedalyahu*. *Or ha-Chaim* analyzes the activities demanded of the Israelites in setting up the Tabernacle, and finds parallel actions that were performed in creating and worshipping the golden calf. Every positive act was designed to atone, in a manner of speaking, for the parallel negative act in connection with the golden calf.

Or Gedalyahu looks at the actions of the Children of Israel in building the Tabernacle as intended to renew the intimate connection between faith in the Almighty and unity of the nation, or in a more specific context—between laws regulating man's behavior in dealing with men as opposed to man's behavior in dealing with G-d. R. Schorr's main theme in *Or Gedalyahu* is that the most important principle in Judaism is unity. Unity must exist between man and G-d, as well as between man and man, and in the long run, it cannot exist on only one of these two planes.

First Overview: The Intellectual Development of the Jewish People

In *The Ethics of Genesis*,[139] it was proposed that the intellectual evolution of the Jewish nation may be looked upon as occurring in three stages—the Primitive Stage, the Universal Stage, and the Particularistic Stage. In the Primitive Stage, man behaved no differently than a wild beast, functioning instinctively to satisfy his physical urges. Only in the Universal Stage did an awareness of higher, universal values dawn upon man, and these values became codified as the seven Noahide laws. These laws, meant for all of mankind, were also the first step in the gradual development of Jewish law, meant only for the Jews and hence called the Particularistic Stage. In this section, the evolution of Jewish law, from the Noahide laws until the culmination of the process with the revelation of the Torah at Mt. Sinai, will be presented.

The Seven Noahide Laws

The Universal Stage was initiated when Adam heard a powerful voice emanating from space, issuing orders that limited the

---

139. Abba Engelberg. *The Ethics of Genesis* (2014), pp. 223-227.

freedom of action to which he had become accustomed, as described in chapter 2 of Genesis:

> And the Lord G-d commanded the man, saying: "Of every tree of the garden you may freely eat, but of the tree of the knowledge of good and evil, you shall not eat of it; for on the day that you eat thereof you shall surely die" (Gen. 2:16-17).

Interestingly, these are the exact verses from which the Talmud derives the seven Noahide laws that characterize this stage, namely: social laws (the establishment of courts which operate on the basis of a set of laws) and refraining from blasphemy, idolatry, adultery, bloodshed, robbery, and eating flesh from a living animal. The Talmud describes how the seven laws are derived:

> R. Johanan answered: The verse says: "And the Lord G-d commanded the man, saying: 'Of every tree of the garden you may freely eat.'" 'And [He] *commanded*' refers to [the observance of] social laws, and so it says: "For I know him, that he will *command* his children and his household after him, and they shall keep the way of the Lord, to do justice and judgment" (Gen. 18:19). 'The *Lord*' is [a prohibition against] blasphemy, and thus it is written, "and he that blasphemes the name of the *Lord* shall be put to death" (Lev. 24:16). '*G-d*' is [an injunction against] idolatry, and thus it is written, "You shall have no other *gods* before Me" (Exod. 20:2). 'The *man*' refers to bloodshed [murder], and thus it is written, "He who sheds *man's* blood, by man shall his blood be shed" (Gen. 9:6). '*Saying*' refers to adultery, and thus it is written, "*They say*, if a man sends away his wife, and she left him, and became the wife of another man" (Jer. 3:1).

'*Of every tree* of the garden' but not stolen [fruit]. 'You may *freely* [extra word] eat' but not flesh cut from a *living animal* (BT *Sanhedrin* 56b).

Why were these specific laws deemed to be so basic that they merited being commanded at an earlier stage than the remaining laws of the Torah? *Torah Temimah* postulates:

> All of these commands are built for and the basis of the existence of the world, the habitation of countries in a manner that allows a secure life, maintenance of possessions, and merciful and empathetic feelings toward other creatures, as is obvious to all (Exod. 21, note 277).

In a second location, *Torah Temimah* adds:

> The absence of these commandments, i.e., behaving in the opposite fashion, leads to decimation and destruction, and the termination of all life (Gen. 2, note 39).

Torah Temimah continues by pointing out that these laws were not necessarily all transmitted to Adam (as will be seen to be the view of Rambam as well), and so he states:

> The simple meaning of the verse does not indicate all of these commands... and the Sages wisely gathered them in one place and related them to the words used in a single verse of the Torah in order to ease memorization.

Since man began his existence as a primitive being not especially different from the beasts of the land, from an educational standpoint it was necessary to introduce commandments gradually, and also to repeat them periodically in order to successfully embed them in man's consciousness. Rambam describes the process as follows:

> Adam was commanded with respect to six items: idolatry, blasphemy, bloodshed, adultery, robbery, and social laws. Even though all of these laws have been transmitted to us by Moses our teacher, *and the mind tends to accept them instinctively*, Torah tradition would seem to imply that he [Adam] was commanded with respect to them, [and G-d] added to Noah the prohibition of eating flesh from a living animal, leading to seven commandments. So was the situation in the entire world until Abraham. When Abraham appeared, he was commanded, in addition to the aforementioned, concerning circumcision, and he prayed the morning prayer [apparently of his own volition]; Isaac tithed his grain and added another prayer in the afternoon; and Jacob added the prohibition of eating an animal's sciatic nerve, and prayed the evening supplication; and in Egypt, Amram [father of Moses] was given some additional *mitzvot*, until Moses our teacher came, and the Torah was completed under his aegis (*Hilchot Melachim* 9:1).

According to Rambam, six of the seven Noahide laws were given to Adam, and the prohibition of eating live flesh was delayed until the time of Noah for a simple reason. The Talmud (BT *Sanhedrin* 59b) explains that until then, it was forbidden to eat meat altogether. The implication of the prohibition of eating live flesh is that it *is* permitted to eat the flesh of a non-living animal, and that was appropriate only from the time of Noah. As previously noted, *Torah Temimah* looks upon the derivation of all seven Noahide laws from the command to Adam to refrain from eating of the Tree of Knowledge as a mnemonic device not to be taken literally, and this flows from the words of Rambam as well: "Torah tradition would *seem* to imply that he was commanded with respect to them." On the other hand, Tosafot (BT *Sanhedrin* 56b) assumes all seven were transmitted to Adam. It justifies the need for the command regarding live flesh by explaining that it is true that Adam was not permitted to slaughter an animal, but if not for the added prohibition, he would have been permitted to eat meat shed of its own accord from a living animal.

Additional Laws Given to Amram

With regard to Rambam's reference to "additional *mitzvot*" given to Amram, two questions have been raised:

1. What is his source?
2. What were these "additional *mitzvot*?"

In answer to the first question, two solutions have been proposed. *Meshech Chochmah* (*Shemot*. s.v. *Elokei*) has based it on the verse describing G-d's first meeting with Moses at the burning bush, which contains the introductory phrase: "I am the G-d of your father [Amram], the G-d of Abraham, the G-d of Isaac, and the G-d of Jacob" (Exod. 3:6). By grouping his father with the patriarchs, the assumption is that he also received instruction in the form of positive commands.

A second possible source is the Midrash (*Mechilta de-Rabbi Yishmael, Yitro, Masechta de-ba-Chodesh, parashah* 3), which speaks of the laws accepted by the nation before Moses ascended

Mt. Sinai (Exod. 24:3), and enumerates the Noahide laws as well as those *commanded in Egypt* and at Marah.

Regarding the second question, R. Yisrael Rubin[140] has found the following possibilities for the laws introduced by Amram:

1. laws of marriage (*Torah Shelemah, Shemot* 2:7);
2. laws pertaining to remarrying one's divorcee (which was relevant to Amram, who had returned to his previously divorced wife Jochebed. See Rashi, Exod. 2:1);
3. laws pertaining to abortion, relating to Pharaoh's request to kill the newborn male children (Exod. 1:16).

Adding More Mitzvot at Marah

It is important to realize that G-d's purpose in creating the world was to bring about that the Nation of Israel - which was meant to be a light unto the nations - conduct its social life in accordance with the laws of the Torah. Life conducted in this manner would climax after the arrival of the Messiah. To stress the centrality and relatedness of these notions, the Midrash states that six objects preceded the creation of the world, and among them were Israel, the Torah, and the name of the Messiah. The pre-existence of the Torah is mentioned in Proverbs as well, where the Torah, so to speak, is quoted as saying: "When He established the heavens, I was there" (Prov. 8:27). The Midrash continues:

> R. Huna and R. Yirmiyah… said: Contemplating the existence of Israel preceded everything… Had the Lord not foreseen that after twenty-six generations [ten from Adam to

---

140. Israel Rubin. *Amram nitztaveh mitzvot yeterot*, "He'arot u-Bi'urim" (5766), vol. 912 (www.haoros.com).

Intellectual Development in Exodus

Noah, ten from Noah to Abraham, followed by Isaac, Jacob, Levi, Kohath, Amram, and Moses (*Maharzo*)] Israel would receive the Torah, He would not have written in the Torah [which existed before creation] "command the Children of Israel," "speak to the Children of Israel" (*Gen. Rabbah* 1:4).

At every stage, the Almighty wished to stimulate mankind to progress in the direction of the final objective. Immediately upon creation of Adam, G-d commanded him to fulfill the Noahide laws, which are mostly moral in content.

G-d actually wanted to present Adam with more commandments. With regard to the verse: "And the Lord G-d took the man, and placed him [*va-yanichehu*] in the garden of Eden to work it [*le-ovda*] and to guard it [*u-le-shomra*]" (Gen. 2:15), the Midrash (*Gen. Rabbah* 16:5) says:

> *Va-yanichehu* — G-d gave him the commandment to observe the Sabbath, as it says: And he rested [*va-yanach* – based on the same Hebrew root] on the seventh day (Exod. 20:11). *Le-ovdah* — six days should you work [*taavod*] (Exod. 20:9). *U-le-shomra* — guard [*shmor*] the Sabbath and sanctify it (Deut. 5:12). Another exegesis: to work it [*le-ovda*] and to guard it [*u-le-shomra*] — this refers to the sacrifices, as it says: you shall serve [*taavdun*] G-d (Exod. 3:12), and it also says: you shall guard it [*tishmeru*] to offer it to Me at the proper time (Num. 28:2).

In another place, the Midrash goes further and states that G-d initially wished to give the entire Torah to Adam, as is implied by the verse: "This is the book of the generations of Adam. On the day that G-d created Adam, He made him in the likeness of

G-d" (Gen. 5:1). According to the Midrash (*Gen. Rabbah* 24:5), the book being referred to is the Torah scroll, and the verse indicates that G-d had intended to present it to mankind on the day He created Adam, since man was made in the likeness of G-d, with the wisdom, strength, and diligence to fulfill its commands. But when G-d realized, so to speak, that man had failed to obey even the six Noahide laws of which he was already cognizant, He swiftly changed His plan and decided to transmit the Torah in its entirety only to the future "generations of Adam."

Initially, not only was mankind unable to progress at the speed desired by G-d, but he was not even moving in the right direction, and as is well known, G-d was compelled to practically wipe out mankind and start afresh. In their reconstituted state, after 210 years of enslavement, the Hebrews were so depressed and demoralized that they were incapable of believing in redemption, whether by natural or supernatural means, and they were certainly incapable of comprehending abstractions such as the existence of G-d. It was therefore necessary to re-institute the seven laws that had previously been given to Adam, and then add a few.

The previously quoted excerpt from Rambam (*Hilchot Melachim* 9:1) refers to these laws as being such that "the mind tends to accept them instinctively." The nation of Israel was in need of intensive preparation to achieve the level required to accept the Torah, and it is possible that what occurred at Marah was part of the preparatory process which attempted to first habituate them to fulfill those laws whose purpose and necessity were more readily understandable.

Intellectual Development in Exodus

The Laws Transmitted at Marah – Including Social Legislation

The following external Tannaitic source (Baraita, BT *Sanhedrin* 56b) was quoted in the portion of *Beshallach*:

> The Israelites were given ten precepts at Marah, seven of which had already been accepted by the children of Noah, to which were added at Marah social legislation, the Sabbath, and *honoring one's parents*.

Rashi, based on this Talmudic source, states: "In Marah He gave them a few sections of the Torah to deal with: Shabbat, the *red heifer*, and the administration of justice" (Exod. 15:25).

It will be noted that Rashi replaced *honoring one's parents*, as stated in the Talmud, with the *red heifer*. It is possible that Rashi had a different version of the Talmudic source. At the end of the portion of *Mishpatim* (Exod. 24:3), however, Rashi states that at Marah four commands were given: *Shabbat, honoring one's parents, the red heifer, and the administration of justice*, thus combining the list that appears in the Babylonian Talmud with that which he himself presented in the portion of *Beshallach*.

The Talmudic source strengthens the claim that the progression toward receiving the Torah was not linear, but cyclical, with frequent reviews of previously imparted information. In Marah, therefore, it was necessary to refresh their knowledge of the seven Noahide laws, which were well known by that time, but not necessarily well practiced.

Two questions will be addressed:

1. How is it possible that one of the three laws introduced at Marah was the establishment of courts (social legislation), when this command was already included among the seven Noahide laws?
2. Why were the specific laws introduced at Marah chosen, as opposed to any of the other laws, which were only given later at Mt. Sinai?

Answering the First Question – Wasn't Social Legislation One of the Seven Noahide Laws?

The question is not original, since it was asked as part of the Talmudic discussion in BT *Sanhedrin* 56b. One answer is that the determination that social laws were added at Marah is in accordance with the opinion of the School of Manasseh (*De-Vei Menasheh*), which deletes *social laws* and *blasphemy* from the list of Noahide laws, and substitutes *emasculation* (*serus*) and *forbidden mixtures* in agriculture (*kilayim*). The view of the School of Manasseh is understandable, since the prohibition of *blasphemy* is redundant, being that it is included in the sin of idolatry. A code of *social laws* may not have been included at that stage because it would have been too sophisticated. Unlike the other Noahide prohibitions, which involve a single command, *social laws* imply an entire legislative system. In their stead, the School of Manasseh introduced two laws that forbid attempts to change the natural world as it was presented by G-d to humanity, since the Almighty prefers that man attempt to improve and perfect the world in its pristine form.

Another possible answer to this question hinges on the exact definition of *social laws*. According to Rambam (*Hilchot Melachim* 9:14), the command requires the Israelites to elect judges to sit in every town and deal with transgressors of the Noahide laws. According to Ramban (Gen. 34:13), the scope of this mitzvah is much greater, and it involves framing an entire system of law that encompasses every possible felony and misdemeanor, including robbery, fraud, embezzlement, exploitation of salaried workers, guardianship, rape, seduction, torts, commercial violations, etc. According to Rambam, one might say that the seven Noahide laws include social laws in their more limited form, i.e. those that relate to the enforcement of the other six Noahide laws. The broader definition, which includes formulation of an entire legal system, is the extension which was given at Marah.

Answering the Second Question – What Characterizes the Specific Laws Given at Marah?

The question that arises is, if the Lord wished to present the Children of Israel with a preview of the Torah, of all of the 613 commands, why were the specific laws pertaining to Shabbat and social laws chosen? Abarbanel (on Exod. 15) notes that Shabbat, which is referred to in the evening *kiddush* (sanctification over wine) as *a reminder of the act of creation*, stresses the existence of G-d as the Creator of the world and his ability to change the rhythm of nature, if He so desires. Jurisprudence emphasizes G-d's way of running the world, which is to compensate each person in accordance with his deeds (i.e., reward and punishment), which in turn illustrates G-d's concern for the destiny of each individual.

G-d chose to reveal at Marah those commands that were most suited to serve as an introduction to the acceptance of the yolk of Divine kingship and the requirement to fulfill His commands. The existence of G-d and the concept of reward and punishment are the first two of the three principles of faith proposed by R. Yosef Albo (*Sefer ha-Ikkarim*, introduction to Article 1), while the third principle—the revelation at Mt. Sinai—was to be realized before the entire congregation of Israel six weeks hence.

If the third law given at Marah is honoring one's parents, this supports the thesis that the process of accepting the *mitzvot* is a gradual one. After the laws of Shabbat and establishing a legal system demonstrated the foundations of the religion, G-d added another law that is both ethical and logical. Only after becoming accustomed to observing the laws regulating man's behavior toward his fellow man would it be appropriate to issue more esoteric laws, which is what took place at Mt. Sinai.

If the third law is the statute of the red heifer, one might relate the significance of its being given at Marah to a distinction made by the Abarbanel in the portion of *Mishpatim*, where he divides all of the 613 commandments into three categories:

> Some of them are called *testimonies*, and they are *mitzvot* which testify to the true beliefs and to the wonders of G-d, such as Shabbat, the laws connected with Passover and *matzah*, the Festival of Tabernacles, and the like, whose reason is known, for they commemorate G-d's wondrous deeds. And some of the *mitzvot* are of a different type called *statutes*, whose reason and explanation are concealed from us, and we don't know them, and so we say that they are the King's decrees… but the third type

of *mitzvot* relate to *inter-personal laws* and decisions... for no community of people can exist without inter-personal decisions (Exodus 21).

Based on this categorization, one can say that at Marah Israel was given a command of each type—Shabbat is of the testimony type, the red heifer is of the statute type, and social laws are of the inter-personal type—in order to prepare the nation of Israel for the different types of commands that they would encounter upon receipt of the Torah.

THE GIVING OF THE TORAH – ITS PURPOSE

The goal of the Torah itself is to engender peace in the world. If people succeed in loving—or at least in not hating—others, it will be possible to achieve peace. Rambam, at the end of his laws of Hanukkah, relates to the situation that might arise if an indigent person has enough money to purchase candles either for Hanukkah or for Shabbat, but not for both of them. He states (*Hilchot Megillah ve-Chanukah* 4:14):

> [In such a case] Shabbat candles take precedence, to promote peace within the household, since G-d's name is erased in order to advance peace between a man and his wife [to allow a woman suspected of adultery to prove her innocence (Num. 5:23)]. Great is peace, since the entire Torah was given to make peace in the world, as it says: Her ways are ways of pleasantness, and all her paths are peace (Prov. 3:17).

According to R. Eliezer Berkovits (*G-d, Man and History* [1965], p. 109), even ritual laws, such as those restraining sexual and culinary appetites, serve to train one in self-restraint, so that when one must control himself in dealing with his compatriots, he will be well prepared.

THE GIVING OF THE TORAH AT MT. SINAI – WHAT WAS GIVEN AND WHAT WAS RECORDED?

Each *mitzvah* may be divided in two sections—its general description and definition, and the body of its details, some of which are included in the written law, and others of which are included in the oral law.

Were both sections transmitted to Moses at Mt. Sinai, or just the general description, with the rest being filled in by G-d during the long journey through the desert in the Tent of Meeting or at the end of the trek on the plains of Moab? There is a Tannaitic dispute with regard to this question (BT *Zevachim* 115b; BT *Chagigah* 6a):

> R. Ishmael said: The general laws were stated at Sinai [e.g., "You shall make an altar of earth for me, and you shall sacrifice your burnt offerings and peace offerings on it" (Exod. 20:21)] and the details were given in the Tent of Meeting [e.g., that the burnt offering was to be skinned and dismembered (Lev. 1:6); hence, until the Tent of Meeting was constructed, it was not required that burnt offerings be skinned and dismembered]. R. Akiva said: Both the general laws and the details were given at Sinai, repeated in the Tent of Meeting, and reiterated once more on the plains of Moab (Deut. 1:5).

Intellectual Development in Exodus

A number of verses with apparent redundancies (in italics) have been explicated in keeping with the view of R. Akiva, as listed below:

1. The verse from the end of *Mishpatim*: "And the Lord said unto Moses: 'Come up to Me on the mountain and remain there; and I will give you *the tablets of stone, and the law and the commandment, which I have written in order that you teach it to them*" (Exod. 24:12).

   The Talmud resolves the repetitive references to the content of the transmission to Moses as follows:

   "Tablets of stone" — these are the ten commandments; "the law" — this is the Pentateuch; "the commandment" — this is the Mishnah; "which I have written" — these are the Prophets and the Hagiographa; "that you may teach them" — this is the Gemara (BT *Berachot* 5a).

   According to this exegetical interpretation, the Talmudic details as well as the general description were conveyed to Moses at Mt. Sinai.

2. The verse from Leviticus, "And the Lord spoke to Moses on Mt. Sinai saying" (Lev. 25:1), unnecessarily mentions that the Sabbatical laws were given at Mt. Sinai. Since these laws are not explicated in any other location (such as Deuteronomy), they must have been given in their entirety at Mt. Sinai. Accordingly, Rashi understands that the extraneous mention of Mt. Sinai teaches that just as both the generalities and the details of the Sabbatical year were transmitted at Sinai, so were they both transmitted regarding every other command given at Sinai.

3. Another wordy verse is found in Deuteronomy: "And the Lord gave me the two tablets of stone written with the finger of G-d; and *on them* all of the words that the Lord spoke with you on the mountain out of the midst of the fire on the day of the assembly" (Deut. 9:10). The second half of the verse seems superfluous. The Talmud, in the following segment, understands the extraneous words *on them* to imply that Moses was taught everything that would ever be said about what was written on the tablets:

It teaches us that the Holy One, blessed be He, showed Moses homiletical lessons based on the Torah, and homiletical lessons derived by the Scribes, and innovations that would be introduced by the Scribes. What does this refer to? The reading of the Megillah (BT *Megillah* 19b).

This section from the Talmud goes further than both R. Akiva himself and the previously quoted exegesis, by saying that Moses was not only taught all of the details of every law given at Mt. Sinai, but he was also informed of future Talmudic discussions and even rabbinical enactments. *Torah Temimah* (Exod. 24:12) has difficulty accepting the thesis that every future derivation was revealed to Moses. He interprets the Talmud to mean that beyond the written law, the only laws taught explicitly to Moses were those (perhaps even rabbinical) for which there was no clear-cut source in the text of the Pentateuch (*halachot le-Moshe mi-Sinai*), as well as the thirteen hermeneutical principles, while lessons derivable hermeneutically were not transmitted to Moses, but were rather left for future generations. *Tosafot Yom Tov* (in the introduction to his commentary on the Mishnah) explains that while Moses may have been shown prophetically and ephemerally all of the future Talmudic exegesis, he did not fully absorb it, nor did he pass it on to Joshua.

A difference between the view of *Torah Temimah* and *Tosafot Yom Tov* might occur with respect to one of the four species associated with Sukkot (Tabernacles). On that holiday, the Torah commands one to take "the fruit of goodly trees" (Lev. 23:40), understood to be an elegant citron (*etrog*). But how is "elegance" defined? According to the Talmudic commentator *Ran*,[141] the Torah did not specify, but rather relied on the sages to stipulate specific requirements. In this case, *Tosafot Yom Tov* might say that these details were initially transmitted to Moses, but went no further. The Rabbis formulated them independently at a later stage. *Torah Temimah*, on the other hand, would say that these enactments first appeared only later, along with other rabinically-derived laws.

Of course, there also exist Midrashim that support the view of R. Ishmael. Regarding the verse "And He gave Moses, when He finished speaking with him upon Mt. Sinai, two tablets of the testimony, tablets of stone, written with the finger of G-d" (Exod. 31:18), the Midrash (*Exod. Rabbah* 41:6) notes that the Hebrew word used for the phrase "when He finished speaking with him" (*ke-chaloto*) could also mean "He outlined." The Midrash goes on to say that it would have been impossible to teach Moses the details "of all of the laws in the Torah in just forty days." After all, the breadth of Torah knowledge has been described as longer than the earth and broader than the sea (Job 11:9). G-d must have, therefore, only taught Moses each *mitzvah* in outline form.

---

141. Ran on Rif, BT *Sukkah* 13b s.v. *u-mihu*.

In addition, there are four instances in the Torah where Moses was unable to answer a halachic question, and had to communicate with the Lord to obtain the solution. The four queries concerned: *Pesach Sheni* (Num. 9), the Sabbath wood-gatherer (Num. 15), the daughters of Zelophehad (Num. 27), and the blasphemer of the Almighty (Lev. 24). The simplest explanation of Moses' inablility to respond unassisted is that he had not yet learned the details of these halachic issues, in accordance with the view of R. Ishmael.

It must be stressed that even though R. Ishmael believes that only the basics were taught to Moses at Sinai, he agrees that eventually he was taught the details as well in the Tent of Meeting or on the plains of Moab. R. Akiva accepts the latter point, just that in his opinion, it was not the first time he was exposed to this material. Also, even though R. Akiva believes that all the details were given at Sinai, he too agrees that they were transmitted orally.

So when was the entire Torah actually transcribed in writing? On this question, R. Johanan and Resh Lakish argue. The former says that every time Moses enlarged upon the details of a specific command during their travels in the desert, that portion was written on parchment, and after forty years all of the separate scrolls were sewn together to form the complete Torah scroll. The latter says that nothing was put into writing throughout their travels in the desert. Only at the conclusion of their forty-year trek was the entire Torah written at one sitting, as described in the Talmud:

> R. Johanan said in the name of R. Banaah: The Torah was transmitted in separate scrolls, as it says in Psalms, "Then I said I am included, in the scroll of the book it is written of me" (Ps. 40:8) [implying that the book was initially composed of separate scrolls, and a reference to David is

prophetically found in one of them]. R. Simeon b. Lakish said: The Torah was transmitted entire, as it says, "Take this book of the law" (Deut. 31:26) [implying its first appearance was as a complete book] (BT *Gittin* 60a).

Tosafot *(*BT *Gittin* 60a, s.v. *Torah chatuma nitna)* suggests that according to both opinions, parts of the Torah were put in writing during their travels. The argument is only if every part was written immediately. According to the alternative view, those sections that actually occurred earlier, but were to appear in the Torah after a later event, were not committed to writing until the later event transpired, so that a single Torah scroll could be filled in sequentially.

Frequency of Torah Reading

The following excerpt from the Talmud, which denigrates the activities of the Israelites during the three-day journey to Marah, is used as a source for establishing the frequency of the public reading of the Torah.

> The [following] ten enactments were ordained by Ezra: That the law be read [publicly] in the afternoon service on Shabbat; that the law be read [publicly] on Mondays and Thursdays.... That the law be read [publicly] in the afternoon service on Shabbat, on account of shopkeepers [who on weekdays have no time to hear the reading of the law]. That the law be read [publicly] on Mondays and Thursdays, but was this ordained by Ezra? Was this not ordained even before him? For it was taught: "And they

went three days in the wilderness and found no water," upon which those who expound verses metaphorically [*dorshei reshumot*] said: "Water can only mean Torah, as it says: 'Let everyone who is thirsty go to the water' (Isa. 55:1)." It thus means that as they went three days without Torah, they immediately became exhausted. The prophets among them thereupon rose and enacted that they should publicly read the law on Shabbat, make a break on Sunday, read again on Monday, make a break again on Tuesday and Wednesday, read again on Thursday, and then make a break on Friday, so that they should not be kept for three days without Torah. [So why then was it necessary for Ezra to enact this, being that it had been the custom ever since revelation?] Originally, it was ordained that one man should read three verses or that three men should together read three verses [one verse each], corresponding to priests, Levites, and Israelites. Then Ezra came and ordained that three men should be called up to read, and that ten verses should be read, corresponding to the ten members [*batlanim*] of the community for the maintenance of religious services.[142] [By reading ten verses in honor of the ten *batlanim*, they are granted well-deserved honor, since it is only on their account that there is a quorum (*minyan*) to read the Torah in the first place] (BT *Bava Kama* 82a).

Tosafot[143] asks why Monday and Thursday were specifically chosen for reading the Torah, leading to the following gaps: Shabbat to

---

142. BT *Megilla* 21b indicates that the number ten is especially meaningful in Judaism. Reading ten verses may also be said to be reminiscent of the Ten Commandments and the ten statements with which the world was created (Ethics of the Fathers 5:1).

143. BT *Bava Kama* 82a, s.v. *She-lo yalinu gimel yamim be-lo Torah*.

Monday (1), Monday to Thursday (2), Thursday to Shabbat (1). The gaps in many possible arrangements would have also met the requirement of a three-day maximum, for example: Shabbat to Tuesday (2), Tuesday to Wednesday (0), Wednesday to Shabbat (2). Tosafot answers that according to tradition, Moses ascended Mt. Sinai to receive the second set of tablets on a Thursday.[144] The fortieth day hence, when Moses descended, would then be a Monday. Since those forty days symbolized a period of grace, their beneficence is commemorated every week by reading the Torah on Monday and Thursday.

The Talmud quotes its source as "those who expound verses metaphorically" (*dorshei reshumot*). *Iyun Yaakov* (*Ein Yaakov*, *Bava Kamma* 82a) explains that this expression implies that the stated derivation is to be treated as homiletic exegesis rather than as literal derivation, since in actuality the Torah was not yet given, so how could the people have been expected to have studied it on their journey?

Torah Temimah (Exod. 15:22) has the same question as *Iyun Yaakov*, and he extends it to the reason proffered by Tosafot for reading the Torah on Monday and Thursday, namely that these were the days on which Moses ascended and descended Mt. Sinai, where he beseeched the Lord. Since that event was also part of the process of receiving the Torah, it too occurred at a much later stage than the three-day trip through the desert.

Torah Temimah asks another question based on the Talmud's relating the enactment to read the Torah on Mondays and Thursdays to "the prophets among them." But who would those

---

144. Traditionally, revelation was on Shabbat. Moses ascended for 40 days on Sunday, but the count started only on Monday (Rashi, Exod. 32:1). He then descended on Friday, ascended again on Shabbat for the intermediary 40 days, descended on Wednesday, and went up for the second set of tablets on Thursday.

prophets be? The most straightforward assumption is that the Talmud is referring to the greatest prophet ever, Moses our teacher. This is in fact the view of Rambam, who summarizes the entire Talmudic script in simplified form, in his inimitable manner:

> Moses our teacher enacted for Israel that they read the Torah publicly on Shabbat and during the morning service on Monday and Thursday, in order that three days not elapse without hearing [words of] Torah. Ezra the scribe enacted that they should read in the afternoon service on Shabbat on account of shopkeepers, and he also enacted that on Mondays and Thursdays they call three people [to the Torah], and that they should not read less than ten verses (*Hilchot Tefillah* 12:1).

However, if "the prophets among them" refers to Moses, why was his identity hidden? The Talmud describes quite explicitly a number of enactments made by Moses in various locations, for example:

> R. Nahman said: Moses instituted for Israel the first benediction of the grace at the time when manna descended for them (BT *Berachot* 48b).

> Our Rabbis taught: Moses enacted for the Israelites that they should inquire about and discuss the subject of the day — the laws of Passover on Passover, the laws of Pentecost on Pentecost, and the laws of Tabernacles on Tabernacles (BT *Megillah* 32a).

Torah Temimah suggests an original answer. He says that the decision to read the Torah at intervals not separated by more than three days was made at a much later stage, perhaps when the Jews were in exile in Babylonia, or about to be exiled. To strengthen the attachment of the people to Torah study and observance, a number of enactments were instituted by the prophets, including the one presently under discussion. The Talmud records a number of prophetic enactments, such as the law to take the willow-branch on Hoshana Rabbah (BT *Sukkah* 44a).

Torah Temimah's answer validates the wording of the Talmud, which ascribes the enactment to "the prophets among them." But more important, it provides a basis more firm than an anachronistic interpretation of Scripture for the practice of thrice-weekly Torah readings.

Second Overview: The Tabernacle-Oriented Portions

The book of Exodus is divided into eleven weekly portions. The last five, almost half of the book, relate to the holy Tabernacle (*Mishkan*), which was to be used for prayer and sacrifice, and administered by the priests, as well as to the special garments to be worn by those priests. The portion of *Terumah*, the seventh in Exodus, describes the design of the structure itself and the vessels contained therein, while *Tetzaveh*, the eighth, provides instructions for sewing the priestly garments. The tenth and eleventh portions in Exodus, *Vayakhel* and *Pekudei*, document the collection of the building materials for the *Mishkan*, the manufacture of its vessels and the sewing of the priestly garments, respectively. Sandwiched in between is the portion of *Ki Tissa*, which appropriately starts with a description of additional items and commodities needed for the functioning of the *Mishkan*, instructions with regard to their preparation, and the appointment of the craftsmen who would be responsible for the successful execution of the entire project. However, the majority of the portion of *Ki Tissa* is devoted to a detailed narration of the story of the golden calf and its ramifications. At first blush, the story of the golden calf is an independent event, unrelated to the construction of the Tabernacle.

The Tabernacle-Oriented Portions

Why is it placed between the description of the design of the *Mishkan* (in the seventh and eighth portions) and the construction of the *Mishkan*, the production of its utensils, and the sewing of the priests' garments (in the tenth and eleventh portions)?

Ramban – (Almost) Everything Is in Its Proper Order

According to Ramban (Exod. 35:1), the story of the golden calf appears between the command to build the *Mishkan* and its actual construction for a very simple reason—that is when it occurred. Many activities were involved in the process of setting up the *Mishkan* and its inauguration, and they are described from the portion of *Terumah* until the portion of *Shemini* in the book of Leviticus. An ordered list of these activities appears below:

1. G-d orders the building of a Tabernacle: "And they shall make Me a sanctuary, so that I may dwell among them" (Exod. 25:8).
2. At the beginning of the portions of *Terumah* (Exod. 25:1-7) and *Ki Tissa* (Exod. 30:11-15), G-d commanded the Children of Israel to contribute silver and other materials with which to build the Tabernacle and sew the priestly garments. Rashi (Exod. 30:15) explains that there were three calls to contribute. The first contribution of a half-shekel was intended for use in making the silver sockets that held the panels that served as the walls of the *Mishkan*. The second contribution of a half-shekel was needed in order to purchase animals for communal sacrifices (and this was the only contribution that was preserved as a mandatory fee throughout the generations, until the destruction of the Second Temple). Both of these

donations were required of all males over the age of twenty at the time of the construction of the Tabernacle (Exod. 30:14). The list at the beginning of *Terumah* includes materials that would be used in building the *Mishkan* and preparing its accessories. All members of the congregation were invited to voluntarily donate as much as they wanted of these items, and this was the third potential contribution.

3. The portions of *Terumah*, *Tetzaveh*, and the beginning of *Ki Tissa* (until the end of chapter 31) contain a description of the *Mishkan* and the priestly garments.

4. Chapter 29 in the portion of *Tetzaveh* describes the ceremony associated with the inauguration of the *kohanim* (priests), which would take place eventually. The chapter opens with the verse, "And this is the thing that you [Moses] should do to them [Aaron and his sons] to make them holy," which implies that it will be Moses who will be conducting the ceremony. The ceremony, when it took place, was to include animal sacrifices and meal offerings, bodily ablutions, wearing priestly garments, and anointing the *kohanim* (Exod. 29:41). It was to be repeated every day for a week, as the verse says, "for seven days you should consecrate them," and Rashi comments, "in this manner and by means of these sacrifices on every day" (Exod. 29:35).

5. The remainder of *Ki Tissa* (chapters 32-34) tells the stories of the golden calf, the breaking of the tablets, Moses' successful prayer to save the nation from the threat of Divine destruction, and Moses' ascent of the mountain for the third time (the first ascent was to receive the first set of tablets, and the second to seek forgiveness for the sin of the golden calf) to receive the Ten Commandments on a new set of tablets (Rashi on Exod. 33:11).

6. The portions of *Vayakhel* and *Pekudei* come next. Ramban explains: "Since the Lord relented, and gave him the second tablets and made a new covenant with him that G-d would walk among them, things returned to their previous state and to the love of their betrothal, and with the knowledge that His Presence would rest among them just as it was initially commanded [planned]… and for this reason Moses commanded them now concerning all matters that he had commanded them before [hence the repetition]." In these portions the donations were received, and the vessels and clothes were made. These events could have occurred at any time between Yom Kippur and the end of the month of Adar, and perhaps throughout that period.
7. After all of the materials needed for constructing the Tabernacle were assembled, and all of the vessels and garments were completed, Moses was told to set up the structure on the first of the Hebrew month of Nisan, as it says: "On the first day of the first month you should set up the Tabernacle of the Tent of Meeting" (Exod. 40:2).
8. The text describes the location and anointment of the vessels after the Tabernacle was standing (Exod. 40:3-11).
9. The inauguration of the *kohanim* is described (Exod. 40:12-15). As Ramban noted, this is a repeat of certain verses that appeared previously,[145] for the purpose of reassuring the people that in spite of the heinous sin of the golden calf, the plans for the *Mishkan* were back on track.
10. "And Moses did according to all that the Lord commanded him, so did he" (Exod. 40:16). This verse serves as an introduction

---

145. Exod. 40:12 parallels 29:4, 40:13 parallels 29:5, and 40:14 parallels 29:8. Verse 40:15 does not have a parallel in chapter 29, possibly because regular priests would not have to be anointed in the future (Saadiah Gaon).

to what follows, the setting up of the entire *Mishkan* (Exod. 40:17-33).

11. The Tabernacle was set up, but Moses could not enter, because it was enveloped in the Divine Presence, as it says: "And Moses was not able to enter the Tent of Meeting, because the cloud rested on it, and the glory of the Lord filled the Tabernacle" (Exod. 40:35). Leviticus begins with the phrase, "And the Lord called Moses and spoke to him from the Tent of Meeting" (Lev. 1:1), apparently to tell him that the cloud had dissipated and he could now enter the Tent of Meeting. Another possibility is that Moses did not enter the Tent of Meeting, but rather heard the voice of the Lord emanating from it. A third option is that the verse describing the glory of the Lord served as the introduction to an event that actually occurred later (on the eighth day of consecration).

12. Having previously described the inauguration in detail and then in summary form (points 4 and 9), the actual implementation occurs only in the book of Leviticus, where the tragic events that took place on the eighth and last day (the deaths of Nadab and Abihu) are also delineated (Lev. 8:1-10:7).

13. In addition to the inauguration of the priests, another event was tied to the completion of the *Mishkan*, namely the gifts presented by the princes of each of the twelve tribes, as described in the book of Numbers, which starts as follows: "And it came to pass on the day that Moses finished setting up the Tabernacle, and had anointed it and sanctified it, and all of its furniture, and the altar and all of its vessels, and had anointed them and sanctified them; that the princes of Israel… brought their offering before the Lord… each prince on his day" (Num. 7:1-11).

The Tabernacle-Oriented Portions

Adding a Time-Line

The Tabernacle was set up on the first of the Hebrew month of Nisan (point 7 in the previous section). Clearly, the inauguration could not have occurred before the *Mishkan* was in place, since the ceremony involved bringing sacrifices on its altar, and for that reason its implementation is described later in the book of Leviticus (point 12). Ibn Ezra describes the situation as follows:

> On the first day of the first month putting up the Mishkan was initiated (Exod. 40:17)… and on this day Moses anointed the *Mishkan* and all of the vessels, and the burnt offering altar and all its vessels, and the laver and its base; and the congregation gathered at the entrance of the Tent of Meeting, and they washed Aaron and his sons with water, and he [Moses] dressed Aaron in holy garments, and he also dressed his sons, and they were anointed with holy oil. And he brought the bullock and two rams… so he did for the seven days of consecration (Lev. 8:10-36). And it says, "And it came to pass on the day that Moses finished setting up the Tabernacle and had anointed it" (Num. 7:1), and he had sanctified the altar on the seven days of consecration. Then the princes started sacrificing for the inauguration of the altar (Num. 7:2-88)… and behold the inauguration of the altar was completed after nineteen days of the first month (Exod. 40:2).

Concisely, the schedule was:

1. 1 Nisan: the Tabernacle was set up.
2. 1-7 Nisan: the Tabernacle and the priests were consecrated.

3. 8 Nisan: the eighth day of consecration; Nadab and Abihu were burned to death (Lev. 9:1-10:7).
4. 8-19 Nisan: each day one of the twelve princes brought his offering.

The chronology proposed by Ibn Ezra seems to follow from a straightforward perusal of the relevant verses, and the chronological sequence follows the order of Scripture. Nevertheless, since there are Tannaitic sources that present different sequences, Ibn Ezra feels compelled to support his opinion. He does so by quoting the Midrash,[146] which cites R. Akiva's view that when the Torah says that there were some people who were impure at the time of Passover and so could not sacrifice the Pascal lamb (Num. 9:6), it was referring to Mishael and Elzaphan. The latter were the sons of Uziel, the brother of Amram, making them the first cousins of Aaron, and thus the first cousins once removed of Aaron's children. Scripture tells how they carried out the bodies of Nadab and Abihu, making themselves impure (Lev. 10:4-5). Since, according to Ibn Ezra, the death of Aaron's sons occurred on the eighth of Nisan, and since it takes seven days to become purified, it is clear that they would still have been impure on the fourteenth of Nisan, when the Pascal lamb was to be slaughtered.

R. Avraham Shama[147] has noted that the general chronology of Ibn Ezra corresponds to the way Josephus understood the Biblical text. Josephus writes:

> But at the beginning of the second year... in the month Nisan, as the Hebrews call it, on the new moon, they

---

146. *Sifrei Behaalotcha* 68, cited in BT *Succah* 25b.
147. Avraham Shama, *Shtei megamot be-chanukat ha-Mishkan*, "Megadim" 2 (1986).

consecrated the Tabernacle and all its vessels... After this manner did he consecrate them and their garments for seven days together... But on the eighth day he appointed a feast for the people, and commanded them to offer sacrifices according to their ability. They offered also gifts to G-d... tribe by tribe... each head of a tribe brought a bowl and a basin and a spoon of ten shekel full of incense... These heads of tribes were twelve days in sacrificing, one sacrificing every day (*Antiquities* 3.8.4-10).

Although he does not say so explicitly, it is possible that according to Josephus, the princes began bringing their gifts on the ninth rather than the eighth of Nisan (when he speaks of a feast taking place), continuing until the twentieth rather than the nineteenth. If that was his view, based on an analysis of the text, it is quite reasonable. The ceremonies on the eighth day were quite different from those on the first seven days (Lev. 8:2). Not only was a different set of sacrifices prescribed, but on the eighth day there was a second set of sacrifices brought on behalf of the nation itself, and of course, G-d's presence was to be manifested (Lev. 9:1-5). So the eighth of Nisan was already an action-packed day, and scheduling more sacrifices for the altar would have caused unnecessary congestion. In addition, the terrible tragedy that befell the sons of Aaron would have made it a very inauspicious day to start offering a series of gifts.

A Second Time-Line

Although Ibn Ezra's approach seems to fit the text quite well, there is one textual problem which apparently induced the Sages to present a different chronology.

At the end of the portion of *Pekudei* it says: "And it came to pass in the first month in the second year, on the first day of the month, that the Tabernacle was set up" (Exod. 40:17). According to Ibn Ezra, that day (the first of Nisan) was the first day of the consecration of the priests, a very reasonable inference, since the consecration involved sacrifices on the altar in the Tabernacle. Immediately after the *Mishkan* was set up, it was to be anointed (i.e., on the same day), as it says: "And you shall take the anointing oil, and anoint the Tabernacle, and all that is in it, and you shall make it holy, and all of its furniture" (Exod. 40:9).[148]

But in Numbers, as previously noted, it says that the princes started bringing their gifts on the same day that the Tabernacle was completed, i.e., on the first of Nisan, with no mention of the seven-day inauguration of the priests intervening. Clearly, the princes could not have brought their animal sacrifices simultaneously with the consecration ceremony.

Ibn Ezra was not bothered by this problem, because he interprets the words in Numbers, "on the day that Moses finished setting up the Tabernacle, and had anointed it and *sanctified* it… that the princes of Israel… brought their offering before the Lord," to mean that the princely gifts were initiated only after the consecration was completed, since that was its sanctification. The time from the anointing to the sanctification spanned a period of seven days.

The Sages, on the other hand, felt that the verse was referring to events which all took place on the same day. But if the princely gifts started on the first of Nisan, as soon as the *Mishkan* was set up, when did the inauguration of the priests take place? The Rabbis concluded that it must have preceded the setting up of the

---

148. Although it doesn't say that Moses fulfilled this command on the same day, there is certainly no reason to assume otherwise.

The Tabernacle-Oriented Portions

Mishkan, i.e., it must have been before the first of Nisan, and this view is expressed in the following Midrash:

> A Tanna taught: That day [the first of Nisan] took ten crowns [was special in ten ways]. It was the first of the Creation [a Sunday], the first for the princes [when their gifts for the dedication of the Tabernacle were initiated], the first for the priesthood [when Aaron began to officiate as a priest, i.e., the eighth day of consecration], the first for [public] sacrifice, the first for the descent of fire [from heaven, which also happened on the eighth day of consecration].[149]

The Midrash[150] explicates the chronology according to this view:

> On the twenty-third of Adar they brought the [sacrifices of] consecration. Twenty-three and seven are thirty. On the first of Nisan they completed the consecration, "for He shall consecrate you seven days" (Lev. 8:33).

But how could the inauguration of the *kohanim* have preceded the setting up of the *Mishkan*, since the latter is needed to bring the sacrifices that were part of the inauguration service? The Midrash solves the problem by stating:

> During each of the seven days of installation, Moses erected the Tabernacle every morning, brought his sacrifices on it [the altar] and [then] dismantled it [the

---

149. The Midrash appears in numerous collections, perhaps the earliest is *Seder Olam Rabbah* 7. Other locations: BT *Shabbat* 87b; *Sifra Shemini, Mechilta de-Milluim* A; *Gen. Rabbah, Bereishit* 3; *Num. Rabbah, Naso* 13.
150. *Sifra Tzav, Mechilta de-Milluim* 36; *Sifrei, Naso* 44.

Tabernacle]. On the eighth [day] he erected it but did not [again] dismantle it. R. Yosi b. Yehudah says that also on the eighth he erected and dismantled it.[151]

One arrives at the following time-line according to this view (also adopted by Ramban[152] and Rashi[153]):

1. 23-29 Adar: Moses consecrated the Tabernacle and the priests. Sacrifices were brought by the *kohanim*. Moses set up the Tabernacle and dismantled it daily.
2. 1 Nisan: Eighth day of consecration. Sacrifices were brought both by the nation and the *kohanim*, and G-d's presence was manifested. Nadab and Abihu were burned to death (Lev. 9:1-10:7).
3. 1-12 Nisan: Each day one of the twelve princes brought his offering.

Ibn Ezra does not accept the view of this Midrash for quite valid reasons. In his words (on Exod. 40:2):

Why didn't the text mention that [every day] Moses erected and dismantled it [the *Mishkan*]? And when it was dismantled, where would the entrance to the Tent of Meeting be located, for the verse states: "And at the door of the Tent of Meeting you shall sit day and night for seven days" (Lev. 8:35)?

---

151. *Sifra Tzav, Mechilta de-Milluim* 36; *Num. Rabbah, Naso* 12:15 cites opinions that Moses erected and dismantled it two or three times a day.
152. Exod. 40:2, Lev. 8:2.
153. Lev. 8:2, 9:1.

The Midrash, however, does find a source for the seven-fold erection and dismantling of the Tabernacle in the previously quoted verse (point 13), which includes the words: "on the day that Moses *finished* setting up the Tabernacle." The Midrash asks why the verse does not simply state "on the day that Moses set up the Tabernacle?" Apparently, the verse teaches that Moses set up the *Mishkan* many times, but on the first of Nisan, he set it up for the last time, i.e., he *finished* setting it up.

Nevertheless, according to the Midrashic approach, the sacrifices of Aaron, the Israelites, and the princes, as well as the public descent of the Divine presence, all occurred on the first of Nissan, while according to Ibn Ezra, one may posit that the princely sacrifices occurred later, which seems more reasonable.

Rashi: "There Is No Earlier or Later in the Torah"

Rashi argues with the principle which Ibn Ezra and Ramban support, that the Torah is ordered chronologically. On the contrary, he maintains that there is no earlier or later regarding events related in the Torah, in Hebrew—*ein mukdam u-me'uchar ba-Torah*. Chronology does play a role, but it is only one of many possible explanations, and it is when other equally valid reasons determine the order of Scripture that the aforementioned principle is invoked.

Immediately before the story of the golden calf, Rashi states:

> The incident of the [golden] calf [in chapter 32] occurred a long time before the commandment to work on the Tabernacle [in chapter 25]—for on the seventeenth

of Tammuz the tablets were broken, and on the Day of Atonement G-d reconciled with Israel, and on the next day they began with the contributions for the Tabernacle, and it was set up on the first of Nisan (Exod. 31:18).

Rashi defines the order of events more explicitly at a later stage, where he states:

> On the seventeenth of Tammuz the tablets were broken, on the eighteenth he burned the calf and judged the offenders, and on the nineteenth he ascended, as it says (Exod. 32:30): "And it came to pass on the next day [after he had punished the offenders] (Exod. 32:26-29) that Moses said to the people: 'You have sinned a great sin; and now I will go up unto the Lord.'" There he spent forty days and requested [of G-d] that He be merciful, as it says, "And I fell down before the Lord, as I did the first time, for forty days and forty nights; I did not eat bread or drink water; because of all your sins which you sinned, by doing that which was evil in the eyes of the Lord, to provoke Him" (Deut. 9:18). On the first of Elul he was told "ascend Mt. Sinai in the morning" (Exod. 34:2) to receive the latter [second] tablets, and he spent forty days there, concerning which it says: "And I stood on the mountain, as on the first days, forty days and forty nights" (Deut. 10:10). Just as the first were with a pleasant demeanor [on the part of G-d, since the Israelites had not sinned as of yet], so were the latter with a pleasant demeanor. Say from here, the intervening forty days were passed in anger [on the part of G-d]. On the tenth of Tishrei, G-d was reconciled with Israel in joy and sincerity and said to Moses, "I have

forgiven as you requested,"[154] and handed him the latter [second] tablets. And he [Moses] descended and began commanding them concerning the work of the Tabernacle, and they did it until the first of Nisan, and from the time it was set up, He [G-d] spoke with him [Moses] only from the Tent of Meeting (Exod. 33:11).

The verses having to do with the consecration of the priests that Ramban found problematic did not disturb Rashi at all. In particular, although the verse: "And it came to pass in the first month in the second year, on the first day of the month, that the Tabernacle was set up" (Exod. 40:17), describing the erection of the *Mishkan* after the seven days of consecration, appears at the end of the book of Exodus, Rashi is not disturbed by the verses that appear afterwards, in the book of Leviticus, describing the first day of the consecration ceremony, namely: "Take Aaron and his sons with him… and assemble all of the congregation at the entrance of the Tent of Meeting" (Lev. 8:2). Rashi simply comments: "This section was said seven days before the erection of the *Mishkan*, because there is no earlier or later in the Torah." This flippant reaction was quoted by Ramban (Lev. 8:2), who was upset enough to state: "Why scramble [the order of] the words of the living G-d?"

WHY DID RASHI CHANGE THE ORDER OF BIBLICAL EVENTS?

Even if Rashi does not require concordance between the Biblical narrative and its chronological order, he must justify the

---

154. Num. 14:20. The citation is actually from Moses' prayers to spare the nation after the sin of the ten spies.

divergence between the two. Why is Rashi unwilling to believe that the portion of *Terumah* could have been among the laws and commands that the Almighty taught Moses before he descended from the mountain and beheld the golden calf? What intrinsic difference is there between the ordinances found at the end of *Yitro* and most of *Mishpatim*, which were taught at Sinai, and the guidelines for constructing the Tabernacle and crafting its vessels described in *Terumah*?

The answer is that Rashi bases himself on a Midrash which says that if not for the sin of the golden calf, G-d would not have commanded the construction of the *Mishkan*. The Midrash states (*Tanchuma, Terumah* 8):

> And you find that on the Day of Atonement they were forgiven [for the sin of the golden calf], and immediately on that day G-d said to them "And let them make Me a sanctuary, that I may dwell among them" (Exod. 25:8), *so that all of the nations should know that they were pardoned for the sin of the golden calf.* And for that reason it is called the Tabernacle of the Testimony, for it gives testimony to mankind that the Almighty dwells in your sanctuary. Said the Lord: "Let the gold in the Tabernacle come and atone for the gold from which the calf was made," concerning which it says, "And all the people broke off the golden rings that were in their ears, and brought them to Aaron" (Exod. 32:3). And therefore they atoned [for their sin] with gold, [as it says] "And this is the offering that you shall take of them: gold…" (Exod. 25:2). Said the Almighty: For I will restore you to health, and I will heal you of your wounds… because they [the hostile nations] have called you an outcast (Jer. 30:17).

The Tabernacle-Oriented Portions

Obviously, the commandment to build the Tabernacle could not precede the sin of the golden calf, for which it was meant to atone. The afore-cited Midrash implies that the sin of the golden calf was fully eradicated, and the *Mishkan*, the Tabernacle of Testimony, was meant to publicize this fact to all of humanity. One might ask, why is this important to other nations and why does it even interest them? Apparently, in order for Israel to serve as "a kingdom of priests and a holy nation" (Exod. 19:6), which sets a positive example for the nations of the world and will lead them to belief in the Almighty, it is necessary for Israel itself to have an intimate relationship with the Lord.

It is thus clear why, in Rashi's opinion, the text of the Bible is not in chronological order. However, one may still ask why the story of the golden calf could not have been inserted after *Mishpatim* and before *Terumah*, which introduces the construction of the *Mishkan*? A possible answer may be gleaned from the previously quoted phrase: "For I will restore you to health, and I will heal you of your wounds" (Jer. 30:17). If the *Mishkan* is to serve as a remedy for wounds, which represent sin, it is important to show that the remedy preceded the sin and so Israel need not despair. G-d's encouragement and support lest Israel be disheartened is displayed in the Midrash on the following verse from the Song of Songs: "I am sleeping, but my heart is awake. My beloved knocks [saying]: 'Open for me, my sister, my love, my dove, my undefiled; for my head is filled with dew, my locks with the drops of the night'" (Songs 5:2). As is well known, the Midrash considers the Song of Songs to represent a love song between the Divine Spirit (the suitor) and the Jewish people (the damsel). The Midrashic exegesis of this particular verse is as follows:

I am sleeping — because of the golden calf incident [I—the Nation of Israel—have lost hope that G-d will ever forgive me for the grave sin of the golden calf].
But my heart is awake. My beloved (the Lord) [who is the heart of the Children of Israel] *knocks* — saying: They should take an offering for me.
Open for me, my sister, my love — [G-d figuratively stands outside and calls to those inside, saying:] Until when shall I walk about homeless?
For my head is filled with dew [as is wont to happen to one who is exposed to the elements]: Therefore, make me a sanctuary, so that I will not be outside (*Exod. Rabbah* 33:3).

Just as the maiden sleeps indoors and does not expect her lover to seek her, so the Nation of Israel fears that all is lost and the Almighty no longer desires an intimate relationship. G-d informs Israel by means of the Tabernacle and the Temple that the relationship can still be renewed, and perhaps even intensified.

Communicating with G-d before the Sin of the Golden Calf

Seforno explains that as soon as the Children of Israel left Egypt and experienced revelation, it was incumbent on every Jew to create a relationship between himself and the Almighty. At this stage, the communication was user-friendly—it could transpire at any place and at any time, in a direct fashion, without intermediaries or symbols. There were no holy sites; rather, the holiness permeated the environment. Seforno found a description of this state of affairs in the verses that appear at the end of *Yitro*:

The Tabernacle-Oriented Portions

- "You shall not make with [in addition to] Me gods of silver, nor should you make for yourselves gods of gold" (Exod. 20:20). Seforno: "Since you have seen that you don't need intermediaries in order to draw close to me, do not make such intermediaries."
- "An altar of earth you shall make for Me, and you shall sacrifice on it your burnt offerings, and your peace offerings, your sheep, and your oxen; in every place where I allow My name to be mentioned, I will come to you and bless you" (Exod. 20:21). Seforno: "And you will also *not* need to make temples of silver and gold and precious stones in order for me to come close to you, but an earth-filled altar will suffice."
- "And if you make Me an altar of stone, you should not build it of hewn stones (Exod. 20:22). Seforno: In order to beautify it; for if you wave your tool over it, you profane it."
- "And you should not ascend using steps on My altar, so that your nakedness not be revealed on it" (Exod. 20:23). Seforno: "Even though I will not trouble you to perform craftsmanship and beautification in order for me to dwell in your midst, nevertheless be careful not to behave frivolously at the altar."

These verses and the appended exegeses relate to the period before the sin of the golden calf, when the assumption was that each individual would be independently responsible for strengthening his character and meeting his own religious needs. In the aftermath of their sin, it became evident that the nation was susceptible to going astray unless properly guided and directed. G-d accordingly decided to institutionalize ritual behavior by appointing public servants (priests and Levites), determining a fixed place of worship (the Tabernacle and later the Temple), and specifying different types of sacrifices and their respective descriptions. These changes manifested themselves in the verses that appear (according to Rashi's opinion) right after the sin, such as:

- And let them make Me a sanctuary, that I may dwell among them (Exod. 25:8).
- And bring near to you Aaron your brother, and his sons with him, from among the Children of Israel, in order to minister to Me as priests (Exod. 28:1).

The Sin of the Generation of the Flood vs. the Sin of the Golden Calf

According to Rashi, it follows that the requirement to build a Tabernacle and later a Temple were, in a manner of speaking, not part of G-d's original plan. Similarly, it was not G-d's original intention to inundate the entire world during the time of Noah. Both were the result of man's poor behavior, which on the one hand G-d could not prevent without depriving man of his freedom of choice, but on the other hand could not ignore without endangering mankind's ability to progress in the desired direction.

There exists a parallel with regard to the consequences of both sins. Both led to a narrowing of the channels of communication between G-d and humanity. Before the flood, the heavenly interface was available to any person in any place. After the deluge, the dynasty of the patriarchs led to the establishment of "a kingdom of priests, and a holy nation" (Exod. 19:6); in other words, the scope of the Divine connection was limited to Israel. The location of the connection was also minimized. If it could originally occur anywhere in the universe, it would now be constricted to the Land of Israel exclusively, as it says: "And I will give to you and your seed after you, the land of your sojournings, all of the land of

Canaan, for an everlasting possession" (Gen. 17:8). After the sin of the golden calf, direct heavenly contact was even more greatly reduced. Instead of being accessible to all of the Children of Israel, it was granted to the tribe of Levi alone. Rather than being able to occur at any place within the boundaries of the Land of Israel, it was limited to the Tabernacle and the Temple.

One should not conclude that the Almighty meant to exclude non-Jews or non-Levites from the realm of direct communication. The changes were administrative measures exclusively—there was to be a transition to a more centralized system and the task of education was to be placed on a particular group (the Israelites), and more specifically, on a group within that group (the tribe of Levi within the twelve tribes)—but the availability of direct personal contact with the Divine was not to be impinged upon. Abarbanel (on Exod. 25:1) presents the following four guidelines that outline this approach:

1. The donation will be accepted "from every man whose heart makes him willing" (Exod. 25:2). Democracy prevails with respect to each person's relationship to the Almighty, Who provides equal opportunities to everyone. The following Midrash emphasizes this point:

    R. Samuel said: When Moses came before the Israelites and said to them: "The Lord told me 'Make Me a Tabernacle,'" the princes replied: "We will make a Tabernacle from our own donations." He [Moses] said to them: "The Lord commanded me: 'Speak to the Children of Israel, that they take for Me an offering from every man.'" The princes immediately withdrew and did not participate with the congregation.[155]

---

155. *Midrash ha-Gadol*, Exod. 35:27 (p. 568).

2. No man should be compelled to donate, as it says: "from every man whose heart makes him willing." Sincere intentions play an important role in creating a meaningful relationship with the Almighty.
3. Nobody should be asked to donate a particular item, as it says, "from every man whose heart makes him willing shall you *take* My offering." You should make no requests of them, but rather you should take what they offer. The desire to communicate with the Lord must emanate from each person's initiative, and not be the result of embarrassment or obligation.
4. If a man wishes to contribute his entire fortune, his donation will not be accepted, because irresponsible extravagance is not a virtue, but a defect. The link to the Almighty must flow from a responsible lifestyle in this world, and out of a desire to advance the standard of living, not from seclusion and asceticism.

The View of Ramban on Sacrifices and the Temple

As noted, Ramban believed that Scripture adheres to chronological order, and therefore the sin of the golden calf in *Ki Tissa* occurred after the instructions for making the Tabernacle, its vessels, and the priestly garments, which were transmitted in the preceding weekly portions. In other words, the aforementioned items reflected G-d's plan for the Children of Israel independent of the grave sin they committed later.

The Tabernacle-Oriented Portions

Functioning of the *Mishkan* before and after the Sin

Based on a question raised by *Meshech Chochmah*, even though Ramban believes that the Tabernacle was part of G-d's original plan, there might still be a difference between its mode of functioning before and after the sin of the golden calf.

At the beginning of *Vayakhel*, preceding the description of the actual production of the holy vessels, the following phrase is found: "on the seventh day you will have a holy day, a Sabbath of solemn rest to the Lord" (Exod. 35:2). Rashi comments: "He mentioned to them the prohibition of [working on] the Sabbath before the command about the building of the Tabernacle to indicate that it [building the Tabernacle] does not override the Sabbath." Asks *Meshech Chochmah*: Why should constructing the Tabernacle on the Sabbath really be prohibited? After all, in the same Tabernacle they will work on the Sabbath and slaughter sacrifices, which is permissible because it is part of the Divine service. Using *a fortiori* logic, how much more so should building the Tabernacle, whose existence enables the aforementioned slaughtering to take place, be permitted on the Sabbath. He answers that before the sin, when the Divine Presence rested in Israel without recourse to the Tabernacle, the *Mishkan* served as a means of strengthening contact with the Almighty, which had already been initiated by each Israelite who was in a sense like a priest. The building of a *Mishkan* by each Israelite at that stage was no different than the slaughtering of animals to be sacrificed by a priest. But after the sin, when holy work was localized to priests in the Tabernacle, until the Tabernacle was built, none of the activities performed were considered to be part of the holy service, and thus did not override the Sabbath.

In a similar fashion, Ramban may have believed that the *Mishkan* was intrinsic to the Jewish plan, but its functioning may have taken on a different hue after the sin of the golden calf.

Ramban's Approach Is in Harmony with His General Understanding of the Essence of Sacrifices

According to Ramban (Lev. 1:9), a sacrifice represents the ultimate expression of recognition that one has performed a sin, and it demonstrates a sincere effort to achieve absolution to the point of self-sacrifice. The Torah describes sacrifices as "a sweet savor to the Lord" (Lev. 1:9), which indicates that sacrifices have an intrinsic value. Ramban was expanding on the view of Judah ha-Levi, who wrote a hundred years before him that sacrifices are "designed to show that G-d is satisfied with the orderly lifestyle of the nation and its priests, and, so to speak, accepts their gifts and dwells in their midst as a means of honoring them" (*Kuzari* 2:25-26).

Ramban had taken issue with Rambam (*Guide* 3:32), who had declared that the main purpose of sacrifices was to wean the Nation of Israel from the widespread practice of worshipping tangible objects, while the real ideal is unadulterated prayer. Rambam contends that just as a baby suckles his mother's breast because he does not yet possess teeth and a digestive system, so the Almighty permitted the sacrificial service, but cleansed it of foreign elements and limited its scope. Specifically, He designated sheep, goats, and cows—which served as the gods of idolaters—as the only acceptable sacrifices; confined the ritual to the holy Temple; and allowed the associated ceremonies to be performed by priests exclusively.

Independent of their approaches from a philosophical point of view, Rambam and Ramban do agree on one point, namely that the requirement of a Tabernacle with the attendant sacrifices predates the sin of the golden calf.

Midrashim that Support Ramban's Approach

The following Midrashic portion (*Exod. Rabbah* 33:1) supports Ramban's view:

> Does there exist such an object that he who sells it, is purchased together with it? The Almighty said to Israel: I have sold you my Torah. I, so to speak, have been sold with it, as it says: And they should take an offering for me (Exod. 25:2) [interpreted as if it says "and they should take me" (*Matnot Kehunah*)]. This is comparable to a king who had an only daughter. One of the kings [of a foreign kingdom] came and took her [as a wife]. He requested to go to his homeland and to take his wife [with him]. He [the local king] said to him: "My daughter whom I gave to you is an only child. To separate from her, I can't; to tell you that you cannot take her [with you], I can't, because she is your wife. But do me this favor. Every place that you go, make me one room where I can live in your house, since I cannot abandon my daughter." Similarly said the Almighty to Israel. "I have given you the Torah. To separate from it I can't. To tell you that you cannot take it, I can't. But every place that you go, make one house for me to live in, as it says, 'And they shall make Me a sanctuary'" (Exod. 25:8).

According to another view,[156] it was not G-d who initiated the intimate relationship manifested in the Tabernacle, but the Israelites. As is well known, at some point when listening to the declaration of the Ten Commandments at Mt. Sinai, the Children of Israel, who had not yet reached a sufficient level of purity and holiness to experience hearing G-d's voice, requested of Moses: "You speak with us, and we will hear; but G-d should not speak with us, lest we die" (Exod. 20:16). The Talmud explains: "[The commandments] 'I' [the first word of the first commandment] and 'You shall not have' [the first words of the second commandment] were heard from the mouth of the Omnipotent," (BT *Horayot* 8a), i.e., the congregation only heard the first two commandments directly from the Lord. On the one hand, the nation could not tolerate G-d's glorious presence. On the other hand, the nation cherished G-d's proximity and intimacy, and wished for them to continue at some level. The Tabernacle option served this purpose. It is accordingly understandable why the first command issued in connection with the *Mishkan* was to make an Ark overlaid by a golden cover upon which stood the Cherubim, concerning which the text states: "I will speak to you from above the Ark-cover, from between the two Cherubim that are on the Ark of the testimony" (Exod. 25:22). The continued link between each Israelite and G-d, with Moses serving as intermediary, provided the Children of Israel with a confidence-building system of support.

It is possible that both approaches are valid. Emotional love engenders longing on the part of both partners. The mutual love between the Almighty and the Nation of Israel is described,

---

156. Menachem Liebtag, "Lessons on the Weekly Portion" (Internet), *Terumah*.

according to the sages, in the Song of Songs. This love was originally kindled by our forefather Abraham, continued to exist during the lives of the patriarchs who followed and the twelve tribes, and was rekindled once more by the events at Mt. Sinai.

Appendix I: Background for Understanding R. Tzadok ha-Kohen

R. Tzadok's explanation (*Pri Tzaddik, Tetzaveh*) of why Moses' name does not appear in the portion of *Tetzaveh* is based on the Talmudic treatment of a Biblical story that occurred during a period of tension between Israel and the Philistines. The book of Samuel describes three heroes in the service of King David, one of whom was named Shammah, whose exploits the Bible portrays as follows:

> And the Philistines were gathered together into a troop, in a plot of ground full of lentils; and the people fled from the Philistines. But he stood in the midst of the plot, and defended it, and slew the Philistines; and the Lord wrought a great victory (2 Sam. 23:11-12).

King David Yearns for Water

The Bible continues with a story of the actions of King David's warriors (when he sought refuge from King Saul by hiding in a cave),[157] which at first blush is independent of the preceding verses.

---

157. 1 Sam. 22:1-2. However, Abarbanel (2 Sam. 23:14) believes this took place after David had been crowned, as does Malbim (2 Sam. 23:13).

Background for Understanding R. Tzadok

And three of the thirty chiefs [or three chiefs of the thirty warriors][158] went down, and came to David in the harvest time to the cave of Adullam; and a company of Philistines was encamped in the valley of Rephaim. And David was then in the stronghold, and the [Philistine] officers[159] were in Bethlehem. And David desired [to drink] and said: "If only someone would give me water to drink from the well of Bethlehem, which is by the gate!" And the three mighty men broke through the Philistine camp, and drew water from the well at the gate of Bethlehem, and they carried it and brought it to David; but he did not want to drink it, and he poured it out to the Lord. And he said: "G-d forbid that I should do this; [shall I drink] the blood of the men that went in jeopardy of their lives?" and he did not want to drink it (2 Sam. 23:13-17).

On a basic exegetical level, as Radak says, this incident is self-contained. The verse states that it took place at harvest time, and this hints at the answer to two questions, namely why was David so unusually thirsty, and what were the Philistines up to? In answer to the first question, at harvest time in Israel the sun shines strongly, and it is quite possible that King David felt faint. As far as the second question is concerned, Abarbanel explains that the fear was that the Philistines intended to prematurely harvest the crops of the Israelites, taking the produce for themselves and causing hunger in Israel. The Israelites also feared that if they rushed to pick the crops without military support, the Philistines would attack them.[160]

---

158. *Metzudat David*, 2 Sam. 23:13.
159. Radak, 2 Sam. 23:14.
160. Abarbanel, 2 Sam. 23:13.

How do we explain David's behavior? Would he ask his officers to endanger themselves by penetrating the Philistine camp just to demonstrate their courage? Furthermore, his pouring the water out must have been quite demeaning to them after they risked their lives to procure it.

Three approaches may be taken. First, one might say that he was actually dying of thirst and in danger of dehydration. Water is not that plentiful in Israel, and being a native of Bethlehem with an intimate knowledge of its geography, David may have simply been pointing out the closest known source of water. However, none of the commentators have chosen this explanation. This might be because the phrase used is that "David desired," and some even translate the Hebrew as "David yearned." In other words, it sounds like it was not a matter of life and death, but a nostalgic wish for the waters of his youth. Also, under any circumstances, it would have been completely irrational of David to waste the life-saving water that had been made available to him. And finally, there do not seem to have been any repercussions from his failure to quench his thirst at this point, so it is unlikely that an emergency is being dealt with.

A second possibility is that David was day-dreaming and recalling the sweet water that he had drunk as a child. The last thing he had in mind was that someone would actually attempt to bring him that water. When he realized that that is exactly what had happened, on the one hand he was flattered at the great love and loyalty of his soldiers, but on the other hand he was quite dismayed at the risk they had taken and felt that anything obtained in such a perilous manner must be devoted to a higher purpose.[161]

Finally, Radak (2 Sam. 23:15-16) says that David actually asked for the water, apparently without properly analyzing the potential

---

161. Abarbanel, 2 Sam. 23:17.

implications of his request. Only when the warriors returned and described their adventures did he realize the potential danger to which they had been exposed, and he sincerely regretted that they had jeopardized their lives. The water may have been for drinking (but then why was it spilled out?), or it may have been needed for the ceremonial libation (pouring of water) performed on the festival of Tabernacles. At any rate, Radak is of the opinion that even the most righteous heroes in Judaism were not necessarily perfect, but were susceptible to sin. In fact, King David's renown is based not on the fact that he never transgressed, but that he was able to confess his sins and sincerely repent (2 Sam. 12:13).

Midrashic Explanation of the Biblical Episode

The Midrash (BT *Bava Kamma* 60b) takes the entire story metaphorically. The stimuli for this approach might be the questions previously enumerated concerning David's strange behavior. An allegorical explanation is readily available, because traditionally Torah has been symbolized by water. In the Bible, this may be seen from the verse "Let all the thirsty go to the water" (Isa. 55:1), that opens a chapter in which the congregation of Israel is urged to draw closer to G-d and renew their covenant with Him. In the Talmud, the verse "and they went three days in the desert and found no water" (Exod. 15:22) is used as the source for the requirement to read the Torah in intervals of three days or less because, as the Talmud says, "water can only mean Torah." (see First Overview: Intellectual Development in Exodus).

If David sought Torah knowledge, he must have had a halachic question. The Midrash accordingly explains the previously quoted words of David as follows: "give me water to drink [an answer to my question of Jewish law] from the well of Bethlehem [from the Jewish court (*bet din*)], which is by the gate [Jewish courts were generally located at the town entrance]."

The Midrash relates the halachic question to the verse preceding David's request, which mentions "a plot of ground full of lentils." The query concerned the extent to which a Jewish-owned field could be damaged, and what amount of compensation was required, if its destruction served a positive function in the military effort.

The Midrash then analyzes the meaning of David's refusal to drink the water, and his pouring it out to the Lord, as follows:

> What is the meaning of "But he would not drink thereof" [why did David not accept the answer to his halachic question]? [The meaning is] that he did not want to quote this teaching in their names [the names of those who crossed enemy lines in order to bring him a decision], for he said: "This has been transmitted to me from the court of law of Samuel of Ramah: Regarding anyone who endangers his life [in order] to attain words of Torah, no halachic matter may be quoted in his name" .... What is [the meaning of] "and he poured it out to the Lord?" — that he repeated this [halachic decision] in the name of the Talmud [general traditional learning] (BT *Bava Kamma* 61a).

Background for Understanding R. Tzadok

The Maharsha's Explanation of the Midrash

The Maharsha explains that the Midrash wishes to show that although in general one should always cite the source of innovative ideas, based on the well-known saying: "Whoever reports something in the name of the one who said it brings redemption to the world" (*Ethics of the Fathers* 6:6), here that maxim does not apply, because in order to obtain the information, the messengers transgressed a Torah law by placing their lives in jeopardy.[162] Another Talmudic principle is: "Merit is revealed [and implemented] by means of the meritorious" (BT *Bava Batra* 119b). Since the carriers of the message had sinned in the very act of transmitting the halachic decision, they were not publicly credited.

The Midrash is laying out a very significant halachic principle, namely that as important as engaging in Torah study is, one is not permitted to endanger his life in order to further his Torah knowledge. By pure logic, one is not permitted to perform any sin in order to study more Torah, because the whole point of Torah study is to purify one's soul and distance himself from sin. In fact, the Sages taught that certain activities which are not even laws of the Torah take precedence over Torah study. For example, the Talmud states:

> The father is required regarding his son to circumcise him, redeem him, teach him Torah, arrange a wife for him, and teach him a craft. Some say, even to teach him to swim. R. Judah said: He who does not teach his son a craft, teaches

---

162. BT *Sanhedrin* 74a; prohibited even if there is only a possible loss of life. See BT *Yoma* 84a.

him thievery. Thievery! Can you really think so? But it is as though he taught him thievery [since he will have no means of supporting himself] (BT *Kiddushin* 29a).

Certainly, teaching one's son a craft or how to swim are not included among the laws of the Torah, yet the father is clearly required to disengage himself from Torah study in order to accomplish these tasks. Although such activities are not *mitzvot*, not performing them could lead to the commission of sins. A broader discussion of the relationship between Torah study and working can be found in *The Ethics of Genesis*.[163]

R. Tzadok ha-Kohen's Explanation of the Midrash

In contradistinction to Maharsha, R. Tzadok ha-Kohen takes the Midrashic statement that "no halachic matter may be quoted in his name" not as censure, but as a compliment. By risking their lives, the chiefs turned into being a part of the Almighty, in a manner of speaking, and they therefore have no personal identity and cannot be cited by name. They can only be referred to as part of traditional yeshiva learning, as if they had become part of the laws taught to Moses on Mt. Sinai.

---

163. Abba Engelberg, *The Ethics of Genesis* (2014), Appendix IV.

Appendix II: Functionaries in Jewish Society in Temple Times (A Mishnah)

Although society at the time of the Temple was class-oriented, the common man still had great opportunity for advancement. The following Mishnah sheds light on the different strata of society:

> R. Simeon said: There are three crowns: the crown of Torah [scholarship], and the crown of priesthood, and the crown of royalty; and the crown of a good name rises above them.[164]

Two simple questions must be answered in order to understand the Mishnah:

1. What is the connection between a crown and Torah or priesthood?
2. Why does the Mishnah mention three crowns, and then list four?

---

164. *Ethics of the Fathers* 4:13. In some versions the reference is 4:17.

Answering the First Question

A crown is worn by a king and represents the respect that one has for a king. There is also a tinge of fear when dealing with a king, which exists even when one is not in the presence of the king, and even when one is discussing royalty in general without reference to a specific king. The Mishnah is stating that respecting the person, even when he is not present, as well as the concept, is appropriate also with regard to Torah and the priesthood. Both the scholar must be respected, as well as the Torah that he studies. Both a priest must be respected, as well as the Temple service and the pursuit of peace[165] that he performs.

Answering the Second Question

Rashi asks the second question in his commentary on this Mishnah. His answer is that the crown of a good name does not refer to an additional class of people, but to those that were mentioned previously (namely Torah scholars, priests, and kings). In the words of R. Hirsch:

> All the other three are without value unless they are linked with a crown of a good name. Any of these three crowns can be truly "crowns" only if he who wears them is deserving also of the crown of a good name, because he shines forth both as a human being and as a Jew, distinguished in moral purity and devotion to duty, and particularly in the exemplary

---

165. *Ethics of the Fathers* 1:12: Be of the disciples of Aaron, loving peace and pursuing peace, loving all (human) creatures and drawing them near to Torah.

fulfillment of those duties and those opportunities to do good that are connected with the station of honor and privilege he occupies.[166]

Rashi's answer may be strengthened by extending another comment that he makes on this Mishnah. It will be noted that the Mishnah first lists an option for every Jew, i.e. to excel in the study of Torah. The next type of person listed is a priest, which is only an option for one born into a priestly family, although many fall in this category (Abarbanel holds that this crown refers to the entire tribe of Levi, i.e., Levites as well as priests, hence an even larger group). Last to be listed is a king, which is a position that can only be occupied by one person in each generation. But after narrowing the scope from many people to only one, the Mishnah speaks of a good name, which might have the greatest scope, being that it requires neither exceptional diligence nor outstanding intelligence. However, had a good name been listed first, one might have thought that it is a category in itself, as are the other items of the Mishnah. By including it last, the author indicates that all of the preceding personages do not deserve to be honored unless, in addition to diligently fulfilling their tasks, they also behave morally and graciously.

Another reason that the crown of Torah is mentioned first could be that it applies to the crowns that follow, i.e., decisions of priests as well as kings must be informed by Torah laws and values. And finally, it should be noted that Rashi considers the crown of Torah to be the greatest of the three, specifically because of its universal availability and applicability.

---

166. *The Hirsch Siddur* (Feldheim, 1978), p. 481.

Sources for the Mishnah

Bartenura quotes the Pentateuchal verses that this Mishnah is based on.

1. Honoring Torah scholars: "You should honor an elder [in the sense of learned] person" (Lev. 19:32).
2. Honoring priests: "You should sanctify him, for he offers the bread of your G-d; he should be holy to you" (Lev. 21:8).
3. Honoring the king: "You should surely set a king over you [over you in the sense that he is feared and respected]" (Deut. 17:15).
4. A good name: "A good name is better than precious oil" (Eccl. 7:1). Rashi explains the verse as referring to Hananiah, Mishael, and Azariah, who performed good deeds, as opposed to Nadab and Abihu, who as priests had been anointed with oil. The latter were burned to death (Lev. 10:2), while the former were spared from the fire (Dan. 3:26).

The Importance of a Good Name

A priest whose behavior is not exemplary cannot properly fulfill his tasks, which may then be fulfilled (at least partially) by others, as shown by the following story:

> Our Rabbis taught: It happened with a high priest that as he left the Temple, all of the people followed him, but when they saw Shemayah and Abtalion [teachers of Hillel and Shammai (*Ethics of the Fathers* 1:12), descendants of non-Jews, who according to one tradition were descendants

of Sennacherib (BT *Gittin* 57b)], they forsook him and went after Shemayah and Abtalion. Eventually Shemayah and Abtalion visited him, to part from the high priest. He said to them: "May the descendants of heathens go in peace [Being jealous of the people's preference, he addressed them facetiously]." They answered him: "May the descendants of the heathen, who do the work of Aaron [i.e., pursuing peace], go in peace, but let the descendant of Aaron, who does not do the work of Aaron, not go in peace" (BT *Yoma* 71b)!

The Sages were even more critical of a Torah scholar who did not have a good name (i.e., one who was immoral, insincere, or had bad personal traits), as shown by the following verse from Proverbs, which seems to denounce those not possessed of intelligence: "What value is money in the hand of a fool, [if he uses it] to buy wisdom [i.e. to buy books or pay for lessons], seeing he has no understanding" (Prov. 17:16)?

The message seems to be antithetical to the Jewish belief that every person should acquire Torah, as well as worldly, knowledge to the maximum of his ability. The verse may be interpreted to mean that one should be aware of his own capacity and not waste time or money attempting to achieve goals for which he has no aptitude. Nevertheless, the rabbis felt uncomfortable putting a damper on efforts at self-improvement expended by laymen, especially since the following verse from the book of Psalms implies that even those of lesser intelligence should study Torah, so that they will become more astute: "The testimony [i.e., the Torah] of the Lord is everlasting, making the simple wise" (Ps. 19:8).

In order to reconcile the contradiction, the Talmud takes "wisdom" in the first verse to mean Torah knowledge, and "understanding" to mean moral behavior, leading to the following interpretation of the verse: "What value is money in the hand of a fool, [if he uses it] to buy *wisdom* [Torah knowledge], seeing he has no *understanding* [fear of G-d or moral behavior]." Clearly, he doesn't really understand the deeper meaning of the Torah (and is thus a fool in some sense of the word) if he doesn't realize that Torah only has value if one abides by its rules. In the words of the Talmud:

> Woe unto the enemies of the scholars [a euphemism for scholars] who occupy themselves with the Torah, but have no fear of heaven! R. Jannai proclaimed: Woe unto he who has no court, but makes a gateway for his court (BT *Yoma* 72b).

The court refers to the desired goal, i.e., fear of G-d, moral behavior, and observing the *mitzvot*. The gateway refers to the Torah learning that is supposed to pave the way to achieve that goal. The analogy to a court is especially relevant to the Jewish religion, which is unique in requiring all of its members to study Jewish law, even if they have no intention of becoming rabbis or legal counselors.

Not only is Torah knowledge not beneficial if it does not make one into a moral person—it is even deleterious. This idea is brought out by the continuation of the Talmudic discussion:

> R. Joshua b. Levi said: What is the meaning of the Scriptural verse: And this is *the law that Moses placed* [before the Children of Israel] (Deut. 4:44)? If he is meritorious, it becomes for him a medicine of life, if not, a deadly poison. That is what Rava [meant when he] said: If he uses it the right way, it is a medicine of life; if he does not use it the right way, it is a medicine of death [poison].

Maharsha explains that the Talmud is baffled by the phrase "the law that Moses placed." It should have said the law that Moses taught. The word "placed" implies that one is speaking of a physical object, while even the written law was mostly transmitted orally, and Moses must have spent most of his time explaining the meaning of the various regulations. The Talmud therefore concludes that the word "placed" must have been chosen because of some lesson that it wishes to teach. It turns out that the Hebrew word for "placed" is *sam*, which can also mean "medicine" or "drug" (with a slightly different spelling), and this serves as the basis of the Talmudic homily.

Appendix III: Incense and the Priestly Mission

Incense as a Remedy

The book of Numbers describes the rebellion of Korah and his company, and the subsequent destruction of the families of the rebels and 250 of Korah's followers. When the congregation then accused Moses and Aaron of being responsible for the great loss of life, G-d, so to say, lost patience and threatened to annihilate the entire nation, at which point the text states:

> And Moses said unto Aaron: "Take the censer, and put fire in it from the altar, and add incense, and take it quickly to the congregation, and make atonement for them; for anger has issued from the Lord: the plague has begun." And Aaron took [the censer] as Moses spoke, and ran into the midst of the assembly; and, behold, the plague had begun [to strike] among the people; and he put the incense on it, and made atonement for the people. And he stood between the dead and the living, and the plague was stopped. And the [number of] dead by the plague were fourteen thousand and seven hundred, besides the dead

Incense and the Priestly Mission

in the matter of Korah. And Aaron returned to Moses to the door of the Tent of Meeting, and the plague had been stopped (Num. 7:11-15).

The Talmud (BT *Shabbat* 88b-89a), wondering how Moses knew the remedy for the deadly plague, presents the following Midrash:

> R. Joshua b. Levi also said: When Moses ascended to heaven, the ministering angels said to the Lord, "Sovereign of the universe, what is one born of a woman doing among us?" He said to them, "He has come to receive the Torah." They said to Him, "That secret treasure, which has been hidden by You for nine hundred and seventy-four generations before the world was created, You wish to give to flesh and blood?" ... The Lord said to Moses "Give them an answer" ... He spoke before Him: "Sovereign of the universe, the Torah that You are giving me, what is written in it? 'I am the Lord your G-d, who brought you out of the Land of Egypt' (Exod. 20:2). He said to them [the angels], 'Did you go down to Egypt? Were you enslaved to Pharaoh? Why should the Torah be yours? Again, what is written in it? 'You shall have no other gods' (Exod. 20:3). Do you dwell among peoples who engage in idol-worship? Again, what is written in it? 'Remember the Sabbath day, to keep it holy' (Exod. 20:8). Do you then perform work, that you need to rest? Again what is written in it? 'You shall not take [the name of the Lord your G-d in vain]' (Exod. 20:7). Are there business dealings among you [in connection with which you might swear falsely]? Again, what is written in it? 'Honor your father and your mother' (Exod. 20:12). Have you fathers and mothers? Again,

what is written in it? 'You shall not murder. You shall not commit adultery. You shall not steal' (Exod. 20:13-15). Is there jealousy among you? Is the evil inclination [*yetzer hara*] found among you?" They immediately conceded to the Lord.... Immediately each one started loving him [Moses] and gave him something.... Also the angel of death gave him something, for it says: "and he put the incense on it, and made atonement for the people" (Num. 17:12) and it says: "and he stood between the dead and the living" (Num. 17:13). Had he [the angel of death] not told it to him [Moses], would he have known it?

In short, Moses was informed of the ability of incense to serve as a remedy by the angel of death himself, all of which demonstrates that Satan and the angel of death represent no more than G-d's outstretched arm.

INCENSE AS A SYMBOL

The Talmud states:

Any fast in which none of the sinners of Israel participate, is no fast [i.e., they may not be excluded as unworthy of joining their fellow-Jews in prayer], for behold the odor of galbanum is unpleasant, and yet it was included among the spices for the incense (BT *Keritot* 6b).

The galbanum accordingly represents the transgressors of Israel, and Aaron was assigned the task of befriending them and serving as a positive influence. The beginning of *Tetzaveh* speaks of olive

Incense and the Priestly Mission

oil used for light. As previously mentioned, light symbolizes Torah, whose content Aaron is here requested to spread among all strata of the congregation.

In the words of R. Tzadok:

> As is known, out of the eleven ingredients of the incense, galbanum has an unpleasant odor, and by mixing it with the ten ingredients having a pleasant odor, the galbanum itself turns into being sweet-smelling, and from here it was learned to include the sinners of Israel in the prayer gatherings on fast days, and this is because even a soul that has already degenerated into evil [like the galbanum] can be changed into being good by joining a company [*minyan*] of Israel in fellowship, which is made up of ten [symbolized by the sweet-smelling ingredients].... And behold this portion records all of the preparations of Aaron the priest to bring the souls of Israel closer by implanting in their hearts the light of holiness for each soul, in proportion to his willingness and desire to come close to holiness with the commandment as a candle, and the Torah as light (Prov. 6:23), and this is [explains] the beginning of the portion [of *Tetzaveh*] with oil and candle, so it seems to me. And it finishes with the section describing the incense altar and this represents the goal of also bringing close to holiness the souls that have sunk into evil [ways] and their hearts don't turn toward holiness. Still, there is hope that they will return to being good by joining them with [those who encourage] holiness, and this is the attribute of Aaron: loving peace... and drawing them near to Torah (*Ethics of the Fathers* 1:12), and therefore a crown was made for it [the incense altar], which alludes to the crown

of the priesthood, which Aaron was awarded forever and always (*Pri Tzaddik, Tetzaveh* 11).

Interestingly, incense is here shown to embody G-d's attribute of mercy, in spite of the fact that with regard to Nadab and Abihu, the same incense manifested G-d's attribute of strict justice.[167] Perhaps R. Tzadok understands this conundrum to imply that just as Nadab and Abihu were not allowed to deviate from their instructions, so Aaron was forbidden to deviate from his instructions, which were that he be the merciful intermediary between the nation and G-d.

---

167. As Rashi (Num. 17:13) says, this indicates that it was not the incense that killed them, but the sin. The idea of the same object being prohibited in one place and permitted in another has already been seen with regard to the Cherubim, which were graven images; the priestly garments, which could be made of *shaatnez*; and the slaughter of animals on the Sabbath for the daily sacrifices.

Appendix IV: Arbitration in Jewish Law – Moses vs. Aaron

Arbitration (*pesharah*) is defined as a process of settling an argument or disagreement in which the people on both sides present their opinions and ideas to a third party, who then tries to find a resolution acceptable to both sides. At first blush, one would assume that Judaism, which highly values peace and harmony among mankind (Rambam, *Hilchot Chanukah* 4:14), would very much favor this method of settling arguments. But things are not that simple. Judaism is peculiar when compared to other religions in that its laws, both people-oriented and G-d-oriented, serve as the centerpiece of the religion, and one of the laws, which is actually unlimited in scope, is to spend as much time as possible studying all of the other laws, as well as that law itself. But arbitration means neglecting to seek a decision based on the letter of the law, and instead looking for a solution that satisfies both disputants. By arbitrating, one is in a certain sense slighting the law, and in another sense weakening the motivation, as well as the benefit, of studying the law.

The Talmudic Discussion

The Talmud (BT *Sanhedrin* 6b) contrasts the method used by Moses to settle civil disagreements with that which was typically used by his brother Aaron. The Biblical phrase chosen to reflect the approach of Moses is, translated literally: "He who praises the robber, disgraces the Almighty" (Ps. 10:3). The Talmud, for its purposes, translates it metaphorically as: "He who praises the arbitrator, disgraces the Almighty." In other words, it is preferable to adhere to the minutiae of *halachah* (Jewish law) than to reach a compromise. The justification for replacing the Hebrew word for "robber" with "arbitrator" is that by arbitrating, one who lawfully should get a certain amount is now (according to the terms of the arbitration) losing that money, i.e., it is as if the arbitrator stole from one of the litigants and gave to the other.[168]

Aaron, on the other hand, is characterized by a verse from the prophet Malachi that describes the desired behavior of priests (*kohanim*): "Instruction of truth was in his mouth, and injustice was not found in his lips; *he walked with Me in peace and integrity,* and returned many from sin" (Mal. 2:6). The Talmud's view is that arbitration is more likely to lead to peace than a court decision, since it is based on the mutual agreement of the litigants. In reference to the previously cited verses, the Talmud states:

> R. Eliezer the son of R. Jose the Galilean says: It is forbidden to arbitrate, and anyone who arbitrates is a sinner, and whoever praises the arbitrator disgraces the Almighty, for it is written: "He who praises the arbiter, disgraces the Almighty," but let the law cut through the mountain [i.e., take its course, even if it is harsh]. And so Moses was wont to say: "Let the law cut through the mountain, as is written, 'For the judgment is G-d's'" (Deut. 1:17). But Aaron loved peace and pursued peace and made peace between one man and his friend, as it is written: "Instruction of truth

---

168. Rif, *Ein Yaakov*, Sanhedrin 6b.

was in his mouth, and injustice was not found in his lips; he walked with Me in peace and integrity, and returned many from sin" (BT *Sanhedrin* 6b).

On the simplest level, Moses and Aaron differed as to whether arbitration is permitted. In actuality, however, the gap between them was much smaller and limited itself to a difference in outlook. Clearly, before approaching a court, arbitration was permitted (even if Moses was not overjoyed by the prospect). Hence, they both agreed that Aaron had a right to mollify disputants before they ever went to court (Rashi's view), or even after, as the prohibition was only for judges, and Aaron was not a judge (Tosafot). Furthermore, even Aaron would have agreed that after a court issues a verdict, arbitration is inappropriate. The only stage at which they disagreed was after the litigants had arrived in court, but before the final verdict was issued.

The following passage clarifies the Talmudic view that peace and strict halachic decisions are not usually compatible.

> R. Joshua b. Korcha says: Settlement by arbitration is a mitzvah, for it is written: "Truth and peaceful judgment should be executed in your gates" (Zech. 8:16). Surely, where there is strict justice there is no peace, and where there is peace, there is no strict justice! But what is that kind of justice which is also peaceful? One must say: It is arbitration. And so, regarding David it says "And David executed justice and charity towards all his people" (2 Sam. 8:15). But every place where there is strict justice, there is no charity, and [where there is] charity there is no justice! But what is that kind of justice which is also peaceful? One must say: It is arbitration... Rav says: the *halachah* is in agreement with R. Joshua b. Korcha (BT *Sanhedrin* 6b).

The Talmud has arrived at a strange conclusion. On the one hand, the finalized law is that even after arriving in court, it is not only permitted, but recommended, that the judges inform the litigants of the possibility of arbitration. On the other hand, Moses is said to have looked askance at this option. Would the Rabbis negate the opinion of Moses? Netziv explains that once the basic outline of the final decision is clear, arbitration is not acceptable even according to R. Joshua. But Moses was so knowledgeable and brilliant that once the litigants presented their arguments, he immediately knew what the appropriate decision was, and therefore arbitration was improper. For almost everyone else, that clarity of knowledge does not exist, and there is thus ample opportunity to resort to arbitration.[169]

The Talmud then relates to Aaron's behavior with the golden calf. Before delving into the Talmudic discussion, it is suggested that one read Appendix V: THE DESTRUCTION OF THE TEMPLE WAS IN RETRIBUTION FOR KILLING A PROPHET.

The Talmud claims that Aaron was, in a sense, making a compromise:

> R. Tanhum b. Hanilai says: this verse [see next section, RASHI VS. TOSAFOT, for a discussion of which verse is being referred to] was said only with reference to the story of the golden calf, for it says: "And Aaron saw and built an altar before it" (Exod. 32:5). What did he actually see? R. Benjamin b. Japhet says that R. Elazar said: He saw Hur lying slain before him,[170] and said [to himself]: If I do

---

169. Netziv, *Harchev Davar*, Exod. 18:23.
170. The Hebrew words in the verse quoted are *va-yiven mizbe'ach*, "he built an altar." They can also be read *va-yiven mi-zavu'ach*, "he understood from he who had been slain."

not listen to them now, they will do to me as they did to Hur, and it will be fulfilled in me [the words of Jeremiah], "Shall the priest and the prophet be slain in the Sanctuary of G-d?" (Lam. 2:20),[171] and they will never be forgiven. Better they should worship the golden calf, perhaps they will achieve forgiveness through repentance.

The Talmud is explaining Aaron's involvement with the golden calf. In concurrence with previously cited Midrashim, there is no suspicion that Aaron attached any sanctity to it. His belief in G-d was not inferior to that of Moses. He also did not fear dying a martyr's death in the same manner as Miriam's son, his nephew Hur, who was killed by the mob. His only worry concerned the negative consequences that would accrue to Israel as a result of their rebellion. There exists a principle that was apparently already established at this early stage, namely, that the sin of killing a priest is unforgivable. On the other hand, as bad as it is to worship idols, doing so constitutes a sin for which one may repent and be forgiven. Aaron therefore chose to permit Israel to transgress the latter sin, which held out the possibility of repentance, which is what Aaron hoped would eventually occur.

Regarding the prohibition of killing a priest, *Iyun Yaakov* (BT *Sanhedrin* 6b) asks a simple question. As has been noted, the Temple service was originally designated for the firstborn. Everything changed after the sin of the golden calf. But at this stage, the sin had not even taken place, which means that Aaron was not yet a priest, and so the prohibition had not yet taken effect. He answers that in fact the high priesthood was transferred from

---

171. The series of events leading to the destruction of the First Temple is said to have been initiated by the slaying of a priest. See BT *Gittin* 57b, *Sanhedrin* 96b.

Moses to Aaron from the time that Moses had been reluctant to fulfill his G-d-given mission to lead the Children of Israel out of Egypt,[172] which took place before the exodus. At that stage, Aaron's helpers were meant to be the firstborn, and that is what changed as a result of the sin. Instead of the firstborn being the common priests, it was the descendants of Aaron who served that function.

Rashi vs. Tosafot

A very important question is, which verse does R. Tanhum use to characterize the creation of the golden calf? Is it the one associated with Moses, which condemns the arbitrator ("He who praises the arbitrator, disgraces the Almighty"), or is it the one associated with Aaron, which praises the arbitrator ("he walked with Me in peace and integrity")? The answer will determine whether compromise is highly acclaimed, even with regard to questions of religious practice, or whether it is applicable only to financial disputes between people. The former view is supported by Tosafot, while the latter approach is taken by Rashi.

Rashi's View

Me'iri succinctly summarizes Rashi's viewpoint: "Although compromise is recommended with respect to monetary disputes, regarding religious prohibitions this is not so, and the judge should not say we will permit him [to eat] this so that he won't eat that" (on BT *Sanhedrin* 7a).

Me'iri distinguishes between money matters, regarding which one can concede his own material wealth for the higher purpose of

---

172. BT *Zevachim* 102a, based on Exod. 4:14.

promulgating peace in this world, as opposed to spiritual matters, concerning which proper behavior has been legislated by G-d, and which are therefore not in the purview of any individual to amend.

One may ask, however, regarding what sin was Aaron attempting to compromise? It would seem that he was not required to rebuke the nation as his nephew Hur did, for it is written: "Just as it is a *mitzvah* for a person to rebuke his friend and tell him something that he is likely to accept [and obey], so it is a *mitzvah* not to tell him something that he is unlikely to accept" (BT *Yevamot* 65b). After murdering Hur, it was quite evident that the nation was not in a mood to act positively as a result of Aaron's censure, so the Talmudic maxim that the right thing to do is to refrain from rebuke seems perfectly reasonable.

Note, however, that independent of any warning which Aaron should or should not have conveyed to the nation, he himself was forbidden to help create the golden calf, even if he had no intention of worshipping it, since doing so falls in the category of manufacturing accessories to be used for idol-worship. Even though such acts are not punishable by death, if an attempt is made to force one to produce such items, the Code of Law[173] (*Shulchan Aruch*) requires one not to submit, even upon threat of death. In addition, the law is the same also with respect to minor sins that one is forced to commit in the public domain.[174] It is thus clear which sin Aaron transgressed.

Tosafot's View

Tosafot believes that Aaron acted properly, explaining: "He stimulated many to repent from a sin for which repentance

---

173. *Yoreh De'ah* 157:1.
174. BT *Sanhedrin* 74a. See also *Iyun Yaakov* on *Sanhedrin* 7a.

is available." The meaning of Tosafot is that Aaron was not compromising on what G-d expects of man, but attempting to meet His expectation. In this particular situation, there was an apparent conflict between two commands—that which forbids the worshipping of idols and that which commands one to love his fellow man, certainly not to kill him, and even more—not to do so if he is a priest or a prophet. When forced to choose between them, Aaron chose to permit the transgression of the more serious sin, but the one for which it was possible to repent, and he did so because of his great love for his fellow man.[175]

Tosafot is illustrating an important concept in Judaism, namely that Jews are not in a contest with each other to see who arrives in the next world with the most points, but rather are involved in a group effort to maximize the observance of G-d's commands in this world, and this is what the Sages meant when they coined the phrase: "All Jews are responsible for each other."[176] And this is the idea that *Iyun Yaakov*,[177] when explaining Tosafot, wishes to stress when he justifies Aaron's actions because they were meant to save the Nation of Israel, even if they seemingly weakened his own personal balance of *mitzvot*.

Tosafot, as it appears in *Ein Yaakov* (collection of aggadic material in the Talmud), notes that according to Rashi, Aaron is being criticized; yet the Talmudic passage at no point expresses disapproval of his behavior, which would imply that the Talmud agrees with the approach of Tosafot. R. Yoshiyahu Pinto[178] goes even further by interpreting R. Eliezer, who contrasts the behavior of Moses and Aaron, as intending to emphasize that Moses and

---

175. Yuval Cherlo, "*Ha-titachen pesharah be-dinei shamayim?*" (Internet).
176. BT *Sanhedrin* 27b; *Sifra Bechukotai* 7:5.
177. BT *Sanhedrin* 7a.
178. *Rif, Ein Yaakov, Sanhedrin* 6b.

Aaron did not at all argue, since Moses spurned arbitration in monetary cases, while Aaron encouraged it specifically in spiritual matters, where it was appropriate in his opinion.

Of course, Rashi's view is that in spite of the emotional appeal of Tosafot's logic, the law states explicitly that one must allow himself to be killed rather than perform one of the three cardinal sins. Indeed, according to Tosafot, when is martyrdom applicable? Based on the afore-cited *Iyun Yaakov*, one might answer that martyrdom is only appropriate if the enforcer is a Gentile. If the enforcer is a Jew (here the entire nation), one must take into account what is best for him (or them)—as was done in this case, where Aaron considered their welfare as well as his own.

Another commentator[179] distinguishes between a typical case of martyrdom and the case of Aaron. In the present situation, even if Aaron would have been killed, the sin of the golden calf would have taken place. In essence, the difference is between the case of one being forced to worship idols, where the idols will not be worshipped if he is killed, and the case of being forced to help someone else worship idols, where the idol will be worshipped no matter what, so nothing is to be gained by martyrdom.

Modern Applications

Most modern day adjudicators tend toward the approach of Rashi, and do not allow compromises on religious matters, even if there is a possibility that such a compromise would be good in the long run for the Jewish religion. For example, it has been asked whether a religious political party in Israel could support legislation prohibiting work-related activities on the Sabbath, but allowing

---

179. Chanoch Gebhard, *Shiurim be-Aggadot Chazal*.

public transportation and places of entertainment to be open. When such a question was posed to R. Isaac Herzog, chief rabbi of Israel (1936-59), he replied that *halachah* knows of only one situation which allows desecrating the Sabbath, and that is where there is danger to life. Nevertheless, based on the assumption that such legislation would actually reduce the amount of Sabbath desecration, while making life for the non-Orthodox population more bearable, he was willing to allow political representatives of Orthodox parties to support such laws.[180]

A second case occurred in New York in 1964, when R. Shlomo Riskin was offered the position of rabbi at the Lincoln Square Synagogue, which did not have a *mechitzah*, the partition between the men's and women's sections. After consulting with R. J.B. Soloveitchik, it was decided that for a period of six months the rabbi would pray at an early service in a completely Orthodox synagogue, and only afterwards would he lead the service at Lincoln Square, where he would deliver a sermon and officiate as rabbi. If by the end of the trial period he had not convinced the congregation to set up the required barrier, he would resign. The project succeeded, and not only did that *shul* become one of the leading Orthodox synagogues in America, but a significant number of congregants moved to Israel with their rabbi and established a successful community that is today a large and important city in Israel called Efrat.[181]

It should be noted that in the aforementioned cases, the rabbis involved did not permit a forbidden act. They merely allowed borderline behavior that would not normally be tolerated had there not been a good reason to do so.

---

180. Ohad Fixler, *Pesharah she-einah be-dinei mamonot*, VBM.
181. Shlomo Riskin, *Listening to G-d* (2010).

Appendix V: The Destruction of the Temple Was in Retribution for Killing a Prophet

Review of Some Biblical Events

Soon after the First Temple was built, the kingdom split into two. In the kingdom of Judea, the kings were of the Davidic dynasty, each king generally being succeeded by one of his sons. In the kingdom of Israel, which originated when Jeroboam revolted against Solomon's son, Rehoboam, the dynasties rarely lasted more than three generations, since most of the kings were wicked and the Lord did not allow their families to rule in peace for long. The initiator of one of these lines of descent was a military hero named Omri (ca. 887 BCE) and it continued with his son Ahab, followed by Ahab's son Ahaziah, who died after two years and was succeeded by his brother Jehoram. The prophetic author of the book of Kings, Jeremiah, considered all of the kings of this line (as well as most of the other lines) to be wicked, but Ahab was declared the most wicked of all (1 Kings 16:30), and his depraved wife Jezebel, under whose influence he committed the atrocity against Naboth the Jezreelite, made things even worse.

The Ethics of Exodus

Meanwhile, in the Judean kingdom, kingship was passed from father to son. Following Rehoboam were Abijam, who reigned for three years, Asa (forty-one years), and Jehoshaphat (twenty-five years). The former two were not considered to be righteous, but the latter two were. However, Jehoshaphat did make one serious error, which had long-term repercussions. He joined forces with Ahab in battling the king of Aram (1 Kings 22:4), thus initiating a close relationship with the evil Kingdom of Israel. This eventually led to the marriage of Joram, the son and heir of Jehoshaphat, to Athaliah, the daughter of King Ahab and Jezebel (2 Kings 8:18). Not surprisingly, Joram, influenced by his wife and her family, did not follow in the path of his father and grandfather. When Joram died, his son Ahaziah became the next king of Judea. When Ahaziah went to visit Jehoram, king of Israel, after the latter had been injured in battle against Hazael, king of Aram, both Ahaziah and Jehoram were assassinated by Jehu, who then became king of Israel.[182]

At this stage, Athaliah had lost her husband the king, and her stepson the king, and she herself craved dominion. In order to improve her chances of eventually ruling, since she was not in the line of succession, she decided to kill anyone with a legitimate claim, e.g. the brothers of her husband Joram and of her stepson Ahaziah, possibly including children or grandchildren of her own. Ahaziah had an infant son, Joash, who was saved from Athaliah's wrath by Ahaziah's full sister, named Jehosheba (2 Kings 11:1-3). Her husband, Jehoiada, being the high priest, had access to the Temple, where Joash was hidden until he was seven years old, at which time he was crowned king and Athaliah was killed. This seems to be the first incident in which priests assumed a political, and not merely a clerical, function. Having been brought up

---
182. 2 Kings 8:28-29, 9:24-29.

under the guidance of the high priest, Joash became a righteous king (2 Kings 12:3).

According to the book of Kings, Joash was assassinated at the age of forty-seven, with no explanation offered (2 Kings 12:21). The missing details are supplied by a Midrash and a number of verses in the book of Chronicles.

The Midrash[183] states:

> You find that all of the time that Jehoiada was alive, Joash obeyed the will of his Creator, for it says: "And Joash did that which was right in the eyes of the Lord all his days, as Jehoiada the priest had instructed him" (2 Kings 12:3).

The Midrash sees a link between the good behavior of Joash and the instruction supplied by Jehoiada, implying that when the latter was no longer living, the former's good deeds also ceased, as if the words "all his days" refer to all the days of Jehoiada.

But where does Scripture imply that Joash sinned? In discussing the last years of the life of Joash, the Bible states: "And after the death of Jehoiada, the princes of Judea came, and prostrated themselves before the king. Then the king listened to them" (2 Chron. 24:17).

When the verse says that "the king listened to them," the Midrash[184] wonders, what was there to listen to? All that the princes had done was bow down to him; no verbal exchange is mentioned. The Midrash comes to the conclusion that they must have said something related to the fact that they prostrated themselves. The Midrash continues:

---

183. *Tanchuma, Masei* 12; *Num. Rabbah* 23:13.
184. *Exod. Rabbah* 8:2.

They made him into a god. They said to him, "If you were not a god, you would not have been able to emerge alive after seven years in the Holy of Holies." He said to them, "So it is," and he took it upon himself to be made into a god, and so corrupted his soul.

Joash had been hidden in the Holy of Holies until he was seven. Now the princes said to him: [It says in the Torah that] "the commoner who comes near [to the Holy of Holies] will die."[185] Furthermore, even the high priest could only enter on the Day of Atonement in a cloud of incense and prayer, in special garments and after being ritually immersed. They told him, "If you survived without all of that, you must indeed be a god."[186]

How was his soul corrupted? First, it was corrupted by what he did. Second, it was corrupted by the depraved punishment that was visited upon him (see further).

THE SINS OF JOASH

Making Joash into a god cleared the way for the princes' complete retrogression to idol-worship, with the nation following soon after. This obviously angered the Almighty: "And they forsook the house of the Lord, the G-d of their fathers, and they served the Asherim and the idols; and [G-d's] wrath came upon Judea and Jerusalem for this, their guiltiness" (2 Chron. 24:18).

G-d warned them to cease their destructive behavior, to no avail: "And He sent prophets to them, to bring them back to the Lord; and they admonished them, but they did not listen" (2 Chron. 24:19).

---

185. Num. 1:51, 3:10, 3:38, 18:7.
186. *Matnot Kehunah*, Exod. Rabbah 8:2.

Temple's Destruction as Retribution

In addition to the prophets whom G-d had sent, Zechariah the son of Jehoiada (the benefactor of Joash) felt urged by a G-dly spirit to reprimand the people: "And the spirit of G-d came upon Zechariah the son of Jehoiada the priest; and he stood above the people, and said to them: 'So says G-d: Why do you transgress the commandments of the Lord, and you will not succeed? Because you have forsaken the Lord, He has also forsaken you'" (2 Chron. 24:20).

After initiating their decline to idol-worship, Joash compounded his sins by instigating the murder of Zechariah: "And they conspired against him, and they stoned him with stones at the commandment of the king in the court of the house of the Lord" (2 Chron. 24:21).

In addition to idol-worship and murder, Joash displayed a total lack of gratitude by murdering the son of his savior Jehoiada. Zechariah, on his death bed, demanded that G-d avenge his death. These points are summarized in the following verse:

> And Joash the king did not remember the kindness that Jehoiada his father had done to him, but he slew his son. And when he died, he [Zechariah] said: "The Lord should look upon it [my murder], and demand [punishment of its perpetrators]" (2 Chron. 24:22).

The Punishment of Joash

Aram then viciously attacked the nation, as indicated below:

> And next year the army of the Arameans came up against him; and they came to Judea and Jerusalem, and destroyed [only] the princes of the people from among [all of] the

people, and they sent all of their spoils to the king of Damascus (2 Chron. 24:23).

The following verse introduces a miraculous element to the defeat of Judea, namely that it was accomplished by an unusually small force, as if to emphasize that it was not a natural occurrence, but a preternatural one, implemented by G-d as punishment for Joash's three sins (idol-worship, murder, and lack of gratitude):

> For the army of the Arameans came with a small company of men; and the Lord delivered into their hand a very great host, because they had forsaken the Lord, the G-d of their fathers (2 Chron. 24:24).

The Midrash explains that the judgment executed upon Joash was particularly demeaning. He was said to have been the victim of homosexual rape:[187] "and they executed judgment upon Joash… they left him with great diseases" (2 Chron. 24:24-25). The Midrash links the word "diseases" with desecration of his honor.

The Arameans violated and fatally injured him, but it was his servants who finished the job, as the verse states:

> And when they were departed from him… his own servants conspired against him for the blood of the sons [note the plural[188]] of Jehoiada the priest, and slew him on his bed, and he died (2 Chron. 24:25).

---

187. *Mechilta Beshallach, Masechta de-Amalek, parashah* Aleph.
188. Radak intimates that Joash may have killed other sons of Jehoiada in addition to Zechariah.

In addition to being tortured and defiled before death, he was punished after death by not being accorded a king's burial: "and they buried him in the city of David, but they did not bury him in the sepulchers of the kings" (2 Chron. 24:25).

Talmudic and Midrashic Sources Relating to the Killing of Zechariah

The Midrash makes two points about the killing of Zechariah.

1. It took place in the holiest area of the Temple, namely the priestly court (the court where the sanctuary and outer altar stood, where only priests were allowed entry, as opposed to the courts where non-priests were permitted to tread). In addition to the severity of the deed, the Midrash stresses the disrespect for the Jewish religion and its holiest sites.
2. A second sign of disgraceful behavior was the condition in which the body was abandoned. The Midrash states:

> They did not treat his blood even as the blood of the gazelle or the blood of the hart, regarding which the Torah states "He should pour out its blood and cover it with dust" (Lev. 17:13), but with respect to Zechariah the righteous… they poured it on the stones.[189]

The Midrash stresses once more the intimate connection between laws relating to G-d and those relating to man. Neglecting or transgressing one in the first category (e.g., the deification of Joash) quickly leads to contempt of those in the second (e.g., the slaying of Zechariah), and vice versa.

---
189. *Eccl. Rabbah* 3:16.

The Importance of Being Modest

An interesting aside is that although one's sympathy is with Zechariah, whom the previous Midrash designated as "the righteous," it did not refrain from criticizing negative attributes that it found in his persona, independent of how great he was considered to be. Accordingly, in examining the phrase used when Zechariah chastised the people, namely "and he stood above the people" (2 Chron. 24:20), the Midrash has the following to say:

> Did he then walk above people's heads? But he saw himself as greater than the populace, as a cousin of the king [his mother being the aunt of Joash], a priest, a prophet, and a judge. He started speaking condescendingly, and said to them: "Why do you transgress the commandments of the Lord, and you will not succeed? Because you have forsaken the Lord, He has also forsaken you" (2 Chron. 24:20). Immediately [the next verse states] And they conspired against him, and they stoned him with stones at the commandment of the king in the court of the house of the Lord.[190]

Rambam, after incorporating in his code of law that "the right way is the middle degree of each trait among those common to humanity" (*Hilchot De'ot* 1:4), proceeds to declare (*Hilchot De'ot* 2:3):

> There are some traits for which it is forbidden for a person to merely keep to the middle path, but he should distance

---
190. *Eccl. Rabbah* 10:4.

himself to the opposite extreme, and such [a trait] is pride, for the right way is not that a person should just be modest, but that he should be humble-minded and lowly of spirit to the utmost. And therefore it said of Moses that he was "exceedingly modest" (Num. 12:3), not merely that he was "modest." Hence, our sages exhorted us: "Be most exceedingly humble-minded" (*Ethics of the Fathers* 4:4). They also said that anyone who permits his heart to swell with haughtiness has denied the essential principle of our religion, as it says: "And your heart will be proud, and you will forget the Lord your G-d" (Deut. 8:14).

The Destruction of the First Temple

The Talmud relates the story of the murder of Zechariah to the destruction of the First Temple, as described in the following narrative:

> R. Hiya b. Abin said in the name of R. Joshua b. Korhah: An old man, from the inhabitants of Jerusalem, told me that in this valley Nebuzaradan, the master butcher, killed two hundred and eleven myriads [2,110,000], and in Jerusalem he killed ninety-four myriads [940,000] on one stone, until their blood went and joined that of Zechariah, to fulfill the words, "Blood touched blood."[191] He noticed the blood of Zechariah boiling and bubbling. He said: "What is this?" They said: "It is the blood of the sacrifices that spilled." He had some blood brought, but it was not similar. He [then] said to them: "If you tell me [the

---

191. Hos. 4:2. The blood of those murdered in Jerusalem flowed into the blood of those killed in the valley, as well as into the blood of Zechariah.

truth], good, but if not, I will tear your flesh with combs of iron." They said: "What can we say to you? There was a prophet among us who used to reprove us with words from heaven; we rose up against him and killed him, and for many years his blood has not stopped [bubbling]." He said to them: "I will appease him." He brought the great Sanhedrin [of 71] and the small Sanhedrin [of 23] and killed them for [the injustice done to] him, but it did not stop [i.e., it continued bubbling]. Young men and women he slaughtered for him, but it did not stop. He brought school-children and slaughtered them for him, but it did not stop. He said: "Zechariah, Zechariah. The best of them I have destroyed; do you want me to destroy them all?" When he said this to him, it stopped. At that moment Nebuzaradan thought in his mind to repent. He said to himself: "If such is the penalty for slaying one soul, what will happen to a person [me] who has slain such multitudes?" He ran away, sent home a will to dispose of his effects, and became a convert (BT *Gittin* 57b).

The Talmud proceeds to enumerate a number of former enemies whose progeny converted and became great scholars, such as the grandsons of Haman, who are said to have learned Torah in Bnei Berak; Sisera, whose descendants taught children in Jerusalem; and Shemaya and Abtalion, who were descendants of Sennacherib and gave public expositions of the Torah. Perhaps the moral is that any person can repent, find the right path, and be forgiven, if he only tries hard enough. Of course, if people who are essentially good persecuted Israel, that also indicates that in some sense they must have been G-d's messengers to exact the punishment that G-d wished to mete out.

The link between the murder of Zechariah and the destruction of the Temple is introduced in the following Midrashic text:

> It was told concerning Doeg b. Joseph, who passed away, leaving a small son to [be taken care of by] his mother, that she would measure him by handbreadths every year and would give his [extra] weight in gold to the Sanctuary. And when Jerusalem was besieged, she slaughtered him with her own hands and ate him, and concerning her Jeremiah lamented: "Shall the women eat their fruit, their children that are still in their hands?" (Lam. 2:20). Whereupon the Holy Spirit replied [the continuation of the verse], saying: "Shall a priest and a prophet be slain in the Sanctuary of the Lord?" — this is Zechariah b. Jehoiada.[192]

Concerning the slaying of Zechariah, the Midrash magnifies the enormity of the act when it states:

> R. Yuden said: They transgressed seven sins on that day: they killed a priest, and a prophet, and a judge, and they spilled innocent blood, they defiled the sanctuary, and it was Sabbath and it was the Day of Atonement.[193]

The connection between the child and his weight in gold shows how precious he was to his mother, and serves to emphasize the great degree of desperation she must have felt in order to perform such an act.

The verse quoted by the Midrash in denigrating the murder of Zechariah is the same verse (Lam. 2:20) that the Talmud (BT

---

192. *Sifra Bechukotai* 2:6.
193. *Eccl. Rabbah* 10:5.

Sanhedrin 7a) attributes to Aaron at the time of the golden calf, in explanation of why he helped in its construction rather than permitting himself to be martyred. Just as G-d did not allow the sin of killing Zechariah to be rectified, and the Temple was in fact destroyed, similarly the Jewish nation would have been annihilated in its infancy had it been responsible for the unjustified murder of Aaron.

Appendix VI: What Happened to the Holy Ark?

According to tradition, the Ark constructed in the time of Moses for the Tabernacle was still in existence at the time of the First Temple, where it was placed in the Holy of Holies. However, it eventually disappeared, and was not to be found in the Second Temple. In fact, no new Ark was constructed, and the Second Temple functioned without an Ark. In an attempt to trace its whereabouts, a short synopsis of various Biblical events is required.

The Later Kings of the Kingdom of Judea

According to the Biblical account, the kings of Israel were all considered to be wicked. Many of the kings of Judea, on the other hand, were considered to be righteous, although interestingly, their own fathers or sons were frequently not so.

The following table gives a short review of the last nine kings of Judea:

King	Reigned	Description
Ahaz	735 BCE	Wicked. Passed his son through fire.
Hezekiah	720 BCE	Righteous. Destroyed altars and copper serpent.
Manasseh	692 BCE	Wicked. Idols, witchcraft. Spilled innocent blood.
Amon	638 BCE	Wicked. Was assassinated.
Josiah	637 BCE	Righteous. High priest Hilkiah (some say father of Jeremiah) found Torah scroll.
Jehoahaz	607 BCE	Wicked. Second son of Josiah and Hamutal, daughter of Jeremiah. Pro-Assyrian. Deposed by Pharaoh after 3 months.
Jehoiakim	607 BCE	Wicked. Older son of Josiah. Pro-Egyptian. Deposed by Nebuchadnezzar.
Jehoiachin	597 BCE	Wicked. Son of Jehoiakim. Exiled to Babylon by Nebuchadnezzar.
Zedekiah	597 BCE	Wicked. Son of Josiah. Chosen by Nebuchadnezzar.

Regarding the idol-worship of the Judean kings, the Talmud demonstrates how the evil kings exacerbated the level of iniquity displayed by their wicked ancestors:

> Ahaz set it [an idol] in an upper chamber [of the Temple], as it is written [regarding the righteous king Josiah who destroyed the idols of his predecessors], "And the altars [and hence the idols] that were on the roof of the upper chamber of Ahaz... the king smashed [as required by the law of the Torah[194]]" (2 Kings 23:12). Manasseh [intensified the sin and] placed it [an idol] in the Temple [and not

---
194. Exod. 34:13; Deut. 7:5, 12:3.

just in the Temple's upper chamber], as it says, "And he placed a graven image of the Asherah that he had made in the house concerning which the Lord had said to David, and to Solomon his son, 'In this house and in Jerusalem, which I have chosen out of all tribes of Israel, will I put my name forever.'"[195] Amon [magnified the sin when he] introduced it [an idol] into the Holy of Holies, as it says, "For the bed is too short for a man to stretch out in, and the covering narrower than that needed to wrap himself in it" (Isa. 28:20). What is [meant by] "For the bed is too short for a man to stretch out in?" R. Samuel b. Nahmani said in the name of R. Jonathan: For this bed [the Temple] is too short to be ruled by two entities [the marital bed, being the most intimate place of contact, symbolizes the Holy of Holies, while the two entities are the true G-d and an idol. There is not enough room in the Holy of Holies for both. Although not mentioned explicitly, the verse is understood to refer to Amon, whom the Bible says was even more wicked than Manasseh (2 Chron. 33:23)] (BT *Sanhedrin* 103b and Maharsha thereon).

Talmudic Dispute Regarding the Fate of the Ark

The following Talmudic passage (BT *Yoma* 53b) discusses the displacement of the Ark after the time of the First Temple:

R. Eliezer said: The Ark was exiled to Babylon, for it says: "In the following year [after deposing King Jehoiakim],

---

195. 2 Kings 21:7. See also 2 Chron. 33:3.

King Nebuchadnezzar sent [for Jehoiachin] and had him brought to Babylonia together with the precious vessels [including the Ark] of the house of the Lord" (2 Chron. 36:10). R. Simeon b. Yohai [also] said: The Ark was exiled to Babylon, for it says: "Behold, the days will come when all that is in your house, and that which your fathers have stored until this day, will be carried to Babylon; not a *thing* will be left, says the Lord [In Hebrew 'thing' can also mean 'commandment']" (Isa. 39:6). Those are the Ten Commandments contained in it [the Ark. Isaiah informed Hezekiah that he would be punished in kind for displaying his treasures to the Babylonian king]. R. Judah b. Ilai[196] said: The Ark was hidden [buried] in its own place, as it says: "And the poles [for carrying the Ark] were so long that the ends of the poles were seen [protruding] from the holy place, from the fore [the eastern side] of the Sanctuary; but they could not be seen without [since they were hidden from view by the curtain]; and they are there until this very day [implying forever—even after the Temple was destroyed]" (1 Kings 8:8).

Both R. Eliezer and R. Simeon b. Yohai say that the Ark was taken to Babylon, just that the former says it was taken in the exile of Jehoiachin (together with Ezekiel [Rashi on Ezek. 1:3] and Mordechai or his ancestors [Esth. 2:5-6]), while the latter says it was taken in the exile of Zedekiah.

R. Judah b. Ilai, on the other hand, says it was not taken by Nebuchadnezzar; rather, it was hidden by the righteous King Josiah. But why would he do that? The Talmud (BT *Yoma* 52b) explains:

---

196. Corrected by Soncino, Tractate *Yoma*, p. 253. Was Lakish.

What Happened to the Holy Ark?

(1) He saw the Scriptural passage: "The Lord will bring you, and the king whom you will set over you, to a nation that you have not known" (Deut. 28:36). Therefore he hid it, (2) as it says: "And he [King Josiah] said to the Levites, that taught all Israel, that were holy unto the Lord: Put the holy Ark into the house that Solomon, the son of David King of Israel, built" (2 Chron. 35:3).

This section may be divided into two parts. The first part provides the reason for hiding the Ark, and the second describes the mechanics of actually hiding it. These two parts will now be examined in detail.

1. Why Was the Ark Hidden?

Josiah had seen the attachment to idol-worship increasing, to the point that an idol was introduced by his own father into the Holy of Holies, as described in BT *Sanhedrin* 103b. After the priest Hilkiah found a hidden Torah scroll, the king realized immediately that the nation had been in violation of many religious laws. Also, the Scriptural passage from Deuteronomy made it clear that a possible penalty for such misbehavior was exile from the Land of Israel, which would mean that the safety of the Ark was in danger. The only remaining question was whether degeneration had proceeded to the extent that punishment was imminent. That question was answered when Josiah sent a delegation to the prophetess Hulda, who was a relative of the prophet Jeremiah (BT *Megillah* 14b). The prophetess confirmed Josiah's conjecture that the time of reckoning was indeed near. Because of Josiah's righteousness, however, a gesture would be made on his behalf and the fulfillment of the curses would not take place in his lifetime.[197]

The Talmud (BT *Megillah* 14b) suggests two reasons that Hilkiah went to Hulda rather than to her more famous relative. One is that Jeremiah had left Israel on a mission (that was successful) to return the members of the ten lost tribes. The second is that women are in general more empathetic than men, and he was hoping that the nation would suffer a weaker reprimand. When Josiah saw that leniency was not an option, he must have realized that the time had come to hide the Ark (together with bottles containing manna and water to be sprinkled on the ritually impure, the staff of Aaron which had blossomed, and the chest that the Philistines had sent as a gift to the G-d of Israel [BT *Yoma* 52b]).

2. Where Was the Ark Hidden?

This question will be dealt with by examining the source of the claim that the Ark was in fact hidden by Josiah. The verse from Chronicles quoted above refers to Josiah's preparation for celebrating Passover, and its simple meaning is that the Levites were requested to place the Ark in the Temple (2 Chron. 35:13). However, as R. Yitzchak Levi[198] points out, the Ark had been in the Temple since the time of Solomon, some three hundred years prior, so why was it necessary to move it into place at this late stage? The Talmud concludes that a different move is being referred to—a move from its standard location to a secret hiding place. Rambam (*Hilchot Beit ha-Bechirah*

---

197. 2 Chron. 34:14-28; 2 Kings 22:8-20.
198. Yitzchak Levi, *Genizat ha-Aron*, VBM. A number of the sources and explanations quoted here are found in this article.

4:1)¹⁹⁹ fills in some missing details by explaining that at the time that Solomon built the Temple, he knew prophetically that it would eventually be destroyed, and accordingly dug a deep and circuitous underground tunnel at the time of its construction to preserve the holiest objects for eternity. That the hiding place was secret may be understood from the fact that the Ark was to be hidden, in the words of the verse, by "the Levites, that taught all Israel, that were holy unto the Lord," implying that only a select group of the Levites were privy to the details of the location, and this knowledge was discreetly transmitted from generation to generation.

As far as the location of the repository, R. Judah b. Ilai held that it "was hidden in its own place," i.e. below the Holy of Holies. However, the Talmud does bring an alternative view: "R. Nahman said: It was taught that the Ark was hidden away in the Chamber of the Woodshed [where wood for burning on the altar was kept, in the northeast corner of the women's section, i.e. the northeast corner of the courtyard]" (BT *Yoma* 54a).

That the location was meant to be kept secret follows from the continuation of the Talmudic text:

> It happened to a certain priest who was whiling away his time [light-heartedly] that he saw a block of pavement that was different [raised a bit] from the others, and he went to inform his friend, but before he could complete his words, his soul departed. Thus they knew definitely that the Ark was hidden there. What had he been doing [to incur such a punishment]? R. Helbo said: He was playing with his ax.

---

199. Solomon's foreknowledge of the eventual destruction was noted by Rashi (1 Kings 7:51) as the reason that Solomon did not use gold captured by David in the construction of the Temple, so that Israel's enemies would not be able to claim that the Temple was destroyed because it utilized stolen materials.

Clearly, this event occurred in the woodshed. The priest was punished either because of his disrespectful attitude, or because he should have realized that the data that he had deciphered was classified. Of course, the punishment meted out also revealed its hiding place, but its severity must have made those present realize that such information should go no further.

A second version of the story gives the impression that even if the priest was innocent of wrongdoing, the overarching holiness of the cache, or perhaps the absolute requirement to keep its location secret was sufficient to necessitate the removal of the priest:

> The school of R. Ishmael taught: Two blemished priests [who don't participate in sacrificial service] were removing worms from wood [for the altar, which must be worm-free] when the ax of one of them slipped from his hand and fell on that place [where the Ark was hidden], whereupon a flame burst forth and consumed him.

Alternative Viewpoints

As previously mentioned, some Tannaim felt that the Ark was not hidden, but transported to Babylon. How do they interpret the words "Put the holy Ark into the house that Solomon… built," being that it was already there? Rashi (2 Chron. 35:3) explains that the wicked king Manasseh had removed the Ark from the Holy of Holies and replaced it with an idol; Josiah, the righteous king, destroyed the idol and returned the Ark to its proper location. This approach fits in with the opinions of R. Eliezer and Simeon b. Yohai, both of whom said that the Ark was taken to Babylon, where it disappeared.

What Happened to the Holy Ark?

Rashi's interpretation in Chronicles differs from the previously quoted Talmudic text that states that Manasseh brought an idol into the sanctuary, since Rashi makes it clear that he brought an idol into the Holy of Holies itself. This approach fits in with numerous verses that relate the destruction of the Temple specifically to the heinous deeds of Manasseh, rather than his son Amon, such as:

> But the Lord did not return from His great wrath, from his anger against Judea, because of all of the provocations with which Manasseh had provoked Him (2 Kings 23:26).

> Surely it was by the commandment of the Lord with respect to Judea, to remove them out of His sight because of the sins of Manasseh, for all that he did; and also for the innocent blood that he shed; and he filled Jerusalem with innocent blood, and the Lord was not willing to pardon it (2 Kings 24:3-4).

The last verse stresses not only Manasseh's religious behavior, but his interpersonal behavior as well.

Perhaps on the basis of these verses and Rashi's description of Manasseh's actions, Prof. Yehuda Amitzur[200] concluded that the Ark was already concealed by the priests in the lifetime of Manasseh, and remained so permanently. However, this would seem to contradict both of the previously suggested interpretations of the words "Put the holy Ark into the house that Solomon... built." One might say that it was hidden temporarily during the reign of Manasseh, taken out for Passover by Josiah, and finally stored in a permanent hiding place.

---

200. Yehuda Amitzur, *Pulmus Aron ha-Brit bi-Yemei Yoshiyah*, cited in Yitzchak Levi, *Genizat ha-Aron*, VBM.

In spite of the many verses maligning Manasseh and painting him as the most wicked of all the kings, and the one responsible for the eventual destruction of the Temple and Babylonian exile, it is interesting that according to the book of Chronicles (but not Kings), Manasseh repented at the end of his life and was even able to serve as a positive influence on the Children of Israel, as described in the following verses:

> And when he was in distress, he implored the Lord his G-d, and humbled himself greatly before the G-d of his fathers. And he prayed to Him; and He acceded to him, and He heard his supplication, and brought him back to Jerusalem to his kingdom. Then Manasseh knew that the Lord was G-d…. And he took away the strange gods, and the idol out of the house of the Lord, and all the altars [for idol-worship] that he had built on the mountain of the house of the Lord and in Jerusalem, and he cast them out of the city. And he built up the altar of the Lord, and he offered on it peace offerings and thanksgiving offerings, and he commanded Judea to serve the Lord, the G-d of Israel. But the people still sacrificed on the high places, but only to the Lord their G-d (2 Chron. 33:12-17).

Manasseh became a G-d-fearing Jew and was even successful in dissuading the nation from worshipping idols. He apparently also attempted to limit sacrifices to the Temple, rather than allowing them to be brought on forbidden altars as well. This is a requirement of *halachah*, and many of the righteous kings tried unsuccessfully to enforce this restriction. Although Manasseh was not able to inculcate proper behavior in this respect, he is given credit for weaning the nation from idol-worship and trying to overcome this last stumbling block.

What Happened to the Holy Ark?

Radak (2 Chron. 35:3, 2 Kings 22:8) notes that Manasseh even removed the idol from the Temple. He asks, if that is the case, why didn't he restore the Ark to its proper location? Why did that have to wait for Josiah? Perhaps one can answer that the Ark's hiding place was known to only a small coterie of righteous Levites. Since Manasseh had lived most of his life as a wicked person, he may not have been on the best terms with the devout Levites, and may not have even known to whom such a request should be addressed.

The Hidden Temple Gates

Not only was the Ark hidden, but the Temple gates were as well. On the words in Lamentations describing the destruction of the Temple, "Its gates sunk into the ground" (Lam. 2:9), the Midrash comments: "Because the gates [of the Temple] gave honor to the Ark, the enemy did not prevail over them" (*Lam. Rabbah* 2:13).

Another Midrash[201] explains how the gates honored the Ark. Solomon constructed an Ark ten cubits in width to protect the original Ark that had been in the *Mishkan*, which was smaller and fit inside of it.[202] But the entrance to Solomon's sanctuary was also ten cubits wide, so the new Ark could not fit through the passageway. In his desperation, the Midrash imagines Solomon calling David up from his grave, and crying out the following verse, which appears as part of Solomon's prayer at the inauguration of his Temple: "Do not turn away the face of Your anointed one [implying that David was reincarnated]; remember the good deeds of your servant David" (2 Chron. 6:42).

David was in fact cognizant of the fact that he would be disturbed from his eternal slumber when he wrote in Psalms: "O Lord, You

---
201. *Exod. Rabbah* 8:1.
202. *Etz Yosef, Tanchuma, Va'era* 7.

brought up my soul from the nether-world; You rejuvenated me from those who had descended to the pit" (Ps. 30:4).

Inspired by his father's presence, Solomon was empowered to say: "Lift up your heads, you gates; and be lifted up, you everlasting doors; so that the King of glory may come in" (Ps. 24:7).

At this stage, the gates suspected that when Solomon requested them to rise miraculously, his justification for asking that nature be subverted was that he considered himself to be "the King of glory," leading them to query him immediately, saying: "Who then is the King of glory?" (Ps. 24:10).

Whereupon Solomon gave the right answer: "The Lord of hosts, He is the King of glory!" This answer allayed the fears of the Divine spirit within the gates, who admitted that had Solomon ascribed the glory to himself, the gates were primed to crush his skull.

Solomon had accomplished his mission thanks to his father's revival, which led the heavenly voice quoted by Solomon in the book of Ecclesiastes to call out: "I praised the dead that are already dead, more than the living that are still alive" (Eccl. 4:2).

In summary, there exist Midrashim that speak of both the Ark and the Temple gates as having survived the destruction of the Temple and having been buried in the ground until needed once more, when the Third Temple comes into being.

As with the Ark, so with the Temple gates. Both are quietly waiting in their state of interment to be redeemed and renewed at the advent of the Third Temple in Messianic times.

Source Material

Akedat Yitzchak — Classical work of ritual matters and moralizing legends by R. Yitzchak Arama.

Avot de-Rabbi Natan — Tannaitic work by R. Natan, parallels *Ethics of the Fathers*.

Baal ha-Turim — Commentary on Torah by the halachist Yaakov b. Asher, called *Tur*.

Be'er Mayim Chayim — Novellae on the Pentateuch by R. Chaim Tirar of Chernovitz.

Ben le-Oshri Beracha Meshuleshet — Commentary of Rav Yitzchak ha-Kohen Huberman, Tzaddik of Raanana, on Torah and holidays, using approach of Pardes (*pshat* - simple meaning, *drush* - derived meaning, *remez* - allusions, *sod* - secrets).

Chen Tov — Commentary on the Pentateuch by R. Tuvia Halevi, student of R. Shlomo Sagis in Safed in the 16th century.

Derech Chayim Tochachat Musar — Homiletic work by the Shlah.

Divrei Eliyahu — Commentary on Torah and Talmud by R. Eliyahu of Vilna (the Gaon).

Ein Yaakov — Compilation of all the aggadic material in the Talmud, with commentaries by R. Yaakov ibn Habib and (after his death) by his son, R. Levi ibn Habib.

Emunot ve-De'ot — First systematic attempt to integrate Jewish theology with components of Greek philosophy. Written by Saadia Gaon.

G-d, Man, and History — Basic Jewish philosophy by Dr. Eliezer Berkovits.

Guide for the Perplexed — Basic Jewish philosophy by Rambam.

Haggada — Manual with prayers and customs for conducting the Passover Seder.

Hagut be-Parshiot ha-Torah — Commentary on Torah by R. Yehuda Nachshoni.

Harchev Davar — Commentary on the author's Haamek Davar, both written by Naftali Zvi Yehuda Berlin.

Kuzari — Basic Jewish philosophy by Yehudah ha-Levi.

Likkutei Moharan — Chassidic interpretations of Biblical and Midrashic stories by R. Nachman of Breslav, published and disseminated after his death by his disciple, Reb Nosson. Moharan stands for Moreinu ha-Rav Nachman.

Matnot Kehunah — Simple, well-documented commentary on Midrash Rabbah by R. Yissocher Ber ha-Kohen Katz.

Mechilta de-Rabbi Yishmael — Halachic Midrash on Exodus. Based on the teachings of R. Ishmael b. Elisha, R. Akiva's contemporary, and redacted by Rav.

Mechilta de-Rashbi (R. Shimon b. Yochai) — Halachic Midrash on Exodus. Based on the teachings of R. Akiva. Compiled in fifth century.

Meshech Chochmah — Torah commentary by R. Meir Simcha Ha-Kohen of Dvinsk. *Inter alia*, warns of the danger of living in Europe.

Midrash Lekach Tov — See Pesikta Zutrata.

Source Material

Midrash Rabbah — Name given to ten sets of Midrashim on Torah and the five *Megillot*. Compiled and edited between sixth and tenth centuries.

Midrash Tadshe — Attributed to R. Pinchas b. Yair (Tanna). Some scholars attribute it to R. Moshe ha-Darshan. Tadshe means "Let the earth put forth grass" — the first words of the Midrash. *Gematria* of *Tadshe* and *Pinchas b. Yair* are similar.

Minchah Belulah — Commentary on Torah, based on Midrashim, by Menachem b. Yaakov ha-Kohen Rapoport.

Mizrachi — Super-commentary on Rashi, written by R. Eliyahu Mizrachi.

Netivot Shalom — Series of books by the Slonimer Rebbe, R. Shalom Noach Berezovsky, on the Torah, holidays, chassidism, and Talmud.

Or Gedalyahu — Essays by R. Gedalia Schorr on weekly portions and holidays.

Or ha-Chaim — Commentary on the Torah written by R. Chaim Ben Attar.

Orot ha-Kodesh — Philosophical (*Chochmat ha-Kodesh*) and ethical (*Musar ha-Kodesh*) writings of R. Kook.

Otzar Yisrael — Judah Eisenstein's Jewish encyclopedia, completed in 1913.

Oznayim la-Torah — Commentary on the Torah by R. Zalman Sorotzkin.

Parpera'ot le-Parshat ha-Shavua — Weekly Torah sheet by R. Gershon Steinberg.

Perush ha-Rosh al ha-Torah — Commentary of Rabbenu Asher on the Torah, found in *Hadar Zekenim* together with the commentary of Tosafot.

Pesikta de-Rav Kahana — Aggadic Midrash with homilies for special Shabbatot. Some quoted in the name of Rav Kahana. Compiled between fifth and seventh centuries.

Pesikta Zutrata — Also called *Lekach Tov*. Each homily starts with "tov." Written by Tuvia b. Eliezer, Rashi's contemporary. Explains weekly portions and *Megillot*.

Pirkei de-Rabbi Eliezer — 54-chapter Midrash aggadah. Retells Biblical stories. Traditionally ascribed to R. Eliezer b. Hyrcanus, but Zunz claims it was written in the eighth century in an Islamic country.

Pri Tzaddik — Transcription of the public classes given on Shabbat and holidays by R. Tzadok ha-Kohen.

Rif — Hebrew acronym for R. Yoshiyahu Pinto, the author of the eponymous commentary on *Ein Yaakov*.

Seder Olam Rabbah — Chronological record from Adam to Bar Kochba, attributed to the Tanna Yosi b. Chalafta (ca. 160). Quoted in Talmud, Mishnah, Mechilta, Sifra, Sifrei.

Sefer ha-Ikkarim — Written by Yosef Albo. Proposes three principles of faith - existence of G-d, revelation, and Divine justice (i.e. reward and punishment).

Shittah Mekubbetzet — Anthology of commentaries on various Talmudic tractates, prepared by R. Bezalel Ashkenazi.

Sifra (Torat Kohanim) — *Midrash halachah* (legal Biblical exegesis) on Leviticus. Rambam attributes it to Rav, and Malbim to R. Chiya. From school of R. Akiva. Quoted frequently in Talmud.

Siftei Chachamim — Super-commentary on Rashi's commentary on the Pentateuch, gathered from earlier exegeses on Rashi. Written by Shabtai ben Yosef Bass. Considered so essential that there exists a concise summary, *Ikkar Siftei Chachamim*, which appears with Rashi.

Source Material

Siftei Kohen — Allegoric-kabbalistic commentary on Torah, by renowned Kabbalist R. Mordechai ha-Kohen of Safed, with Kabbalistic explanations and *gematriot*.

Tanna de-Vei Eliyahu — Midrash taught to third-century Amora, Anan, by Elijah (BT *Ketubot* 106a). Consists of *Seder Eliyahu Rabbah* (larger) and *Seder Eliyahu Zuta* (smaller). Final redaction was at end of the tenth century. Describes evolution of the world, Jewish history.

Tanchuma — Aggadic interpretations of the weekly portions, attributed to R. Tanchuma. Edited in fifth century, before Midrash Rabbah and Talmud, which quotes it.

Targum Onkelos — Official translation when reading the Torah in Talmudic times (and today for Yemenites). Tradition: conveyed to Moshe at Sinai, but forgotten and re-recorded by Onkelos the convert. "Reading the weekly portion twice and targum once" refers to Targum Onkelos.

Targum Yonatan — Official translation of prophets, ascribed to Yonatan b. Uziel. Targum Yonatan on the Torah (pseudo-Yonatan) composed in seventh or eighth century.

Tiferet Yisrael — Commentary on Mishnah, composed by R. Yisrael Lifshitz, in two parts (after the two Temple pillars): *Yachin* is the basic explanation; *Boaz* contains new ideas and is more analytical.

Torah Or — Chassidic explanations of the weekly Torah portions and holidays, written by *Baal ha-Tanya*.

Torah Temimah — Collection of Talmudic and Midrashic teachings related to the verses of the Torah, with commentary. Prepared by R. Baruch ha-Levi Epstein.

Tosafot Yom Tov — Mishnah commentary by R. Yom Tov Lipmann Heller. Comparable to Tosafot on the Talmud, just as Bartenura's Mishnah commentary is comparable to Rashi.

Tzeror ha-Mor — Kabbalistic and Midrashic commentary on the Torah by R. Avraham Saba. First printed in Venice in 1523.

Yad ha-Chazakah — Code of law containing 14 books (the Hebrew numerical value of *Yad* is 14), written by Rambam. Also called *Mishneh Torah*, "the repetition of the Torah."

Zohar — Literally, "splendor." Foundational work of Jewish mystical thought known as Kabbalah. Discusses the nature of G-d, structure of the universe, nature of souls.

Commentators

Abarbanel, Isaac (1437-1508) — Born to a wealthy family in Lisbon, Portugal. Wrote three types of works: exegesis of Bible and Haggadah, philosophy, and apologetics.

Albo, Yosef (1380-1444) — Born in Monreal, Aragon. Student of Hasdai Crescas. Had medical knowledge. Versed in Aristotle. Wrote *Sefer ha-Ikkarim*.

Alshich, Moshe (1508-1593) — Student of Yosef Karo, from whom he received ordination (true *semichah*) with Sanhedrin, and teacher of R. Yitzchak Luria (Arizal). Wrote Torat Moshe on Torah.

Arama, Yitzchak (1420-1494) — Born in Spain. Talmudist, philosopher. Wrote *Akedat Yitzchak* ("Binding of Isaac"), a philosophical, homiletic commentary on Torah.

Asevilli, Yom Tov b. Avraham (1250-1330) — Born in Seville, Spain (Asevilli, from Seville). Student of Raah and Rashba. Became rabbi of Saragossa. Famous for his commentary on the Talmud. Known as the Ritva (Hebrew acronym of his name).

Asher b. Yechiel (Rosh, Rabbenu Asher) (1250-1328) — Born in Germany. Great-grandson of Raavan (Tosafist). Student of Meir of Rothenburg. Worked in money-lending, wealthy. Fled to Toledo, became rabbi after being recommended by Rashba. His *magnum opus* is an abstract of Talmudic law.

Ashkenazi, Bezalel (1520-1592) — Student of Radbaz and teacher of Arizal in Egypt. Wrote *Shittah Mekubbetzet* on numerous tractates. Moved to Israel and became the rabbi of Jerusalem.

Ashkenazi, Issachar Baerman — See Katz, Yissocher Ber ha-Kohen.

Baal ha-Tanya — See Borukhovich, Shneur Zalman.

Baal ha-Turim — See Yaakov b. Asher.

Bachya b. Asher ibn Halawa (1255-1340) — Born in Saragossa. Student of Rashba. Like Ramban, used Kabbalah to interpret the Bible. Principal work: commentary on Torah called Rabbenu Bachya, which refers, *inter alia*, to *Sefer ha-Bahir, Zohar*.

Bass, Shabtai ben Yosef (1641–1718) — Born in Kalisz, Poland. Wrote *Siftei Chachamim*. Studied Talmud, singing. Appointed bass singer at Prague Altneuschule (where he got his name).

Ben Attar, Chaim (1696-1743) — Born in Meknes, Morocco. Talmudist, Kabbalist. Wrote the *Or ha-Chaim* commentary on Torah. One of four called holy (*kadosh*), in addition to Ari, Alshich, Shlah. Teacher of Chidah. Buried on Mount of Olives.

Berezovsky, Shalom Noach (1911-2000) — Born in Baranovitch, Belarus. Moved to Israel in 1936. Re-established Slonimer *chasidut* after WWII, became rebbe in 1981. Magnum opus - *Netivot Shalom*.

Berkovits, Eliezer (1908-1992) — Born in Hungary. Ordination from R. Akiva Glasner (*Dor Revi'i*) and R. Yechiel Weinberg at Hildesheimer. Ph.D. in Philosophy, U. of Berlin. Wrote *Tnai be-Nisu'im u-ve-Get*; *G-d, Man, and History*.

Berlin, Naftali Zvi (*Netziv*, 1816-1893) — Born and learned in Mir, Belarus. First wife was daughter of R. Yitzchok of Volozhin; second wife was his niece, daughter of R. Y.M. Epstein (*Aruch ha-Shulchan*). Rosh Yeshiva of Volozhin, 1854-92. Wrote: *Haamek She'eilah* (on *She'iltot*), *Haamek Davar* (on Torah).

Commentators

Borukhovich, Shneur Zalman (Shneur Zalman of Liadi, the Alter Rebbe, 1745-1812) — Born in Poland. Great-grandson of Maharal. Wrote *Shulchan Aruch ha-Rav*, *Tanya* (exposition of chasidic philosophy), *Torah Or*, and *Likkutei Torah* on weekly portion. Founder of Chabad dynasty in Liadi.

Botchko, Moshe (1917-2010) — Modern Orthodox Rosh Yeshiva in Montreaux, Switzerland. In 1986 established the hesder yeshiva Heichal Eliyahu in Jerusalem, later in Kochav Yaakov. Author of *Hegyonei Moshe*.

Chaim of Chernovitz — See Tirar, Chaim.

Chizkuni (Chizkiya b. Mano'ach, 1250-1310) — Born in France. Wrote Chizkuni, based on Rashi, but used twenty other commentaries. Wandered the world to find proper explanations. Quotes by name only Rashi, Dunash ben Labrat, *Yosippon*, and *Physica*.

Eidels, Shmuel Eliezer ha-Levi (Maharsha, 1555-1631) — Born in Poland to Maharal and Klonymus families. Mother-in-law, Eidel, supported him. Wrote commentary on Tosafot and aggadic parts of Talmud. Knew Kabbalah. Believed in reincarnation.

Eisenstein, Yehuda David (1854-1956) — Born in Congress Poland, moved to US in 1872, called *Baal ha-Otzarot* ("master of anthologies") because of his encyclopedic works, including *Otzar Yisrael* and *Otzar Midrashim*. Translated U.S. constitution into Hebrew.

Epstein, Baruch ha-Levi (*Torah Temimah*, 1860-1941) — Lithuanian rabbi, son of author of *Aruch ha-Shulchan*. Learned in Volozhin under his uncle the Netziv. Wrote the *Torah Temimah* commentary on Torah and *Megillot*, citing Talmud and Midrash on each verse, with explanations.

Frand, Yissocher — Born in Seattle. Educated at Ner Yisroel in Baltimore, where he became a senior lecturer. Skilled orator. Author of numerous books on Jewish topics, especially the weekly portion.

Ha-Kohen, Meir Simcha (1843-1926) — Born in Lithuania. Rabbi in Dvinsk, together with R. Joseph Rozin (Rogatchover) of chasidic community. Wrote *Or Same'ach* on Rambam. *Meshech Chochmah* on Pentateuch published posthumously.

Ha-Kohen, Mordechai (1523-1598) — Born in Safed. Student of Moshe di Trani (Mabit) and Yosef Karo, contemporary of R. Yosef di Trani (Maharit, son of Mabit). Wrote *Siftei Kohen* on Torah. Left Safed for financial reasons, became rabbi in Aleppo (1570).

ha-Levi, R. Yehudah (1075-1141) — Born in Spain. Student of Moses Ibn Ezra, Rif. Educated in Jewish scholarship, philosophy, medicine. Knew Avraham Ibn Ezra. Wrote poetry, *Kuzari*. According to legend, he was killed by Arab horseman on arrival in Jerusalem.

Heller, Yom Tov Lipmann ha-Levi (1579-1664) — Born in Bavaria. Studied under Maharal. Wrote Tosafot Yom Tov on Mishnah, *Maadanei Yom Tov* on Rosh. Rabbi in Krakow. Ancestor of Arye Leib Heller (*Ketzot ha-Choshen*) and his brother Yehuda Heller Kahana (*Kuntras ha-Sefeikot*).

Hirsch, Samson Raphael (1808-1888) — Born in Hamburg. Student of R. Jacob Ettlinger. Rabbi in Frankfurt. Father of Torah with *derech eretz*. Wrote *Nineteen Letters of Ben Uziel* (defense of tradition); *Horeb* (explanation of *mitzvot*); commentary on the Torah.

Hoberman, Yitzchak ha-Kohen (1896-1977) — Born in Tomashov, Poland. Mastered Talmud in youth; deported to Siberia (1940); relocated to Raanana (1950). Follower of Ger (*Sefat Emet*), learned Kabbalah with the Rebbe. Wrote *Ben le-Oshri Berachah Meshulleshet*.

Horovitz, Yeshayahu (1565-1630) — Born in Prague. Magnum opus is *Shnei Luchot ha-Brit* (basis of the acronym, *Shlah ha-Kadosh*), an encyclopedic compilation of ritual, ethics, and mysticism. Moved to Palestine in 1621.

COMMENTATORS

Ibn Ezra, Avraham (1089-1167) — Born in Tudela. Excelled in philosophy, astronomy/astrology, mathematics, poetry, linguistics, and Biblical exegesis. In Granada, met his friend (and perhaps father-in-law) Yehudah ha-Levi. Wrote Biblical commentary.

Ibn Habib, Yaakov (1460 –1516) — Born in Spain. After expulsion, settled in Salonika. Collected all *aggadot* from Babylonian Talmud, many from Jerusalem Talmud. Died after two of six orders printed. Son, Levi, completed it, without *aggadot* of Jerusalem Talmud.

Katz, Yissocher Ber ha-Kohen (1500s) — Born in Poland. Wrote Matnot Kehuna on Midrash Rabbah, *Mar'eh Kohen* on Zohar and Jewish theology. Student of Rama. Knew medicine, astronomy.

Kimchi, David (Radak, 1160-1235) — Born in Provence. Wrote commentaries on Prophets, Genesis (seeks historical, ethical underpinnings), Psalms, Chronicles. Influenced by Ibn Ezra, Rambam; favored the latter in controversy regarding his works. Delved into philosophy, science.

Kook, Avraham Yitzchak (1865-1935) — Born in Latvia, student of Netziv, son-in-law of Aderet; became rabbi of Yafo (1904); became first Israeli chief rabbi (1921); founded Mercaz HaRav (1924). Close with secular, religious, Zionist, and Charedi communities. Wrote on Talmud, Jewish thought.

Kramer, Eliyahu (Vilna Gaon, 1720-1797) — Born in Grodno. Teacher: Moses Margalit, author of *Pnei Moshe*. Talmudist, halachist, Kabbalist. Encouraged study of secular sciences. Main students: Chaim of Volozhin, Yisroel of Shklov, and Hillel Rivlin (descendants founded neighborhoods in Jerusalem).

Leibowitz, Nechama (1905-1997) — Born in Riga. Elder brother was Yeshayahu Leibowitz; Ph.D. in Germany (1930), emigrated to Israel, became professor of Bible at Tel Aviv University; Israel Prize (1956); Bialik Prize (1983). Wrote *New Studies in the Weekly Parsha*.

Levi, Yitzchak (b. 1951) — Served in Intelligence Corps in the IDF, studied in kollel of Yeshivat Har Etzion, where he serves as spiritual guide. Earned BA in Jewish history and archeology. Teaches at Herzog College.

Lifshitz, Yisrael (1782-1861) — Grandson of rabbi who aranged Cleves get. Born in Danzig, became head of local Bet Din. Wrote *Tiferet Yisrael* on Mishnah, *Shvilei de-Rakiya* on rabbinical astronomy, and *Derush Or ha-Chaim* on age of universe.

Luntschitz, Shlomo Ephraim (1550-1619) — Born in Luntschitz, Poland. Student of Maharshal. Rosh yeshiva in Lvov. Rabbi of Prague after Maharal. Students include Sheftel Horowitz, son of the *Shlah*. Wrote *Kli Yakar* (magnum opus) and *Olelot Ephraim* (sermons).

Luria, David (Radal, 1798-1855) — Born in Belarus. Child prodigy. Scion of wealthy family (Maharshal). Knew science, medicine, foreign languages. Wrote responsa and commentaries on Mishnah, Talmud, Midrash Rabbah (*Chiddushei ha-Radal*), Zohar.

Luzzatto, Shmuel David (Shadal, 1800-1865) — Born in Trieste. Wrote popular Torah commentary. Blames Rambam for accepting Aristotelian philosophy. Regarding *Yeshayahu*, maintained whole book written by him; concluded *Kohelet* was written after Shlomo.

Maharsha — See Eidels, Shmuel Eliezer.

Maimonides — See Rambam.

Malbim (Meir Leibush b. Yechiel Michel, 1809-1879) — Born in Ukraine. 1859 - chief rabbi of Bucharest. Argued with upper class, who wanted changes. Imprisoned, then liberated by Montefiore on condition that he leave Romania. Magnum opus is a commentary on Bible known by his acronym, *Malbim*.

Commentators

Mizrachi, Eliyahu (Re'em, 1435-1526) — Born in Turkey. Knew Arabic, Greek. Discovered how to extract square roots; chief rabbi of Turkey (1495). Sensitive to *agunot*, Karaites. Wrote commentary on Rashi (*Re'em*); his responsa used by R. Yosef Karo.

Nachman of Breslav (1772-1810) — Born in Medzhybizh, Ukraine, great-grandson of Baal Shem Tov. Founder of Breslav chasidism. Believed in closeness to G-d, speaking to G-d as with a best friend, and *hitbodedut*—unstructured, spontaneous prayer.

Nachmanides — See Ramban.

Nachshoni (formerly Razmivash)**, Yehuda** (1915-1982) — Born in Marmarosh, Transylvania (Romania). Educated in Jewish texts, thought. Moved to Israel in 1950. Journalist, leader of Po'alei Agudat Yisrael (edited their newspaper, *She'arim*). Wrote *Hagut be-Parshiot ha-Torah* on weekly portions.

Netziv — see Berlin, Naftali Zvi.

Nisim b. Reuven of Gerona (Ran, 1320-1376) — Born in Barcelona. Teacher: R. Peretz ha-Kohen. Physician, astronomer, and scribe. Received queries from entire diaspora. Wrote sermons and commentary on Rif, Talmud, Bible. Students: Rivash, Hasdai Crescas, Yosef Chaviva (*Nimmukei Yosef*).

Onkelos (first century) — Nephew of Hadrian. Converted between 35-120, translated Torah into Aramaic. Contemporary of R. Akiva, R. Yishmael.

Pinto, R. Yoshiyahu (1565-1648) — Born in Damascus. Father was a Spanish refugee who attained wealth, married sister of Chaim Vital. Ordained by R. Yaakov Abulafia, who was ordained by R. Yaakov Beirav II. Wrote *Ma'or Einayim* (Rif) on *Ein Yaakov*, *Kesef Mezukak* on Torah.

Rabbenu Bachya — See Bachya b. Asher ibn Halawa.

Rabinowitz, Tzadok ha-Kohen (1823-1900) — Born in Lithuania. Great-grandson of *Chacham Tzvi*. Child prodigy: at 1, blessed mother's milk; at 3, learned Talmud, Tosafot. Met Ishbitzer, became his *chassid*, and later (against his will) Rebbe of Lublin. Wrote *Pri Tzaddik, Tzidkat ha-Tzaddik*.

Radak — See Kimchi, David.

Radal — See Luria, David.

Rambam (Maimonides, 1138-1205) — Born in Cordoba. Wrote commentary on Mishnah, *Sefer ha-Mitzvot, Yad ha-Chazakah, The Guide for the Perplexed*. Court physician. Buried in Tiberias. Epitaph: From Moshe (Rabbenu) to Moshe (Maimonides) there was none like Moshe.

Ramban (Nachmanides, 1194-1270) — Born and became rabbi in Gerona. Medical doctor. Wrote *Chiddushei ha-Ramban* on Talmud, *Iggeret ha-Kodesh* on marriage, Torah commentary. Students: Rashba, Raah (*Chinuch*). In 1263, won debate with Pablo Christiani, but had to relocate to Israel.

Ran — See Nisim b. Reuven of Gerona.

Rapoport, Menachem ha-Kohen (1520-1596) — Born in Porto. Descendant of Rapa family. Changed name to Rapoport (i.e., Rapa of Porto). Learned Talmud, medicine. Witnessed burning of Talmud in Venice. Rabbi in Verona and Cologne. Wrote *Minchah Belulah*. Edited *Yalkut Shimoni*.

Rashbam (Shmuel b. Meir, 1085-1158) — Born in Ramerupt, Northern France. Mother was Yocheved, Rashi's daughter. Shepherd, vintner. Rashi's student, elder brother of Rabbenu Tam. Earliest Tosafist. Wrote basic commentary on Bible. Completed Rashi's commentary on *Bava Batra, Pesachim*.

Commentators

Rashi (Shlomo Yitzchaki, 1040-1105) — Born in Troyes. Student of Yaakov b. Yakar (Worms), who was student of Rabbenu Gershom. Wrote commentary on Talmud, Tanach (many supercommentaries, including *Gur Aryeh* by Maharal, *Mizrachi* by Re'em, *Yeri'ot Shlomo* by Maharshal).

Ri Migash — See Yosef b. Meir ha-Levi ibn Migash.

Riskin, Shlomo (b. 1940) — Born in Brooklyn. Ordination from YU; Ph.D. from NYU (1982); founding rabbi of Lincoln Square Synagogue (1963); founding chief rabbi of Efrat (1983). Established Ohr Torah Stone Institutions. Wrote *Torah Lights* series, *Listening to G-d*.

Ritva — See Asevilli, Yom Tov b. Avraham.

Saba, Avraham (1440-1508) — Born in Castillia. In Portugal, imprisoned, tortured; children kidnapped and baptized. Escaped to Morocco, then Turkey, where rewrote his books on Torah (*Tzeror ha-Mor*), *Megillot*, holidays, and *Ethics of the Fathers*. Granddaughter married Yosef Karo.

Saadiah b. Yosef Gaon (882-942) — Prominent rabbi, Jewish philosopher, and exegete of the Gaonic period. Active in opposition to Karaism, defense of rabbinic Judaism. Founder of Judeo-Arabic literature. Magnum opus is *Emunot ve-De'ot* (Jewish philosophy).

Schorr, Gedalia (1910-1979) — Born in Poland; went to U.S. (1922); taught in Torah Vodaas under R. Mendelovitz (1931), then studied under R. Kotler in Kletsk until war. Called first American educated gadol by R. Kotler; named Rosh Yeshiva of Torah Vodaas (1958).

Seforno, Ovadia b. Yaakov (1475-1550) — Born in Cesena, Italy. Studied math, philosophy, medicine. Had contact with Reuchlin, Meir Katzenellenbogen, Maharik. Wrote commentary on Torah and *Megillot*, selecting from Rashi, Ibn Ezra, Rashbam, Ramban, adding his own interpretations.

Shadal — See Luzzatto, Samuel David.

Shapira, Avraham (1911-2007) — Born in Jerusalem. Learned at Chevron Yeshiva under Rabbis Moshe Mordechai Epstein, Yechezkel Sarna. Became chief rabbi of Israel, head of Mercaz Harav. In print: *Shiurei Maran ha-Gra Shapira, Minchat Avraham, Morasha*.

Shlah — See Horovitz, Yeshayahu.

Shmulevich, Chaim (1901-1978) — Born in Poland. Student of R. Shimon Shkop. Rosh Yeshiva at Mir in Lithuania, Shanghai (during WWII), and Israel. Married daughter of the Rosh Yeshiva Eliezer Y. Finkel. Composed *Shaarei Chaim* on Talmud, *Sichot Musar*.

Shneur Zalman of Liadi — See Borukhovich, Shneur Zalman.

Soloveitchik, Yosef Dov ha-Levi (1903-1993) — Born in Russia. Descendant of R. Chaim of Volozhin and Tosfot Yom Tov. His mother was a cousin of R. Moshe Feinstein. Wrote *Lonely Man of Faith, Halakhic Man*. Advocated compatibility of Torah and academic scholarship.

Sorotzkin, Zalman (1880-1966) — Born in Lithuania, studied in Slabodka, Volozhin, and Telz. Rabbi of Luzk, Ukraine. Escaped Holocaust to Israel in 1940. Wrote *Oznayim la-Torah, Ha-De'ah ve-ha-Dibbur*. Headed Israeli Council of Sages.

Steinberg, Gershon (1936-2011) — Jerusalem-based educator at the Kaminetz Talmud Torah. Issued a weekly sheet of comments on the Biblical portion, called *Parpera'ot le-Parshat ha-Shavua*.

Tirar, Chaim (1740-1817) — Born in Galicia. Student of Maggid of Mezeritch. Chasidic rabbi, Kabbalist in Mogilev, Chernovitz, etc. 1813 – emigrated to Safed. Wrote *Sidduro shel Shabbat* (Kabbalistic homilies), *Be'er Mayim Chayim*, and novellae on tractate *Berachot*.

Tur - See Yaakov b. Asher.

Commentators

Tzaddik of Raanana - See Hoberman, Yitzchak ha-Kohen.

Tzadok ha-Kohen — See Rabinowitz, Tzadok ha-Kohen.

Vilna Gaon — See Kramer, Eliyahu.

Yaakov b. Asher (*Tur, Baal ha-Turim*, 1269-1343) — Son of Rosh, born in Cologne. Moved to Castile with his father. Wrote *Arbaah Turim* (Code of Law); *Rimzei Baal ha-Turim* (concise Torah commentary); *Perush al ha-Torah*, which quotes Ramban, Saadiah Gaon, Rashi, and Ibn Ezra.

Yosef b. Meir ha-Levi ibn Migash (1077-1141) — Born in Seville. Student of Rif, who chose him (over his own son) as next rosh yeshiva. Taught Maimon, Rambam's father. Wrote *She'elot u-Teshuvot Ri Migash* (quotes Rif and R. Chananel) and Talmudic commentaries.

Yosef, Ovadia (1920-2013) — Born in Baghdad. Studied at Porat Yosef; Israel Prize (1970); Chief Rabbi of Israel (1973-1983); founded Shas Party (1984). Wrote *Yabi'a Omer*, *Yechaveh Daat* (responsa); *Chazon Ovadiah* (on Shabbat and holidays).

www.ingramcontent.com/pod-product-compliance
Lightning Source LLC
Chambersburg PA
CBHW031312160426
43196CB00007B/498